DATE DUE counted.

NOV 1 2 1997			
JAN 0 5 1998			
MAR 1 6 2005			
FEB 0 8 2001			
NOV 2 7 2000			
NOV 0 5 2008			
GAYLORD			PRINTED IN U.S.A.

Mexico

WORLD BIBLIOGRAPHICAL SERIES

General Editors:
Robert G. Neville (Executive Editor)
John J. Horton

Robert A. Myers   Ian Wallace
Hans H. Wellisch   Ralph Lee Woodward, Jr.

John J. Horton is Deputy Librarian of the University of Bradford and currently Chairman of its Academic Board of Studies in Social Sciences. He has maintained a longstanding interest in the discipline of area studies and its associated bibliographical problems, with special reference to European Studies. In particular he has published in the field of Icelandic and of Yugoslav studies, including the two relevant volumes in the World Bibliographical Series.

Robert A. Myers is Associate Professor of Anthropology in the Division of Social Sciences and Director of Study Abroad Programs at Alfred University, Alfred, New York. He has studied post-colonial island nations of the Caribbean and has spent two years in Nigeria on a Fulbright Lectureship. His interests include international public health, historical anthropology and developing societies. In addition to *Amerindians of the Lesser Antilles: a bibliography* (1981), *A Resource Guide to Dominica, 1493-1986* (1987) and numerous articles, he has compiled the World Bibliographical Series volumes on *Dominica* (1987), *Nigeria* (1989) and *Ghana* (1991).

Ian Wallace is Professor of German at the University of Bath. A graduate of Oxford in French and German, he also studied in Tübingen, Heidelberg and Lausanne before taking teaching posts at universities in the USA, Scotland and England. He specializes in contemporary German affairs, especially literature and culture, on which he has published numerous articles and books. In 1979 he founded the journal *GDR Monitor*, which he continues to edit under its new title *German Monitor*.

Hans H. Wellisch is Professor emeritus at the College of Library and Information Services, University of Maryland. He was President of the American Society of Indexers and was a member of the International Federation for Documentation. He is the author of numerous articles and several books on indexing and abstracting, and has published *The Conversion of Scripts, Indexing and Abstracting: an International Bibliography* and *Indexing from A to Z*. He also contributes frequently to *Journal of the American Society for Information Science, The Indexer* and other professional journals.

Ralph Lee Woodward, Jr. is Director of Graduate Studies at Tulane University, New Orleans, where he has been Professor of History since 1970. He is the author of *Central America, a Nation Divided*, 2nd ed. (1985), as well as several monographs and more than sixty scholarly articles on modern Latin America. He has also compiled volumes in the World Bibliographical Series on *Belize* (1980), *Nicaragua* (1983), and *El Salvador* (1988). Dr. Woodward edited the Central American section of the *Research Guide to Central America and the Caribbean* (1985) and is currently editor of the Central American history section of the *Handbook of Latin American Studies*.

VOLUME 48

Mexico
Revised and Expanded Edition

George D. E. Philip

Compiler

CLIO PRESS
OXFORD, ENGLAND · SANTA BARBARA, CALIFORNIA
DENVER, COLORADO

British Library Cataloguing in Publication Data

Mexico. – 2nd ed. – (World bibliographical series; vol. 48)
I. Philip, George D. E.   II. Series
016.972

ISBN 1–85109–198–x

Clio Press Ltd.,
55 St. Thomas' Street,
Oxford OX1 1JG, England.

ABC-CLIO,
130 Cremona Drive,
Santa Barbara,
CA 93116, USA.

Designed by Bernard Crossland.
Typeset by Columns Design and Production Services Ltd, Reading, England.
Printed and bound in Great Britain by
Bookcraft (Bath) Ltd., Midsomer Norton

THE WORLD BIBLIOGRAPHICAL SERIES

This series, which is principally designed for the English speaker, will eventually cover every country (and many of the world's principal regions), each in a separate volume comprising annotated entries on works dealing with its history, geography, economy and politics; and with its people, their culture, customs, religion and social organization. Attention will also be paid to current living conditions – housing, education, newspapers, clothing, etc.– that are all too often ignored in standard bibliographies; and to those particular aspects relevant to individual countries. Each volume seeks to achieve, by use of careful selectivity and critical assessment of the literature, an expression of the country and an appreciation of its nature and national aspirations, to guide the reader towards an understanding of its importance. The keynote of the series is to provide, in a uniform format, an interpretation of each country that will express its culture, its place in the world, and the qualities and background that make it unique. The views expressed in individual volumes, however, are not necessarily those of the publisher.

VOLUMES IN THE SERIES

1 *Yugoslavia*, John J. Horton
2 *Lebanon*, C. H. Bleaney
3 *Lesotho*, Shelagh M. Willet and David Ambrose
4 *Rhodesia/Zimbabwe*, Oliver B. Pollack and Karen Pollack
5 *Saudi Arabia*, Frank A. Clements
6 *USSR*, Anthony Thompson
7 *South Africa*, Reuben Musiker
8 *Malawi*, Robert B. Boeder
9 *Guatemala*, Woodman B. Franklin
10 *Pakistan*, David Taylor
11 *Uganda*, Robert L. Collison
12 *Malaysia*, Ian Brown and Rajeswary Ampalavanar
13 *France*, Frances Chambers
14 *Panama*, Eleanor DeSelms Langstaff
15 *Hungary*, Thomas Kabdebo
16 *USA*, Sheila R. Herstein and Naomi Robbins
17 *Greece*, Richard Clogg and Mary Jo Clogg
18 *New Zealand*, R. F. Grover
19 *Algeria*, Richard I. Lawless
20 *Sri Lanka*, Vijaya Samaraweera
21 *Belize*, Peggy Wright and Brian E. Coutts
23 *Luxembourg*, Carlo Hury and Jul Christophory
24 *Swaziland*, Balam Nyeko
25 *Kenya*, Robert L. Collison
26 *India*, Brijen K. Gupta and Datta S. Kharbas
27 *Turkey*, Merel Güçlü
28 *Cyprus*, P. M. Kitromilides and M. L. Evriviades
29 *Oman*, Frank A. Clements
31 *Finland*, J. E. O. Screen
32 *Poland*, Rev. Ed. George Sanford and Adriana Gozdecka-Sanford
33 *Tunisia*, Allan M. Findlay, Anne M. Findlay and Richard I. Lawless
34 *Scotland*, Eric G. Grant
35 *China*, Peter Cheng
36 *Qatar*, P. T. H. Unwin
37 *Iceland*, John J. Horton
38 *Nepal*, John Whelpton
39 *Haiti*, Frances Chambers
40 *Sudan*, M. W. Daly
41 *Vatican City State*, Michael J. Walsh
42 *Iraq*, A. J. Abdulrahman
43 *United Arab Emirates*, Frank A. Clements
44 *Nicaragua*, Ralph Lee Woodward, Jr.
45 *Jamaica*, K. E. Ingram
46 *Australia*, I. Kepars
47 *Morocco*, Anne M. Findlay, Allan M. Findlay and Richard I. Lawless

48 *Mexico*, George D. E. Philip
49 *Bahrain*, P. T. H. Unwin
50 *The Yemens*, G. Rex Smith
51 *Zambia*, Anne M. Bliss and J. A. Rigg
52 *Puerto Rico*, Elena E. Cevallos
53 *Namibia*, Stanley Schoeman and Elna Schoeman
54 *Tanzania*, Colin Darch
55 *Jordan*, Ian J. Seccombe
56 *Kuwait*, Frank A. Clements
57 *Brazil*, Solena V. Bryant
58 *Israel*, Esther M. Snyder (preliminary compilation E. Kreiner)
59 *Romania*, Andrea Deletant and Dennis Deletant
60 *Spain*, Graham J. Shields
61 *Atlantic Ocean*, H. G. R. King
62 *Canada*, Ernest Ingles
63 *Cameroon*, Mark W. DeLancey and Peter J. Schraeder
64 *Malta*, John Richard Thackrah
65 *Thailand*, Michael Watts
66 *Austria*, Denys Salt with the assistance of Arthur Farrand Radley
67 *Norway*, Leland B. Sather
68 *Czechoslovakia*, David Short
69 *Irish Republic*, Michael Owen Shannon
70 *Pacific Basin and Oceania*, Gerald W. Fry and Rufino Mauricio
71 *Portugal*, P. T. H. Unwin
72 *West Germany*, Donald S. Detwiler and Ilse E. Detwiler
73 *Syria*, Ian J. Seccombe
74 *Trinidad and Tobago*, Frances Chambers
76 *Barbados*, Robert B. Potter and Graham M. S. Dann
77 *East Germany*, Ian Wallace
78 *Mozambique*, Colin Darch
79 *Libya*, Richard I. Lawless
80 *Sweden*, Leland B. Sather and Alan Swanson
81 *Iran*, Reza Navabpour
82 *Dominica*, Robert A. Myers
83 *Denmark*, Kenneth E. Miller
84 *Paraguay*, R. Andrew Nickson
85 *Indian Ocean*, Julia J. Gotthold with the assistance of Donald W. Gotthold
86 *Egypt*, Ragai, N. Makar
87 *Gibraltar*, Graham J. Shields
88 *The Netherlands*, Peter King and Michael Wintle
89 *Bolivia*, Gertrude M. Yeager
90 *Papua New Guinea*, Fraiser McConnell
91 *The Gambia*, David P. Gamble
92 *Somalia*, Mark W. DeLancey, Sheila L. Elliott, December Green, Kenneth J. Menkhaus, Mohammad Haji Moqtar, Peter J. Schraeder
93 *Brunei*, Sylvia C. Engelen Krausse, Gerald H. Krausse
94 *Albania*, William B. Bland
95 *Singapore*, Stella R. Quah, Jon S. T. Quah
96 *Guyana*, Frances Chambers
97 *Chile*, Harold Blakemore
98 *El Salvador*, Ralph Lee Woodward, Jr.
99 *The Arctic*, H.G.R. King
100 *Nigeria*, Robert A. Myers
101 *Ecuador*, David Corkhill
102 *Uruguay*, Henry Finch with the assistance of Alicia Casas de Barrán
103 *Japan*, Frank Joseph Shulman
104 *Belgium*, R.C. Riley
105 *Macau*, Richard Louis Edmonds
106 *Philippines*, Jim Richardson
107 *Bulgaria*, Richard J. Crampton
108 *The Bahamas*, Paul G. Boultbee
109 *Peru*, John Robert Fisher
110 *Venezuela*, D. A. G. Waddell
111 *Dominican Republic*, Kai Schoenhals
112 *Colombia*, Robert H. Davis
113 *Taiwan*, Wei-chin Lee
114 *Switzerland*, Heinz K. Meier and Regula A. Meier
115 *Hong Kong*, Ian Scott
116 *Bhutan*, Ramesh C. Dogra
117 *Suriname*, Rosemarijn Hoefte
118 *Djibouti*, Peter J. Schraeder
119 *Grenada*, Kai Schoenhals
120 *Monaco*, Grace L. Hudson
121 *Guinea-Bissau*, Rosemary Galli
122 *Wales*, Gwilym Huws and D. Hywel E. Roberts
123 *Cape Verde*, Caroline S. Shaw
124 *Ghana*, Robert A. Myers
125 *Greenland*, Kenneth E. Miller

126 *Costa Rica*, Charles L. Stansifer
127 *Siberia*, David N. Collins
128 *Tibet*, John Pinfold
129 *Northern Ireland*, Michael Owen Shannon
130 *Argentina*, Alan Biggins
132 *Burma*, Patricia M. Herbert
133 *Laos*, Helen Cordell
134 *Montserrat*, Riva Berleant-Schiller
135 *Afghanistan*, Schuyler Jones
136 *Equatorial Guinea*, Randall Fegley
137 *Turks and Caicos Islands*, Paul G. Boultbee
138 *Virgin Islands*, Verna Penn Moll
139 *Honduras*, Pamela F. Howard-Reguindin
140 *Mauritius*, Pramila Ramgulam Bennett
141 *Mauritania*, Simonetta Calderini, Delia Cortese, James L. A. Webb, Jr.
142 *Timor*, Ian Rowland
143 *St. Vincent and the Grenadines*, Robert B. Potter
144 *Texas*, James Marten
145 *Burundi*, Morna Daniels

146 *Hawai'i*, Nancy J. Morris, Love Dean
147 *Vietnam*, David Marr, Kristine Alilunas-Rodgers
148 *Sierra Leone*, Margaret Binns, Tony Binns
149 *Gabon*, David Gardinier
150 *Botswana*, John A. Wiseman
151 *Angola*, Richard Black
152 *Central African Republic*, Pierre Kalck
153 *Seychelles*, George Bennett, with collaboration from Pramila Ramgulam Bennett
154 *Rwanda*, Randall Fegley
155 *Berlin*, Ian Wallace
156 *Mongolia*, Judith Nordby
157 *Liberia*, D. Ellwood-Dunn
158 *Maldives*, Christopher H. B. Reynolds
159 *Liechtenstein*, Regula A. Meier
160 *England*, Alan Day
161 *The Baltic States*, Inese A. Smith and Marita V. Grunts
162 *Congo*, Randall Fegley
163 *Armenia*, Vrej Nersessian
165 *Madagascar*, Hilary Bradt

Contents

INTRODUCTION xiii

THE COUNTRY AND ITS PEOPLE 1

TRAVELLERS' ACCOUNTS 4

TOURISM AND TRAVEL GUIDES 9

GEOGRAPHY 13
    General 13
    Maps and atlases 15

FLORA AND FAUNA 17

ARCHAEOLOGY AND PREHISTORY 19
    The Aztecs 19
    The Maya 23
    Other peoples 26
    General works 30

HISTORY 33
    General 33
    The Conquest (1519-70) 35
    Colonial Mexico (1570-1820) 39
        Comparative works 39
        Works on Mexico 39
    From Independence to the Mexican Revolution (1820-1910) 47
    The Revolutionary period (1910-40) 53

ANTHROPOLOGY AND ETHNOGRAPHY 61
    General 61
    Anthropology of Mexico 62

LANGUAGE AND LINGUISTICS 69

Contents

RELIGION 72

SOCIAL SERVICES, HEALTH AND WELFARE 75

SOCIETY 77
Social conditions 77
Social change 79
The rôle of women 81
Migration and related issues 83

GOVERNMENT AND POLITICS 87
The political system 87
Constitution, legal system and local government 96
Interest groups and pressure groups 98
Historical interpretations of politics 100
Foreign relations 102

THE ECONOMY 107
General and recent history 107
Trade 112
Industry and commerce 114

MINING, OIL AND ENERGY 116

AGRICULTURE 120

LABOUR AND TRADE UNIONS 124

THE ENVIRONMENT 126

EDUCATION AND SCIENCE 128

SPORT 130

LITERATURE 132

THE ARTS 136
Painting 136
Architecture, sculpture and other visual arts 138
Music, theatre and film 145

FOLKLORE 147

COSTUME AND DESIGN 149

COOKING 151

MUSEUMS 153

PRESS AND MASS MEDIA 154

STATISTICS 156

BIBLIOGRAPHIES AND REFERENCE WORKS 158

INDEX OF AUTHORS 163

INDEX OF TITLES 171

INDEX OF SUBJECTS 187

MAP OF MEXICO 195

Introduction

In historical terms there is not one Mexico but many, each of them interesting and important in its own right. When the Spaniards arrived in 1519, there were many pre-Columbian civilizations. The Aztec, the Maya, the Olmec and Teotihuacán are only the best known. Furthermore the impressive progress made by archaeological and related disputes during the past two generations has greatly increased the accessibility of some of these pre-Columbian cultures. We have some understanding of their demography, their belief systems, their economic and political structures and their military organizations. After a long period of proper scholarly caution, some authorities have in the very recent past theorized more freely about, at any rate, the Aztec and Maya cultures in order to try to understand them better 'from within' rather than simply assembling an impressive array of facts. However knowledge does not advance in a straight line. There are many points of dispute and controversy, and the literature here tries to give some weight to these as well.

Catholic, colonial, Mexico may at times appear almost equally remote from the present day. It is an important element of official cultural ideology in Mexico to downplay the Spanish element of the country's past in favour of the pre-Columbian. Montezuma is publicly admired far more than Cortés. Yet it is evident that the Spaniards did bring something positive to Mexican culture – as well as the cruelties of conquest and inquisition. There is a great deal of scholarship, much of it North American, on the colonial period. As with pre-Columbian civilizations, we have a far fuller picture available to us now than was the case two generations ago.

Finally, Mexican independence amounted to neither a clean break from the past nor a gradual departure from it. Tragically, it was a bitterly fought, divisive and ultimately inconclusive question. Divisions at that time spilled over into continuous conflict during the first half of the nineteenth century. To add to the problems, Mexico lost more than one half of its territory to the United States following the secession of Texas and the war of 1846–47. Subsequently the French imposed the Emperor Maximilian upon Mexico although on this occasion Mexican resistance ultimately proved successful. Mexico in 1800 was not in every respect an underdeveloped country. Plainly it had by 1870 fallen back into what today would be described as the Third World.

Why was this period of Mexican history so disastrous? Plainly there was a great deal of rural rebellion in Mexico. We do not always know why. The pressures of a rising population on an essentially fixed amount of land must surely have played a part. However, there appears to be no simple correlation between shortages of land or food and rebellion. Instead, a more complex set of processes would appear to have been at work. And how ideological were the conflicts of the nineteenth century? Were the various battles fought out, as Louis Namier might have supposed, by ambitious groups of power seekers using principles simply as a cover for ulterior motives? Or was there real popular feeling about the proper rôle of the Church in post-colonial society? This volume contains recent historical literature on these and other questions, often presenting different points of view and suggesting areas of further investigation.

During the last 125 years the main themes of Mexican history have been authoritarian stability on the one hand, and revolutionary upheaval on the other. The Great Revolution took place during 1910-17, and there was also extensive mobilization during the presidency of Lázaro Cárdenas, 1934-40. These periods saw great advances in terms of social reform, at least in theory and on paper, but at the price of equally great instability. The 1930s were in fact relatively pacific, but many people died during the Revolution itself. Intervening periods were those of enforced stability under authoritarian governments which achieved considerable economic progress but at the price of great inequality. The great question facing Mexico today is how the country can become more democratic, freer and more equal without losing the political and social discipline which was so thoroughly inculcated by the officially Revolutionary party after 1940.

Even today the dominant Mexican political culture expresses a certain ambivalence about its past. Mexico officially applauds its Revolutionary past, which is glorified symbolically at almost every opportunity. The two main streets in Mexico City are called Reforma and Insurgentes. On the other hand real politics is taken up, to a great extent, with a concern for order. The Presidency is an extremely strong institution, and there is a popular willingness to accept strong government even at the expense of some freedom. As recently as the 1960s, the government showed that it had a short and brutal way with dissidents. It must nevertheless be said that there has certainly been a move toward greater pluralism and respect for democratic principles during the past generation although the political questions arising from this greater openness have by no means yet been resolved.

The effect upon Mexico of rapidly changing circumstances can also be seen in terms of its foreign policy. The most important Mexican relationship is that with the United States. Here there have been many changes and there remains some ambivalence. A minority of Mexicans actively dislike the United States, and fear its intervention in Mexican affairs. They point to the wars of aggression fought by the US against Mexico during the nineteenth century, and to heavy-handed acts of intervention and insensitivity at various points during the present century. The majority, however, admire the economic success enjoyed by the United States and wish Mexico to enjoy, as far as possible, the fruits of North American prosperity.

One thing which did divide official Mexican foreign policy from the United States was the difference in their approaches to Cold War questions. Mexico always sought to tolerate its own Marxist Left – at least in principle, if not always in practice. Mexico also refused to break relations with Cuba in the 1960s and, during the Nicaraguan conflict, took a position which was very different from that of the United States. However, with the ending of the Cold War an important area of difference between the two countries ceased to be relevant. A very important step in Mexican–US relations came in 1990 when President Salinas of Mexico and President Bush announced their intention to negotiate a Free Trade Area for North America – in which Canada would also be involved. At the beginning of 1993 this agreement had been signed but not yet ratified.

Mexican geography is almost as diffuse and pluralistic as its history. The north of the country is mostly desert and has much in common with the southwestern states of the United States. These are places to which millions of people have migrated, principally for economic reasons. There are few historical or cultural landmarks, although the flora and fauna are extremely interesting. Further south, the culture of the mountain people is quite distinctive, as is that of people living near the Caribbean and Pacific coasts. However, most Mexicans still live in the central *altiplano* which is dominated by the Federal capital. Mexico City, with its population approaching 20 million, is vibrant, dynamic and full of interest – but it suffers from severe environmental problems. The atmosphere is one of the most polluted in the world and very many inhabitants suffer from respiratory or gastric illnesses which can be blamed directly on the environment. Further south, there is a mainly rural population, principally of Indian extraction, which remains poorer and less well educated than that in the rest of the country. Critics of the system believe that the bureaucratic agencies and welfare services which are such prominent features of local society tend to create dependency and passivity, while the system's supporters believe that the official party has on the whole done well to prevent these parts of Mexico sinking into utter destitution.

Mexico is, of course, not just a product of its history and geography. It is a dynamic and rapidly changing modern society. The population has now reached some 90 million, a huge increase on the 25 million or so in 1940. If it were not for extensive Mexican migration to the United States, both legal and illegal, the population would be greater still.

Most Mexicans now live in cities. This is a historic change which dates back to the 1960s. It means that the countryside, though still very important, is no longer the central social and political factor. Moreover, the social profile of Mexico has changed in other ways as well. The majority of Mexicans are literate, and a large minority are now fairly well educated. There has been a huge expansion of secondary and university education since the 1960s, but the educational system remains unsatisfactory in certain respects, largely as a result of budgetary pressures. The 1980s were a decade of economic crisis, while the demographic profile of the country reflects a young population with a birth rate which is still high despite some significant decline in recent years. It is an impressive fact that Mexico has made significant socio-economic progress despite the challenge of this demographic expansion.

Urban living standards tend to be higher than rural ones, and many rural dwellers have been to some degree left behind by the considerable economic progress which Mexico has made since 1940. Agriculture at present employs some 25 per cent of the Mexican workforce, but produces only 5 per cent of the GDP. One of the difficulties with agriculture is that more modern techniques, and higher productivity, tend to lead to the employment of fewer people. The government is now making efforts to target rural poverty, while trying to discourage as far as possible further large-scale migration to Mexico's large and overcrowded cities.

The Mexican economy, like its society in many ways, is a mixture of the traditional and the very advanced. Mexico has already undergone substantial industrialization, and US companies are increasingly locating in Mexico in order to re-export to the US market. Well over 500,000 people are currently employed in the in-bond export sector (the *maquiladoras*). Mexico is also rich in oil and minerals, and is a substantial exporter of both, but it suffered in the

1980s as a result of allowing itself to become too dependent on oil income and too indebted during 1976-82, and the government is now a great deal more cautious in its attitude towards allowing the rapid expansion of raw material exports. Since the late 1980s, the government has instead put a great deal of emphasis on controlling inflation, and it has been successful, for inflation fell from a high of 135 per cent in 1987 to a low of just over 10 per cent at the beginning of 1993. In return for progress here, the authorities have been content with a relatively modest rate of economic growth.

The pattern of economic management has changed recently in Mexico, just as in many other parts of Latin America. The 1970s were a populist decade in which the government tried hard to improve the distribution of income while caring much less about the principles of orthodox public finance. The populist experiment was sustained for a time by rapidly rising oil income but led to serious crisis and failure in 1982. Thereafter the populist agenda was firmly shelved, and the authorities have continued to develop market-oriented policies involving free trade, privatization and careful financial management.

There is, of course, more to any country than its politics and economics. Mexico has, perhaps more than most other Latin American countries, a vibrant intellectual and artistic life. Mexican murals are world famous, the product of great artistry. The best Mexican literature is world famous also; here one thinks of names such as Octavio Paz, Carlos Fuentes and Carlos Monsivais. There is also much to be said about Mexican architecture, and about the greatly improved quality of Mexican history and social science.

A bibliographer, therefore, is faced with an embarrassment of choice. When making this selection, I have been governed by a simple set of principles. The first of these was balance. Inevitably the literature relating to any country is uneven, in both quality and quantity. There should not be anything in this volume which is actually of poor quality, but it has been necessary to omit a number of works which had some claim to inclusion. This was particularly true of works of colonial and twentieth-century history, anthropology and on Mexican–US relations. By the same token, due weight has been given to books principally of interest to the general reader. There is a focus on works of scholarship, but not an exclusive one.

Secondly, preference has been given to books rather than articles, and to works available in English rather than Spanish. There are so many articles written about Mexico in various academic journals, that it would be possible to compile a bibliography from these alone. These have, however, been used very sparingly. Nevertheless I have found it useful to include a number of articles from edited collections published in book form. This is partly in the interest of brevity. A reader may prefer to acquire some feel for an argument or analysis over twenty pages, rather than finding himself compelled to read three hundred. There is also the point that there are many Mexican authors whose books have not often been translated into English but whose articles have. I have tried to include at least one article in English from each of the most prominent Mexican historians and social scientists.

Thirdly, there has been a bias towards newer works. This essentially means those written in the 1980s, and published either then or at the beginning of the 1990s. It does take time for books to be published, ordered by libraries and described in bibliographies. As a result some important recent themes, the setting up by the government of its anti-poverty Solidarity programme and negotiations with the United States over the NAFTA agreement, have not yet been discussed in book-length works. The reader is advised to wait for the next edition of this bibliography.

This work on Mexico in fact represents an updating, though a substantial one, of Naomi Robbins's book which was number 48 in the series and appeared in 1984. I am grateful to Ms Robbins for providing an excellent foundation stone for my own efforts. I am also grateful to Alan Biggins from the Library of the Institute of Latin American Studies in London for helping to find some references particularly for the sports section. I should also acknowledge help from the Librarian of Canning House in London, and the LSE library.

George Philip
London School of Economics and Political Science
April 1993

The Country and Its People

1 **Los valores de los Mexicanos. México: entre la tradición y la modernidad.**
(Mexican attitudes. Mexico: between tradition and modernity.)
Enrique Alduncín Abitia. Mexico City: Fomento Cultural Banamex,
1986. 262p.

The first scientifically conducted and comprehensive analysis of Mexican attitudes
towards religion, politics, sexual relationships and other matters. The survey indicates
that considerable change has taken place over the past generation. Attitudes have been
influenced by cultural influences imported from the USA, the weakening of religious
influence and modernization generally. Mexicans, however, remain distrustful of their
political authorities.

2 **Mexico: a country guide.**
Compiled by Tom Barry. Albuquerque, New Mexico: Inter-
Hemispheric Education Resource Center, 1992. xxii + 391p.

A very comprehensive handbook covering the economy, society, human rights issues,
US influences, government and politics, and so on. The book is a very competent
summary of existing sources; it is heavily empirical. Coverage is of considerable depth
and the work will be helpful to professionals, diplomats and possibly advanced
students.

3 **The world in view: Mexico.**
Amanda Hopkinson. London: Heinemann Educational, 1988. 94p.

This general survey of Mexico is pitched at a fairly introductory level and aimed
principally at a school audience. The work is well balanced and very empirical. It
covers a range of social, historical and political topics.

1

The Country and Its People

4 **The Mexicans; a personal portrait of a people.**
Patrick Oster. New York: W. Morrow, 1989. 334p. bibliog.
A fairly sophisticated discussion which includes an account of the way in which the economic crisis of the 1980s impacted upon ordinary people in different economic strata. There has been some degree of economic improvement in Mexico since the book went to press.

5 **The labyrinth of solitude: life and thought in Mexico.**
Octavio Paz, translated from the Spanish by Lysander Kemp. New York: Grove Press, 1962. 212p.
This classic work on Mexican culture and identity was originally published in Mexico in 1950 and revised in 1959. The central thesis of the work is that Mexicans suffer from an identity crisis since they have emerged from a union of conquered and conquering people. This makes it difficult for them to relate easily either to purely liberal or collectivist values. This thesis is controversial but it remains influential. Paz has been for many years one of the leading figures in Mexican intellectual life.

6 **Twentieth century Mexico.**
Edited by W. Dirk Raat, William H. Beezley. London: University of Nebraska Press, 1986. 318p. bibliog.
This is a diverse collection of material which includes reprints of articles, political cartoons and original essays. There is a general thematic section and then a broadly chronological presentation.

7 **Profile of man and culture in Mexico.**
Samuel Ramos, translated from the Spanish by Peter G. Earle. Austin, Texas: University of Texas Press, 1969. 3rd ed. 198p. (Texas Pan-American Series).
A study of the Mexican national identity, from a cultural and educational perspective. Ramos offers an important though incomplete insight into the Mexican political culture of a generation ago.

8 **Inside the volcano.**
Alan Riding. London: I. B. Tauris, 1985. 386p. bibliog. (Published in the United States as *Distant Neighbours*).
A well-written and knowledgeable if poorly conceptualized study of Mexico. The author was a foreign correspondent in Mexico for many years. It is heavily flavoured by the period of Mexican history shaped by the oil boom and the debt crisis. There are chapters covering Mexican history, regional issues, the economy, and the political system.

9 **The roots of lo-mexicana: self and society in Mexican thought 1900-1934.**
Henry C. Schmidt. College Station, Texas: Texas A and M University Press, 1978. 195p. bibliog.
A study of the Mexican search for identity and self-awareness, covering the Revolutionary period and the years both before and after. The focus is on cultural history. This is an important period because the post-Revolutionary years saw the first

2

serious attempt to build a Mexican national identity around mass education, official party rule and rejection of political Catholicism.

10 **Mexico.**
New York; London: Time Life Books, 1985. 160p. bibliog.
This illustrated volume combines personal observation with factual analysis. It explores six principal themes: the country's contrasts; the capital city; the Indian heritage; the Revolution; culture and the arts; and Mexican politics.

11 **The dynamics of Mexican nationalism.**
Frederick C. Turner. Chapel Hill, North Carolina: University of North Carolina, 1968. 350p. bibliog.
A slightly dated but nonetheless useful historical study of the origins of Mexican nationalism. It focuses on the Revolution of 1910 and the state-building activities of the Revolutionary intellectuals. Nationalism should in this sense be understood not so much as anti-foreign sentiment but rather as an attempt to develop a specifically Mexican consciousness.

Travellers' Accounts

12   **An American in Maximilian's Mexico, 1865-1866: the diaries of William Marshall Anderson.**
William Marshall Anderson, edited by Ramon Eduardo Ruiz.   San Marino, California: Huntington Library, 1959. 132p. map. bibliog.
The diaries of an American archaeologist in Mexico commissioned by Maximilian in 1865 to survey Coahuila for colonization by the Confederation. An excellent picture of Mexico during the Juárez–Maximilian era.

13   **Lost cities of the Maya: new horizons.**
Claude Baudez, Sydney Picasso, translated from the French by Caroline Palmer.   London: Thames and Hudson, 1992. 173p.
Two French archaeologists have written this account of southeastern Mexico. The book contains some 40 pages of travellers' accounts, a history of the discovery of Yucatán, and many spectacular illustrations in both colour and black and white. Another volume of similar interest is *Incidents of travel in Yucatán*, written by John L. Stephens and illustrated by Frederick Catherwood (Mexico City: Panorama Editorial, 1991. 2nd ed. 368p.) This work was originally published in 1843. Stephens was the explorer who rediscovered the lost cities of the Maya. Here he discusses his visits to the south of Mexico in 1839 and 1841. Catherwood's illustrations add to the work. Stephens provides a graphic account of his discovery although he admits to some bewilderment as to the significance of his findings. The Panorama volume is nicely produced.

14   **Six months' residence and travels in Mexico: containing remarks on the
      present state of New Spain, its natural productions, state of society,
      manufactures, trade, agriculture and antiques etc.**
      William Bullock.   London: J. Murray, 1824. 532p.
The title contains a full description of contents. The British were very keen to take
advantage of Mexican independence, but their commercial and diplomatic efforts
suffered a number of setbacks thereafter.

15   **Life in Mexico during a residence of two years in that country.**
      Mme Fanny Calderón de La Barca with an introduction by Sir Nicholas
      Cheetham.   London; Melbourne; Auckland; Johannesburg: Century
      Hutchinson, 1987. 542p.
This is one of the best of all of Mexico's many travel memoirs; the picture which it
provides is astonishingly vivid, varied and well observed. The Mexico which Fanny
Calderón saw contained some very primitive features and an ever-present threat of
violence, but also some elements of culture and intellectual life. This work was
originally published in 1842. The author was born in Scotland and married a Spanish
diplomat in 1838. She accompanied him when he was posted to Mexico in 1839.

16   **Mexico south; the isthmus of Tehuantepec.**
      Miguel Covarrubias.   London: KPI, 1986. 427p.
This book was first published in 1946 but it has now been re-issued. It contains an
evocative though perhaps idealized account of ordinary life and customs in southern
Mexico, and a history of the native peoples of the region. Covarrubias was a
distinguished intellectual and literary figure in post-war Mexico.

17   **The chronicles of Michoacán.**
      Edited and translated by Eugene R. Crane, Reginald C. Reindorp.
      Norman, Oklahoma: University of Oklahoma Press, 1970. 250p. map.
      bibliog. (Civilization of the American Indian Series, 98).
This is a translation of the *Relación de Michoacán or Description of the Ceremonies,
Rites, Population and Government of the Indians of the Province of Mechuacan*. It was
written between 1529 and 1541 by a Jesuit priest and is a definitive historical source
relating to the conquest of the Tarascan Indians.

18   **The Bernal Díaz chronicle: the true story of the conquest of Mexico.**
      Bernal Díaz del Castillo, translated from the Spanish by Albert Idell.
      Garden City, New York: Doubleday, 1956. 414p. maps.
The chronicles of one of the *conquistadores* who fought with Cortés. Some of the
descriptions in the account are extremely valuable, particularly those relating to the
Valley of Mexico at that time. The pre-Conquest population of Mexico has been
estimated to have been as high as 11 million, with a considerable variety of indigenous
cultures and languages. This translation was based on a modern Spanish version first
published in Mexico in 1950.

19 **Mexican mosaic.**
Rodney Gallop. London: Quiller Press, 1990. 2nd ed. 299p.

Rodney Gallop spent three years in Mexico as a diplomat during the 1930s and first published this account in 1939. While limited in some ways by the perspective of the author, this is nevertheless an important eye-witness account of Mexico in the 1930s. The focus is very much on the character and life of Mexico's Indian communities. The title of the work emphasizes the ethnic diversity of Mexico at the time.

20 **The Lawless Roads.**
Graham Greene. New York; London: Penguin, 1979. 3rd ed. 224p.

In 1938, Graham Greene travelled extensively in Chiapas and Tabasco in southern Mexico. He was interested mainly by the religious issue, and in 1940 he published *The Power and the Glory* which tells the story of a priest caught up in the anti-Catholic persecutions of the period. *The Lawless Roads* is a non-fiction account of his time in Mexico.

21 **Inside Latin America.**
John Gunther. London: Hamish Hamilton, 1942. 375p. bibliog.

John Gunther was, in his day, a prominent American journalist and travel writer. About sixty pages of this book are on Mexico, which he visited in 1941. The account is at times naïve, but at others very perceptive. It provides an account of an interview with President Avila Camacho (1940-46).

22 **Travels in the interior of Mexico in 1825, 1826, 1827 and 1828.**
Robert William Hale Hardy. Glorieta, New Mexico: Rio Grande Press, 1977. 558p. (Rio Grande Classic).

This diary was first published in 1829. It covers the experiences of a commercial traveller based in Baja California in the immediate post-independence period in Mexico.

23 **Beyond the Mexique Bay.**
Aldous Huxley. Aylesbury, England: Triad/Paladin, 1984. 189p.

Huxley was one of several British intellectuals who visited and wrote about Mexico in the 1930s. Most of the account is taken up with the author's travels in southern Mexico, though there are a number of asides on other issues. This is a reprint of a volume originally published in 1934.

24 **Unknown Mexico: explorations in the Sierra Madre and other regions 1890-1898.**
Karl Sofus Lumholtz. New York: Dover Publications, 1987. 2 vols. maps.

Karl Lumholtz was a Norwegian explorer, naturalist and anthropologist. These two volumes provide extensive material on a number of Indian societies in the west and northwest of Mexico. It contains the first illustrations of West Mexican shaft tomb figures and a good deal of information on the languages, lifestyles, customs, myths and traditions of the various Indian tribes.

25 **New trails in Mexico: an account of one year's exploration in northwestern Sonora, Mexico, and southwestern Arizona 1909-10.**
Karl Sofus Lumholtz.   New York: C. Scribner's Sons, 1912. 411p.
A further account by the same author, of travels just over a decade later, covering the far northwest of Mexico.

26 **Into a desert place: a 3000 mile walk around the coast of Baja California.**
Graham Mackintosh.   London: Unwin Hyman, 1988. 312p.
An account of the author's travels and adventures. These include numerous encounters with the local life, including fish, rattlesnakes and scorpions.

27 **The Cora Indians of Baja California; the *relación* of Ignacio Maria Napoli, September 20, 1721.**
Ignacio Maria Napoli, translated from the Spanish and edited by James Robert Moriaty III, Benjamin F. Smith.   Los Angeles, California: Dawson's Book Shop, 1970. 76p. map. bibliog. (Baja California Travels Series, no. 19).
Ignacio Maria Napoli was a Jesuit priest in Mexico in the eighteenth century. This volume is made up of his observations, to which there is added a short biography of the priest.

28 **Missionary in Sonora: the travel reports of Joseph Och S.J., 1755-1767.**
Joseph Och, translated from the German by Theodore E. Treutlein.
San Francisco, California: California Historical Society, 1965. 196p.
A travel account by a German Jesuit missionary. It is particularly rich in its descriptions of Mexico City and the towns along his route to Sonora, and also of the Indians of Sonora.

29 **Sonora: a description of the province.**
Ignaz Pfefferkorn, translated from the German by Theodore Fontana.
Tucson, Arizona: University of Arizona Press, 1989. 329p. map.
Father Ignaz Pfefferkorn was an eighteenth-century Jesuit missionary who spent eleven years in Sonora. His insights into the relations between the Indians, the missionaries and the Spanish are particularly valuable. The work was first translated in 1949 and has now been republished.

30 **The life of Graham Greene. Volume 1, 1904-39.**
Norman Sherry.   London; New York: Penguin, 1990. 783p.
One part of this book, amounting to some 80 pages, deals with Graham Greene's experiences in Mexico. The author re-traces Greene's steps and meets some of the people who appeared, in fictionalized form, in *The Power and the Glory*. The real lives of Greene's original figures were in many cases startlingly different from the fiction.

31 **Anahuac: or Mexico and Mexicans, ancient and modern.**
Edward Burnett Tylor.   New York: Bergman, 1970. 344p. map.
The description of a journey in Mexico made by Edward Tylor and companions, largely on horseback, between March and June 1856. The work was originally published in 1861 and has now been reprinted.

32 **The North American sketches of R.B. Cunninghame Graham.**
Edited by John Walker.   Edinburgh: Handsel Press, 1986. 145p. map. bibliog.
In 1879 Gabriela and Robert Cunninghame Graham spent two years travelling in Mexico and the southwest of the United States. The stories and sketches in this volume date from then, although they were originally published over an extended period between 1890 and 1932.

33 **Robbery under law; the Mexican object lesson.**
Evelyn Waugh.   London: Hutchinson, 1939. 279p.
Waugh eventually felt ashamed of this book because it was commissioned by British oil interests following their expropriation in 1938. In fact Waugh is not very perceptive about oil, but he has a lot to say about Mexican Catholicism, the US tourist trade and a variety of other topics.

Tourism and Travel Guides

34 **Guía de murales del centro histórico de la ciudad de México.** (Guide to
    the murals in the historic centre of Mexico City.)
    Edited by Esther Acevedo (et al.).   Mexico City: Universidad
    Iberoamericana, 1984. 143p. maps.

The editor and her team have investigated every mural in the historic centre of Mexico
City. The essays in the volume are historical rather than critical.

35 **Frommer's '93. Mexico on $50 a day.**
    Marta Adair.   New York; London: Prentice Hall Travel, 1992. 787p.

As can be seen from the number of pages in this guide, the coverage is very extensive
and detailed. The budget of $50 a day is, however, possibly optimistic when one bears
in mind the recent rate of inflation in Mexico.

36 **Birnbaum's Ixtapa and Zihuantejo 1992.**
    Stephen Birnbaum, Alexandra Birnbaum.   New York: Harper Collins,
    1991. 181p. maps.

These Mexican towns rarely get independent treatment, so this introduction is
welcome. Much of the book is a guide about 'how to . . .' rather than 'what there is',
though the latter question is far from ignored.

37 **Birnbaum's Cancún, Cozumel and Isla Mujeres, 1992.**
    Stephen Birnbaum, Alexandra Birnbaum.   New York: Harper Collins,
    1991. 221p. maps.

As with the Birnbaum guide to Ixtapa and Zihuantejo (q.v.), about one half of the
contents of the book are travel tips and advice, and the other half is a guide to the area
itself.

38 **The Insider's Guide to Mexico.**
Peggy Bond, Mike Bond, with photographs by Nick Wheeler.
Ashburne, England: MPC, 1992. 320p. maps.
A standard but full and comprehensive travel guide. It is organized into regional
sections and strengthened by many maps and illustrations.

39 **Mexico and Central American handbook.**
Edited by Ben Box. Bath, England: Trade and Travel Publications,
1993. 3rd ed. 797p. maps.
Information on Mexico used to be included in the *South American Handbook*. This
grew to be too large, however, and now different volumes are produced on South
America and on Mexico and Central America. The work itself is a classic. It is based
almost entirely on travellers' reports of their own experiences.

40 **La ruta *maya*.** (The Maya Road.)
Tom Brosnahan. Victoria, Australia: Lonely Planet, 1991. 531p. maps.
About one half of this book covers Mexico; the rest details further south. It is a
relatively specialized travel work by an experienced traveller. An Australian
contribution to this increasingly popular genre.

41 **Hippocrene companion guide to Mexico.**
Michael Burke. New York: Hippocrene, 1992. 320p. maps.
This is a thematic introduction to Mexico more than just a travel guide. It includes
sections relating to the country's history, geography, society, religion and political
system.

42 **1993, Let's go, Mexico.**
Edited by Rene Celaya (et al.). Cambridge, Massachusetts: [n.p.];
London: Pan. 568p. maps.
The book is mostly about Mexico though it does cover Belize and Guatemala as well.
It is written in part by students from Harvard University and is aimed at low-budget
travellers.

43 **No frills guide to hiking in Mexico.**
Jim Conrad. Chalfont St Peter, England: Bradt, 1991. 150p. maps.
The first half of the book is taken up with general advice about what to bring and so
forth. The second half is a detailed look at hikes in several different parts of Mexico.

44 **The Maya Road: Mexico, Belize, Guatemala.**
Jim Conrad. Chalfont St Peter, England: Bradt, 1992. 274p. maps.
A guide for the more determined hiker or traveller rather than the casual tourist. The
information is detailed and specific.

45 **Fodor's Mexico 93.**
New York: Fodor Trade Travel Press, 1992. 555p. maps.
The usual Fodor mixture of history, reference material, shopping tips, transportation details. The book has been considerably expanded in recent years.

46 **Welcome to Mexico.**
Mona King. London: Collins, 1986. 127p.
A concise and well-illustrated pocket guide to Mexico, focusing largely on places to visit. The book is organized by region.

47 **Cancún handbook, plus Mexico's Caribbean coast.**
Chicki Mallan. Chico, California: Moon, 1990. 257p. maps.
A detailed survey of an increasingly popular tourist destination. One of the more specialized guidebooks.

48 **Fodor's 1993. Cancún, Cozumel, Yucatán Peninsula, with trips to the Mayan ruins.**
Erica Melzer. New York: Fodor Trade Travel Press, 1992. 227p. maps.
A more specialized guide in the Fodor style and covering southeastern Mexico.

49 **Mexico. APA insight guides.**
Karl Muller, Guillermo García Oropeza. New York: APA, 1991. 431p. maps.
A very nicely illustrated work. The book is thematic in places, with a proportion of the book taken up with short essays on music, culture, sport, bullfighting and so on.

50 **Maya missions: exploring the Spanish colonial churches of Yucatán.**
Richard Perry, Rosalind Perry. Santa Barbara, California: Espadana, 1988. 249p.
A practical and detailed guide to the colonial churches of the Yucatán. These churches vary in style from the grand monasteries and town churches to rustic chapels. They were originally built by the Franciscan friars and their Mayan disciples. The guide takes the form of six itineraries.

51 **Fodor's Acapulco, Ixtapa and Zihuantejo: the best of resorts, beaches and hotels.**
Anya Schiffrin, Wendy Ortiz de Montellano. New York: Fodor's Trade and Travel Publications, 1992. 5th ed. 137p.
The title of this guide is self-explanatory. These are the main resort towns of the central Pacific coast. Ixtapa and Zihuantejo have been developed for large-scale tourism relatively recently.

52 **Mexico City.**
Edited by Jutta Schulz.   Singapore: APA, 1991. 278p. maps. (Inslght
City series).

This guidebook is strengthened by a series of short essays from a range of writers including the important Mexican novelist and social critic Elena Ponietowska. The essays cover the city's history, people and places, surroundings, art and culture. This is probably the best guide for anyone intending to spend a significant amount of time in the Federal District.

53 **Ancient Mexico: Aztec, Mistec and Maya landscapes.**
George E. Stewart, Winfield Swanson.   New Brunswick, New Jersey;
London: Rutgers University Press, 1992. 124p.

This is a travel guide written largely by professional geographers. They describe ten different locations or journeys which take in some of the most important archaeological sites. As might be expected, the discussion is well informed and the presentation of the guide somewhat austere.

54 **Mexico.**
Catherine Thompson, Charlotte Thompson.   London: Cadogan
Guides, 1991. 538p. maps.

A regionally organized and competently written guidebook. As well as reporting on what to see and where to stay, the authors do give significant attention to historical and cultural dimensions of Mexico.

55 **Baja California: a survival kit.**
Scott Wayne.   Victoria, Australia: Lonely Planet, 1991. 2nd ed. 227p.
maps.

This is one of the few travel guides to this northwestern part of Mexico, which is much less populous than most of the rest of Mexico. It attracts visitors for its beaches, flora and fauna rather than for its historical monuments.

56 **Living in Mexico: a complete guide.**
Michael Zamba.   Lincolnwood, Illinois: LTC, 1992.

This book is not so much for short-stay travellers as for people thinking of long stays or even retirement in Mexico. There is coverage of the legal system, health care and other issues of concern mainly to residents, as well as sections on golf and travel.

Geography

General

57 **An evaluation of industrial estates in Mexico 1970-85.**
Ismael Aguilar-Barajas. Oxford: Pergamon, 1990. 187p. bibliog.
(Progress in planning, vol. 34, part 2).
The author examines two cases where industrial estates were set up in order to try to decentralize Mexico's manufacturing structure. One of these is Morelia, Michoacán and the other the city of Aguascalientes. The author believes that the policy itself was beneficial, but that it had little effect because of more general pressures making for centralization.

58 **The central desert of Baja California: demography and ecology.**
Homer Aschmann. Riverside, California: Manessier, 1967. 315p.
maps. bibliog.
This study first appeared in 1959, and has therefore dated slightly. However, it contains much useful information. The title is largely self-explanatory.

59 **La ciudad de México 1325-1982.** (Mexico City 1325-1982.)
Fernando Benitez. Mexico City: Salvat, 1981. 3 vols.
A well-illustrated, well-researched and comprehensive study of the evolution of Mexico City during the last half-millennium. The work incorporates a range of viewpoints and a wealth of detail.

60 **Plans and planmaking in the valley of Mexico: the evolution of a planning process.**
Timothy Campbell, David Wilk. Berkeley, California: Institute of Urban and Regional Development, University of California, 1986. 51p. bibliog. maps. (Working Paper 450).
The argument of this study is that Mexico has some well-trained planners but that there remain real problems with planning implementation. This is why the ecological problems facing the federal capital are so severe.

61 **The state of the Rio Grande/Rio Bravo: a study of water resource issues along the Texas/Mexico border.**
David J. Eaton, John M. Andersen. Tucson, Arizona: University of Arizona Press, 1987. 331p. maps. bibliog.
An impressively thorough and comprehensive study of water supply and treatment along the Texas–Mexico border. It considers groundwater as well as surface water, and also discusses the relationship between water supply and disease and the impact of rapid population growth on water supply. There are over 100 pages of tables.

62 **A guide to the historical geography of New Spain.**
Peter Gerhard. Cambridge, England; New York: Cambridge University Press, 1972. 476p. maps. bibliog. (Cambridge Latin American Studies, no. 14).
A historical geography of Mexico between 1521 and 1821, documenting the various changes and adding in considerable detail. The area covered today makes up central and southern Mexico, excluding the Yucatán.

63 **Planning for the international border metropolis: trans-boundary options in the San Diego–Tijuana region.**
Edited by Lawrence Arthur Herzog. San Diego, California: Center for US–Mexican Studies, 1986. 108p. bibliog. (Monograph Series, no. 19).
This work defines and assesses possible responses to problems arising from the emergence of large and very rapidly growing conurbations across the US–Mexican border. The San Diego–Tijuana conurbation is a case in point.

64 **Industrialization and secondary cities in Central Mexico.**
Rene Vleugels. Saarbrücken, Germany; Fort Lauderdale, Texas: Verlag Brietenbach, 1990. 269p. bibliog. (Nijmegen Studies in Development and Cultural Change).
The author considers the period 1940-85. He presents a great deal of data to show that, after around 1970, manufacturing output grew fastest in the cities outside the Federal District. Several regional growth centres, Queretaro, San Luis Potosí, Cuernavaca, formed rapidly. Even rapid industrial growth did not, however, create enough employment for a hugely expanding population.

65 **Mexico City; the production and reproduction of an urban environment.**
Peter Ward. London: Belhaven, 1990. 262p. bibliog.

Mexico City is now one of the largest conurbations in the world. Ward seeks to understand its structure. He considers such issues as social unrest and political control, transportation, the provision of urban services generally. The book can be recommended to the general reader as well as to specialists.

66 **Exports and local development. Mexico's new *maquiladoras*.**
Patricia Ann Wilson. Austin, Texas: University of Texas Press, 1992. 161p. bibliog. map.

The Mexican *maquiladora* sector is based on the export of manufactured goods to the United States under special provisions providing guaranteed access and relatively favourable tax treatment. Patricia Wilson seeks to understand how far the rapidly growing sector has created spin-offs helpful to Mexican development in its broadest sense.

67 **The social ecology and economic development of Ciudad Juárez.**
Edited by Gay Young. Boulder, Colorado: Westview, 1986. 171p. bibliog. (Westview Special Studies on Latin America and the Caribbean).

This is a collection of seven chapters which analyse the Mexican part of a conurbation which stretches across the border in two directions. The contributors analyse the social, economic and physical structure of the city.

Maps and atlases

68 **Atlas geográfico, estadístico e histórico de la república mexicana.**
(Geographical, statistical and historical atlas of the Mexican republic.)
Antonio Garcia y Cubas. Mexico City: Angel Porrua, 1989. 2nd ed. 72p.

This is a facsimile of a work originally produced in 1858. The map covers each of the Mexican states and territories in existence at the time of publication. Each map is bordered by printed text giving information on a range of issues.

69 **Atlas arqueológico del estado de Yucatán.** (Archaeological atlas of Yucatán.)
Silvia Garza Tarazona de Gonzalez, Edward Barna Kurjack Bacso.
Mexico City: INAH, 1980. 249p. bibliog.

An attempt to present all of the main archaeological sites in Yucatán in a comprehensive way. The book also contains detailed analysis of the sites themselves, their settlement patterns and characteristics.

70 **Political essay on the kingdom of New Spain.**
Alexander von Humboldt, translated from the French by John Black.
New York: AMS, 1966. 3 vols. maps.
This is von Humboldt's classic contribution to the geography of Mexico. Von Humboldt spent nearly a year in Mexico during 1803-4, collecting information on social and economic aspects of Mexico, new plants and animals and also on measurements of the territory. This work includes detailed maps based on astronomical as well as mathematical measurement. There is also a description of the silver wealth of Mexico, which led to a considerable increase in European investment, and a passionate denunciation of the system of slavery in Mexico, which had little impact upon contemporaries.

71 **Atlas nacional del medio físico.** (National physical atlas.)
Instituto Nacional de Estadística, Geografía e Informática. Aguas Calientes, Mexico: INEGI, 1981. 224p.
This volume contains eleven specialized maps covering Mexican territory. Sets include topographical, colour relief, geostatistical, climate, mean temperatures, annual rainfall, geological information, soil type, land use and tourist attractions.

72 **Atlas of Mexico.**
James B. Pick, Edgar W. Butler, Elizabeth L. Lanzer. Boulder, Colorado: Westview Press, 1989. 367p. maps.
This is a very extensive database drawn mainly from the 1980 census. There is a wealth of statistical detail on a whole range of different issues – demographic, cultural, economic, social and political. Some of the work could, however, usefully be updated.

73 **Ciudad de México; áreas metropolitana y alrededores.** (Mexico City: the metropolis and its environs.)
Mexico City: Guía Roji, 1990. maps.
Street guide, metro guide and maps, including a large-scale plan (1 to 20,000) of the central streets. This is a very practical and necessary publication for anybody intending to spend considerable time in the federal capital.

74 **Sintesis geográfica de Coahuila.** (A geographical synthesis of Coahuila.)
Secretaria de Planficación y Presupuesto. Mexico City: SPP, 1983. 139p. maps.
A detailed, mainly physical geography of this important northern state of Mexico. Apart from the maps themselves, there are many illustrations.

75 **Map of the ruins of Dzibilshaltan, Yucatán.**
George E. Stuart (et al.). New Orleans, Louisiana: Tulane University Press and National Geographic Society, 1979. 34 maps. (Middle American Research Institute, no. 47).
A thorough and extensive cartographical study of an important Maya site.

Flora and Fauna

76 **A Spanish–English glossary of Mexican flora and fauna.**
Louise L. Choenhals.   Mexico City: Instituto Lingüístico de Verano,
1988. 647p. bibliog.
It is notoriously difficult to translate local names of flora and fauna, but the author has
made a contribution to this field by assembling this compilation of local (Spanish)
names for flora and fauna.

77 **A field guide to the birds of Mexico; including all birds occurring from
the northern border of Mexico to the southern border of Nicaragua.**
Ernest Preston Edwards.   [n.p.]: The author, 1972. 300p. maps.
Over 10,000 Mexican birds are described and illustrated in sketches and colour plates.
Much useful information on colour, voice and habitat, etc. is given in the descriptions.
The birds are arranged by family.

78 **People of the desert and sea: ethnobotany of the Seri Indians.**
Richard S. Fedger, Mary Beck Moser.   Tucson, Arizona: University of
Arizona Press, 1985. 435p. bibliog.
A study of plant life in the area of northwest Mexico occupied by the Seri, followed by
a discussion of the rôle of these herbs in Seri culture. The work is essentially
descriptive, very detailed and heavily illustrated.

79 **90 years and 535 miles: vegetation changes along the Mexican border.**
Roger R. Humphrey.   Albuquerque, New Mexico: University of New
Mexico, 1987. 448p. bibliog.
This book is composed largely of 203 paired photographs which show the nature of
vegetation change along the US border between the Rio Grande and the Colorado
River. The photographs were originally taken in 1892-93 by boundary markers. New
photographs, from the same locations, were taken in 1983-84.

80 **Wildlife of Mexico: the game birds and mammals.**
A. Starker Leopold.   Berkeley, California: University of California Press, 1959. 568p.

An illustrated and extremely extensive work on the distribution of animals in Mexico. This is still in some ways the definitive volume.

81 **A handbook of Mexican roadside flora.**
Charles T. Mason, Patricia B. Mason.   Tucson, Arizona: University of Arizona Press, 1987. 380p. bibliog.

The number of plant species found in Mexico is so great that even a book of 380 pages needs to be very selective. This guide has concentrated mainly on shrubs, trees and other perennials. Local names are given, and there is abundant illustration.

82 **A naturalists' Mexico.**
Roland H. Wauer, foreword by Victor Emmanuel.   College Station, Texas: Texas A and M University Press, 1992. 304p. bibliog.

This is a valuable general account of Mexico's natural environment, organized by region. It includes discussion of the arid lowlands of Mexico, the coastal plains, the highlands and the jungles. The word pictures are vivid and the book also includes photographs in black and white as well as colour. There is no real rival as a general introduction in the English language.

83 **An introduction to the orchids of Mexico.**
Leon Wiard.   Ithaca, New York: Cornell University Press, 1987. 239p. bibliog.

There are 154 species of orchid which grow in Mexico. This book gives information on the geography of Mexico, and the taxonomy of orchids as well as advice on their cultivation. There are also very many colour photographs of the plant and close-ups of individual flowers.

Archaeology and Prehistory

The Aztecs

84 **Aztec sculpture.**
Elizabeth Baquedano.   London: British Museum Publications, 1984.
96p.
This is primarily an account of the origins of the Aztec pantheon and a discussion of its
accompanying theology. Many of the sculptured gods have only recently been
discovered. There are a number of illustrations in black and white.

85 **The Aztecs.**
Frances F. Berdan.   New York: Chelsea House, 1989. 112p. bibliog.
This is a relatively short work intended mainly for the general reader. It is a social and
political history of the Aztecs which covers their architecture, way of life and religion

86 **The Aztecs of central Mexico: an imperial society.**
Frances Berdan.   New York: Holt, Rinehart and Winston, 1982. 195p.
maps. bibliog. (Case Studies in Cultural Anthropology).
A concise description of Aztec society, including discussion of Aztec history,
settlement patterns, economy, social structure, daily life, politics, religion, cultural
achievements and the aftermath of the Spanish Conquest.

87 **The city state in Central Mexico at the time of the Spanish Conquest.**
Warwick Bray.   *Journal of Latin American Studies*, vol. 4, no. 2 (1972),
p. 161-85.
A discussion of the respective value of written sources on the one hand and
archaeological ones on the other. Argues that archaeology is necessary to understand
the more ordinary facts of everyday life, such as the size and character of urban
settlements. Discusses some of the main research under way at the time of writing.

88 **The jade steps; a ritual life of the Aztecs.**
David C. Brundage, foreword by Arthur J. O. Anderson, illustrations by
Newverne Covington.   Salt Lake City, Utah: University of Utah Press,
1986. 280p. bibliog.
A discussion of Aztec religion. The focus is on cults, ritual renewals, definitions of the
divine, temples and idols. There is a discussion of the nature of the priesthood and the
place of human sacrifice.

89 **To change place: Aztec ceremonial landscapes.**
David Carrasco.   Boulder, Colorado: University of Colorado Press,
1991. 254p.
This book is made up of a series of essays resulting from a research project involving
the University of Colorado and the Mexican Instituto Nacional de Antropologia e
Historia. The book concentrates especially on spatial aspects of ceremony and religion.
The studies provide a wider emphasis on the interrelationship between peripheral
ceremonial centres.

90 **Aztecs; an interpretation.**
Inga Clendinnen.   Cambridge, England; New York: Cambridge
University Press, 1991. 365p. bibliog.
An attempt to go beyond the study of human sacrifices in order to understand the
religious context and the social implications of belief systems. The author seeks to
empathize as far as possible with these belief systems. The book is largely made up of
exploratory essays which seek to go to the limit of our contemporary knowledge of
these societies.

91 **The festival cycle of the Aztec Codex Borbonicus.**
Christopher Couch.   Oxford, England: British Archaeological Reports,
1985. 115p.
A heavily illustrated work which discusses the third section of the Codex Borbonicus,
which is essentially a calendar. This section describes Aztec society and religion and
gives particular attention to the annual cycle of Mexican festivals.

92 **The Aztecs; the history of the Indies of New Spain.**
Diego Durán, translated from the Spanish by Doris Heyden, Fernando
Horcasitas.   New York: Orion, 1964. 381p. maps. bibliog.
Diego Durán was a Dominican friar and missionary. He wrote this account between
1574 and 1581. The work then disappeared into an archive in Spain and was only
rediscovered in the nineteenth century. Much of the work, which is principally based
on oral Aztec sources, is taken up with accounts of war and conflict, and includes an
Aztec perspective on the Spanish Conquest.

93 **The Aztecs.**
Brian Fagan.   Oxford, England: W. H. Freeman, 1984. 322p.
The author is primarily an archaeologist, but also writes as a historian in order to
produce a scholarly yet readable account of Aztec history, customs, religion and life in
general. The book also discusses the impact of the Spanish Conquest.

94 **The Aztec kings: the construction of rulership in Mexican history.**
Susan D. Gillespie. Tucson, Arizona: University of Arizona Press,
1989. 272p. bibliog.

Although the Aztec codices offer a wealth of information, one problem is to
distinguish myth from historical fact. This book seeks to use genealogy to understand
rules of succession and intermarriage. The author focuses mainly on the female lines
about which information is more abundant. Dr Gillespie believes that here is to be
found an important key to understanding both history itself and the way in which it was
manipulated to communicate basic ideas about the character of the society.

95 **Aztec warfare: imperial expansion and political control.**
Ross Hassig. Norman, Oklahoma: University of Oklahoma, 1988. 404p.
bibliog. maps. (The Civilization of the American Indian Series, no. 188).

The primary focus of this work is the history of Aztec expansionism. It is heavily
documented. The author also looks at the relationship between politics and war.

96 **Aztec ruins on the Animas: excavated, preserved and interpreted.**
Robert H. Lister, Florence C. Lister. Albuquerque, New Mexico:
University of New Mexico Press, 1987. 120p.

A description of the ruins on the western side of the Río de las Animas Perdidas in
New Mexico. However, as the authors point out, these seem to have been connected
with the Anasazi Indians rather than with the Aztecs as was hitherto believed.

97 **The Great Temple of the Aztecs: treasures of Tenochtitlán.**
Eduardo Matos Moctezuma, translated from the Spanish by Doris
Heyden. London: Thames and Hudson, 1988. 192p. bibliog.

The city of Tenochtitlán was founded by the Aztecs in or around 1325 AD. It became
the most important Aztec city until the Spanish Conquest. Professor Matos is the
Director of the National Museum of Anthropology in Mexico and was in charge of the
excavations of Tenochtitlán. In this much illustrated account he describes the work
undertaken there and explains the significance of some of these findings for the study
of Aztec civilization as a whole.

98 **The Aztecs.**
Eduardo Matos Moctezuma. [n.p.]: Rizzoli International Publications,
1989. 239p.

The author examines the evolution of societies in Mesoamerica, the origin of the
Aztecs, and the reasons for their ascendancy. He also explains Aztec social and
economic organization, their conception of the cosmos and their art.

99 **Law and politics in Aztec Texcoco.**
Jerome Offner. Cambridge, England: Cambridge University Press,
1983. 340p. bibliog. (Cambridge Latin American Studies, no. 44).

Texcoco was the second most important Aztec city. Offner focuses particularly on the
legal organization and procedure of Aztec society. This had serious legal norms; cases
were judged by established legal rules rather than through ordeals or supernatural
guidance. Law was principally a means of social control.

100 **Aztec medicine, health and nutrition.**
Bernard R. Ortiz de Montellano. New Brunswick, New Jersey;
London: Rutgers University Press, 1990. 269p.

An enquiry into the level of health of the Aztecs and into the effectiveness of pre-Hispanic medicine. The author draws on early Spanish written records which tell us a good deal about Aztec medical practices. The author concludes that the Aztecs were reasonably healthy. He discusses a range of concepts such as nutrition and population structure, in addition to the predominantly herbal medicines in use. The book contains a wealth of data and avoids sweeping generalizations.

101 **Aztec thought and culture: a study of the ancient Nahuatl mind.**
Miguel León Portilla. Norman, Oklahoma: University of Oklahoma
Press, 1963. 241p. (Civilization of the American Indian Series, no. 67).

An adaptation of a work, originally published in 1956 under the title *La Filosofía Nahuatl*, which was based on the translation of more than ninety native documents. Aztec ideas on man and religion are also discussed.

102 **The Aztecs.**
Richard F. Townsend. London: Thames and Hudson, 1992. 217p.
bibliog.

This book offers a good general synthesis of our knowledge of the Aztecs. It starts with an account of the Spanish Conquest and then looks backwards to discuss issues involving trade, pre-Hispanic warfare and conquest, and religious observance. The work contains 143 illustrations.

103 **Aztecs of Mexico; origin, rise and fall of the Aztec nation.**
G. C. Valliant, revised by Suzannah B. Valliant. New York:
Doubleday, 1962. rev. ed. 312p. maps. bibliog.

A classic account when first published in 1944, revised and updated by Suzannah Valliant after her husband's death. The first half of the book is broadly chronological while the second deals with social, religious and cultural aspects. There is a final chapter on the Aztecs after the Spanish Conquest.

104 **The Aztec arrangement: the social history of pre-Spanish Mexico.**
Rudolph van Zantwijk. Norman, Oklahoma: University of Oklahoma
Press, 1985. 346p. bibliog.

The author has a somewhat unusual view of the origins of the Aztecs. He argues that their system was formed from the integration of groups from divergent ethnic backgrounds rather than from a single group. The myth of origin from pilgrimage was, the author believes, deliberately created by Itzcoatzin and his co-rulers in or around 1431.

The Maya

105 The origins of Maya civilization.
Edited by Richard E. W. Adams. Albuquerque, New Mexico:
University of New Mexico Press, 1977. 465p. maps. bibliog. (School of
American Research Book, Advanced Seminar Series).
This volume contains discussion of cultural comparisons betwen the Maya and their
neighbours (the Olmec, Mexic-Zoque and Izapa), as well as the early formative stages
of the Maya civilization in different parts of the Maya lowlands.

106 Maya cities; placemaking and urbanization.
George F. Andrews. Norman, Oklahoma: University of Oklahoma
Press, 1975. 468p. bibliog. (Civilization of the American Indian Series,
vol. 131).
The author, an architect, presents an analysis of Mayan cities from the point of view of
their evolution as expressions of the Mayan view of the world. A nicely illustrated
volume, this is a contribution both to archaeology and the study of urbanization.

107 The archaeological ceramics of Becan, Campeche, Mexico.
Joseph W. Ball. New Orleans, Louisiana: Middle American Research
Institute, Tulane University, 1977. 190p. maps. bibliog. (Middle
American Research Institute, Tulane University, Publication no. 423).
An important source work on ceramics from a site in the central Mayan lowlands.

108 The Maya.
Michael D. Coe. London: Thames and Hudson, 1980. 2nd ed. 180p.
maps. bibliog.
A revised and enlarged version of his earlier work which was published in 1966. We
now know considerably more about Mayan hieroglyphic writing and iconography than
we did then. We also understand dynastic history much better. These new insights have
been added to the earlier standard work.

109 Ancient Maya writing and calligraphy.
Michael D. Coe. *Visible Language*, vol. 5, no. 4 (1971), p. 293-307.
This article explains the evolution of Mayan writing from a pictographic system to one
with phonetic-syllabic elements.

**110 *Cemote* of sacrifice: Maya treasures from the sacred well at Chichen
Iztá.**
Clemency Chase Coggins, Orrin C. Shane III. Austin, Texas:
University of texas Press, 1984. 176p. bibliog.
This is a full survey of the objects found at the excavations at the *cemote* of Chichen
Iztá. Over 200 items are illustrated. There are some problems with dating, due to the
shallowness of the soil at Chichen Iztá, but the authors attempt to attribute every piece
presented.

111 **Pre-Columbian population history in the Maya lowlands.**
Edited by Patrick Culbert, Don S. Rice. Albuquerque, New Mexico: University of New Mexico Press, 1990. 395p. maps. bibliog.

A collection of sixteen papers which discuss advances in our knowledge of Maya civilizations since the 1960s. Most of the papers involve discussion of particular mounds. An important if rather narrow study.

112 **Studies in the archaeology of coastal Yucatán and Campeche, Mexico.**
Jack D. Eaton, Joseph W. Ball. New Orleans, Louisiana: Tulane University, Middle American Research Institute, 1978. 146p. maps. (Publication no. 46).

This work contains two studies, one is an archaeological survey of the area, the other describes the archaeological pottery of the region. The period covered extends from the late formative to the colonial era.

113 **Maya: the riddle and rediscovery of a lost civilization.**
Charles Gallenkamp. New York: McKay, 1976. rev. ed. 220p. maps. bibliog.

A book written mainly for the general reader. The author explains recent discoveries which have helped us to understand the origin of the Maya culture, its achievements and its decline.

114 **Maya archaeology and ethnohistory.**
Edited by Norman Hammond, Gordon K. Willey. Austin, Texas: University of Texas Press, 1979. 292p. (Texas Pan-American Series).

A collection of scholarly papers representing research into the civilization of the Mayas, including both fieldwork and analysis of Codices. The papers were presented at the Second Cambridge Symposium on Recent Research in Mesoamerican Archaeology in August 1976.

115 **Maya resistance to Spanish rule and history on a colonial frontier.**
Grant D. Jones. Albuquerque, New Mexico: University of New Mexico Press, 1989. 365p. bibliog.

Jones concentrates on the southern Maya lowlands, which until this work appeared had received little attention. The area covered includes southern Yucatán as well as parts of what are now Guatemala. The author adopts a narrative approach.

116 **Cerro Palenque: power and identity on the Maya periphery.**
Rosemary A. Joyce. Austin, Texas: University of Texas, 1991. 176p. bibliog.

The book refers to excavations carried out in Palenque during 1980-83. It aims to use the information to reconstruct social activity in Palenque, and therefore is fairly broad in focus. Its conclusions are sometimes speculative, but the picture is of a vibrant and relatively complex society.

117 **The ancient Maya.**
Sylvanius Griswald Morley, George W. Brainerd, revised by Robert J.
Sharer. Stanford, California: Stanford University Press, 1983.
4th ed. 708p. bibliog.
This is a further edition of a classic work. Morley was a key figure in developing the
study of the Maya in the early years of this century. Most of his ideas are present in
this volume, the new edition of which is edited and extensively annotated by Robert
Sharer. Sharer introduces new information but tries wherever possible to keep the
original perspective untouched. More recent perspectives, however, place a greater
emphasis on the rôle of war in Mayan life.

118 **The sculpture of Palenque: the cross group, the north group, the**
olvidado **and other pieces.**
Merle Greene Robertson. Princeton, New Jersey: Princeton
University Press, 1991. 110p. bibliog.
A copiously illustrated book which is able to take advantage of recent scholarship in
order to update our knowledge of various aspects of Maya society. The evidence is
archaeological, iconographical and aesthetic.

119 **Late lowland Maya civilization; Classic to post-Classic.**
Edited by Jeremy Sabloff, E. Wyllys Andres. University of New
Mexico, Albuquerque, 1986. 526p. bibliog. (School of American
Research Advanced Seminar Series. A School of American Research
book).
This is a definitive study of what is now known from recent research. The survey covers
the post-800 AD period in the entire Maya lowlands area, as well as introducing some
new interpretations which suggest further directions for research.

120 **The pottery of Mayapan, including studies of ceramic material from**
Uxmal, Kabah and Chichen Itzá.
Robert Eliot Smith. Cambridge, Massachusetts: Peabody Museum of
Archaeology and Ethnology, Harvard University, 1971. 2 vols. bibliog.
(Papers of the Peabody Museum of Archaeology and Ethnology,
Harvard University, vol. 66).
A scholarly work, whose contents are largely explained in the title. Volume one is
made up of text while the second volume contains tables, charts and sketches of the
subject matter itself.

Other peoples

121 **The archaeology of West Mexico.**
Edited by Betty Bell. Ajijic, Mexico: Socieded de Estudios
Avanzados del Occidente de México, 1974. 252p. maps. bibliog.
A collection of papers presented to the Society for American Archaeology symposium
on West Mexico in 1970-71.

122 **Exploraciones arqueológicas en Dainzu, Oaxaca.** (Archaeological
explorations in Dainzu, Oaxaca.)
Ignacio Bernal, Arturo Oliveros. Mexico City: INAH, 1988. 58p.
bibliog.
Report on excavations in Dainzu, which is the western valley of Oaxaca. The site was
occupied from 600 BC to 1200 AD; it includes extensive terracing.

123 **Monte Albán: settlement patterns at the ancient Zapotec capital.**
Richard E. Blanton (et al.). New York: Academic Press, 1978. 451p.
maps. bibliog.
Monte Albán is a prominent series of interconnected hills near Oaxaca, occupied first
by Olmec and later by Zapotec cultures. Here it is analysed as a regional political
capital. Five authors contribute survey data and tabulations to provide conclusions on
the structure of the local population and the social system.

124 **In the land of the Olmec. v.1. The archaeology of San Lorenzo.**
Michael D. Coe, Richard A. Diehl. Austin, Texas: University of
Texas Press, 1980. 416p. maps. bibliog.
San Lorenzo is the earliest known Olmec centre, dating from as early as 1150 BC. At
that time the Olmec were the most advanced culture in Middle America. This study is
the result of a co-operative effort by Yale University, the Instituto Nacional de
Antropologia e Historia and the Instituto de Antropologia de Veracruz. This volume
provides a comprehensive report of the archaeological investigation carried out at the
site. It surveys the ceramics, carved monuments and relates them to the fauna to be
found today. An attempt is made to reconstruct Olmec lifestyles.

125 **In the land of the Olmec. v.2. The people of the river.**
Michael D. Coe, Richard A. Diehl. Austin, Texas: University of
Texas, 1980. 198p. bibliog. maps.
This volume uses photogrammetry to study the soils and vegetation of the Olmec site.
The authors also consider the modern agricultural, hunting-and-gathering patterns and
consider how far these provide us with a model for the Olmec.

126 **Prehistoric social, political and economic development in the area of the Tehuacán Valley: some results of the Palo Blanco project.**
Edited by Robert D. Crennan. Ann Arbor, Michigan: Museum of Anthropology, University of Michigan, 1979. 259p. (Research Reports in Archaeology, Contribution no. 6; Museum of Anthropology, University of Michigan, Technical Report no. 11).
A series of papers in both English and Spanish presenting reports on various aspects of a field study, conducted in the area of the Tehuacán Valley. The object of the study was to understand better how some of these complex societies evolved over time.

127 **The Tloltecs: until the fall of Tula.**
Nigel Davies. Norman, Oklahoma: University of Oklahoma Press, 1977. 533p. maps. bibliog.
The Tloltecs were a Nahuatl-speaking people who originally entered the central valley of Mexico from the north. However much of their history remains obscure. The author has sought to reconstruct Tloltec history from archaeological records and written sources. Where the evidence is contradictory, the author presents both sides. This is a very thorough study.

128 **Chalcatzingo: excavations on the Olmec frontier.**
David Grove. London: Thames and Hudson, 1984. 184p.
Chalcatzingo, located in the central valley of Mexico, was an important trading centre during the period 1500 to 500 BC. It was extensively excavated by the author and his Mexican colleagues during the 1970s. There are strong Olmec connections.

129 **Arqueologia del valle de las cuevas.** (Archaeology of the valley of the caves.)
Arturo Guevara Sanchez. Mexico City: INAH, 1988. 55p. bibliog.
The author gives a short description of caves in the state of Chiapas and of the objects found. There is also a brief description of the Paquime culture to which the discoveries relate.

130 **Cacaxtla: el lugar donde muere la lluvia en la tierra.** (Cacaxtla: the place where the rain dies in the earth.)
Sonia Lombardo de Ruiz (et al.). Mexico City: INAH, 1986. 554p. bibliog.
This is the first major study of this archaeological site, which is in the state of Tlaxcala. The site itself was discovered in the mid-1970s. The work includes an analysis of the main settlement patterns, pottery and ceramic technologies, and there is a lengthy iconography of well-preserved materials.

131 **Debating Oaxaca archaeology.**
Edited by Joyce Markus. Ann Arbor, Michigan: Anthropological
Papers, Museum of Anthropology, University of Michigan Press, 1990.
267p.
There are fifty pages of pictures of the valley of Oaxaca plus 217 pages of text. This is
an interesting example of debate among archaeologists about the significance of the
evidence for explaining the lives of pre-Hispanic Zapotec Indians. One key element of
the dispute concerns the extent of population growth, and its significance in explaining
Zapotec behaviour.

132 **Indian art and history: the testimony of prehispanic rock paintings in
Baja California.**
Clement W. Meighan. Los Angeles, California: Dawson's Book
Shop, 1969. 79p. bibliog. (Baja California Travels Series, no. 13).
An archaeological study of Indian history in Baja California, based on the evidence of
the life-size rock paintings of humans and animals. The volume is enhanced by
numerous photographs and sketches.

133 **Archaeology of the Morett Site, Colima.**
Clement W. Meighan. Berkeley, California: University of California,
1972. 211p. bibliog. (Publications in Anthropology, no. 7).
A report on pottery and figurines found in the area from the early and late periods,
and a discussion of resemblances to pottery from Central and Northern South
America.

134 **Mexica buried offerings: a historical and contextual analysis.**
Debra Nagao. Oxford, England: British Archaeological Reports, 1985.
161p.
The Mexica were a branch of the Aztec people who built a powerful but short-lived
empire around Texcoco, Tlacopan and Tenochtitlán. The author uses various artefacts
from excavations to define and examine Mexica symbolism and religious practices.

135 **The Codex Nuttall: a picture manuscript from ancient Mexico: the
Peabody Museum facsimile.**
Edited by Zelia Nuttall. New York: Dover, 1975. 84p.
A paperback reprint of the Peabody Museum facsimile of a manuscript found in a
Florentine monastery. The manuscript contains historical and genealogical information
on the Mixtec civilization of Oaxaca. Between 1,200 and 1,400 painted figures
represent a visual history of twelfth-century Oaxaca.

136 **The Olmec: mother culture of Mesoamerica.**
Roman Pina Chan, edited by Laura Laurencich Minelli. [n.p.]:
Rizzoli International Publications, 1949. 240p. bibliog.
A relatively early account of the Olmec, by the Mexican archaeologist Roman Pina
Chan. The author advances a theory of the origins of the Olmec and discusses what is

Archaeology and Prehistory. Other peoples

known about their culture, artistic expression, religion and history. Olmec art, with its
simple style and massive form, was the first to appear in Mesoamerica.

137 **The Olmecs: the oldest civilization in Mexico.**
Jacques Soustelle, translated from the French by Helen Lane.
Norman, Oklahoma: University of Oklahoma Press, 1986. 214p.
The Olmecs are one of the oldest pre-Columbian civilizations and one of the least
known. They flourished between *circa* 1200 and 400 BC, mainly on the Gulf coast. Our
knowledge of this civilization is based on the study of artefacts, rock paintings and
ceremonial centres. Soustelle discusses what is currently known about the Olmecs, and
presents various hypotheses of his own.

138 **The Mixtecs in ancient and colonial times.**
Ronald Spores. Norman, Oklahoma: University of Oklahoma, 1984.
263p. bibliog. (The Civilization of the American Indian Series).
The Mixtec Indians lived in the mountainous area of western Oaxaca between 1520 BC
and 1820 AD. They started as small, relatively egalitarian farming communities but
increasingly developed a hereditary ruling class. The author traces the social
transformation brought about by the impact of the Spanish Conquest.

139 **Life and death in the ancient city of Teotihuacán: a modern
paleodemographic synthesis.**
Rebecca Storey. Tuscaloosa, Alabama: University of Alabama Press,
1992. 266p.
Much of this work is taken up with a sophisticated methodology, but the chief general
interest lies in the conclusions. These are that Teotihuacán was a city with a high birth
rate, a high death rate and a high population density. In these respects is was very like
pre-industrial cities in other parts of the world.

140 **The Zapotec princes, priests and peasants.**
Joseph W. Whitecotton. Norman, Oklahoma: University of
Oklahoma Press, 1977. 338p. maps. bibliog. (The Civilization of the
American Indian Series).
An introduction to the archaeology and history of the Zapotec region, covering the
whole period from ancient times to the more recent past.

141 **The shaft tomb figures of west Mexico.**
Hasso Von Winning. Los Angeles, California: Southwest Museum,
1974. 183p. map. bibliog. (Southwest Museum Papers, no. 24).
A study of terracotta figures from the shaft tombs of West Mexico. The objects are
classified according to subject matter, and the reader is provided with some
background into the life and customs of the people who fashioned them.

General works

142 **Prehistoric Mesoamerica.**
Richard E. W. Adams.   Boston, Massachusetts: Little, Brown, 1977.
370p. maps. bibliog.
A well-illustrated, interpretative work on Mesoamerican history which includes Mexico
but also countries to the south. The work is intended for the general and student
readership.

143 **Ancient Mesoamerica: a comparison of change in three regions.**
Richard E. Blanton (et al.).   Cambridge, England; New York:
Cambridge University Press, 1982. 300p. bibliog. (New Studies in
Archaeology).
The societies in three regions – the valleys of Oaxaca and Mexico and the eastern
Maya lowlands – are compared in terms of social history and, particularly, political and
economic development.

144 **A key to the Mesoamerican reckoning of time: the chronology recorded
in native texts.**
Gordon Brotherston.   London: British Museum, 1982. 91p. bibliog.
(Occasional Paper, no. 38).
A study of Mesoamerican chronology which aims to understand internal correlations
between the regional conventions of year-naming.

145 **The ancient kingdoms of Mexico.**
Nigel Davies.   London: Penguin, 1990. 272p. bibliog.
A good general study of Olmec, Teotihuacán, Tloltec and Aztec cultures, discussed in
chronological order. This is a re-issue of an earlier version, published in 1982. The
author is familiar with specialist scholarship but this work is aimed mainly at the
general reader, with a good bibliography which includes advice on further reading.

146 **The God-kings of Mexico.**
Thomas Dickey, Vance Muse, Henry Wieneck.   Chicago, Illinois:
Stonehenge, 1982. 176p. bibliog. (Treasures of the World).
This survey, aimed at the general reader, is illustrated and very factual. It surveys the
history of five pre-Columbian cultures: the Olmec, the Maya, Teotihuacán, the Mixtec
and the Aztec.

147 **Mesoamerica after the decline of Teotihuacán A.D. 700-900.**
Edited by Richard Diehl, Janet Catherine Berlo.   Washington, DC:
Dumbarton Oaks Research Library and Collection, 1989. 244p. bibliog.
This edited collection features the proceedings of a seminar held at Dumbarton Oaks
in 1984 which brought together art historians and archaeologists. The geographical
coverage of the articles encompasses Central Mexico, the Maya area and some parts of
eastern Mexico.

148 **Canal irrigation in prehistoric Mexico; the sequence of technological change.**
William E. Doolittle. Austin, Texas: University of Texas, 1990. 205p.
Doolittle is a geographer who is here relying on data mostly provided by archaeologists. He has provided a detailed study which offers some significant, if controversial, new interpretations of the ecology and technology of pre-Columbian societies.

149 **Land and politics in the valley of Mexico: a two thousand year perspective.**
Edited by H. R. Harvey. Albuquerque, New Mexico: University of New Mexico Press, 1991. 291p.
Despite the title of the book, most chapters refer to the pre-Conquest or early Colonial period. The focus is primarily on non-Aztec civilizations. Pre-Hispanic cultures are treated as complex and in some ways sophisticated structures despite being non-literate.

150 **A guide to ancient Mexican ruins.**
C. Bruce Hunter. Norman, Oklahoma: University of Oklahoma Press, 1977. 261p. bibliog. (Reprinted 1986).
A guide to the ruins of pre-Columbian Mexico, excluding those of the Yucatán. The book is heavily illustrated and non-technical in approach.

151 **Ancient Mexico, an overview.**
Jaime Litvak King. Albuquerque, New Mexico: University of New Mexico Press, 1986. 134p. bibliog.
A short work of synthesis which covers a number of different civilizations. The author is the director of Archaeological Institute at the National Autonomous University of Mexico.

152 **The gods and symbols of ancient Mexico and the Maya: an illustrated dictionary of Mesoamerican religion.**
Mary Miller, Karl Taube. London: Thames and Hudson, 1993. 216p. bibliog.
This is actually more of an encyclopaedia than a dictionary. It is well written and very useful for the general reader, giving detailed accounts of matters relating to the religious principles of the various peoples of Mesoamerica.

153 **Prehistoric settlement patterns in the Texcoco region, Mexico.**
Jeffrey R. R. Parsons. Ann Arbor, Michigan: University of Michigan, 1971. 390p. maps. bibliog. (Memoirs of the Museum of Anthropology, no. 3).
This volume contains site descriptions and comparisons with other regions in the Basin of Mexico. It discusses the results of archaeological research during the 1960s. The appendices include ceramic analyses and descriptions of the mounds.

154 **The Aztecs, Mayas and their predecessors: archaeology of Mesoamerica.**
Muriel Porter Weaver. San Diego, California; New York; Boston,
Massachusetts; London: Academic Press, 1993. 3rd ed. 565p. bibliog.
maps.

The author has now twice updated her earlier general survey of Mesoamerican
civilizations in order to take advantage of new research findings. This is a substantially
revised and generously illustrated volume which updates the previous editions. The
work includes new material on codices, agricultural practices, and the character of pre-
Columbian societies. It also affords a detailed look at the most important pre-
Columbian civilizations. Most of the civilizations discussed, though not all, lie within
the present-day borders of Mexico.

History

General

155 **A concise history of Mexico from Hidalgo to Cárdenas 1805-1940.**
Jan Bazant. Cambridge, England: Cambridge University Press, 1977.
217p.
A standard, and much reprinted, introduction to Mexican history covering most of the
independence period. The account is very lucid and narrative in structure, focusing on
events rather than looking for causes. There is a chronology and references to other
reading.

156 **Mexico.**
Peter Calvert. New York: Praeger; London: Stanley Benn, 1973.
361p. maps. bibliog. (Nations of the Modern World Series).
A work on the history of Mexico aimed at the general reader. This work is particularly
strong in its coverage of the Revolution and the post-Revolutionary period. The author
is very much interested in the so-called Sonoran dynasty which created the post-
Revolutionary political order.

157 **Mexico: class formation, capital accumulation and the state.**
James D. Cockroft. New York: Monthly Review Press, 1983. 384p.
bibliog.
An essentially Marxist approach to Mexican history. The author argues that Mexico
has always had a single power élite, based on ownership of property. The
consequences of political upheavals in Mexico have been to circulate power rather than
to redistribute it.

158 **San José de Gracia: Mexican village in transition.**
Luis Gonzalez, translated from the Spanish by John Upton.   Austin,
Texas: University of Texas Press, 1974. 362p. maps. bibliog.
An excellent local history which won an American Historical Association prize. The
history of San José de Gracia is traced from the 1790s to the present, using written
records, oral accounts, and the author's own memories.

159 **Riot, rebellion and revolution; rural social conflict in Mexico.**
Edited by Friedrich Katz.   Princeton, New Jersey: Princeton
University Press, 1989. 573p.
An attempt to survey comprehensively the course of rural history in Mexico from the
early days of colonial rule to the post-Revolutionary period. There was indeed a great
deal of unrest during this period, and the contributors tend to emphasize a diversity of
factors as being responsible rather than seeking a single all-embracing explanation.

160 **The course of Mexican history.**
Michael Meyer, William Sherman.   New York; Oxford, England:
Oxford University Press, 1987. 4th ed. 711p. maps. bibliog.
A comprehensive survey of Mexican history which covers social and cultural history as
well as its political and economic aspects. Although other periods of Mexican history
are fully covered, there is a particular emphasis on the century between independence
and the outbreak of Revolution in 1910. A comprehensive general introduction which
has undergone several updatings and new editions. The work also contains suggestions
for further reading.

161 **Mexico: a history.**
Robert R. Miller.   Norman, Oklahoma: University of Oklahoma
Press, 1985. 414p. bibliog.
A good general introduction to the history of Mexico. It traces the country from pre-
Columbian times to the beginning of the 1980s.

162 **Triumph and tragedy: a history of the Mexican people.**
Ramon E. Ruiz.   New York; London: W. W. Norton, 1991. 481p.
bibliog.
A long historical essay written in a lucid, rather literary, style. The work covers the
whole period from the Conquest to 1990. There is also a bibliographical essay. The
triumph in the title refers to Mexican achievements in the fields of art, literature and to
some extent political reform. The tragedy lies in the continuing poverty of the majority
of the Mexican people.

The Conquest (1519-70)

163 **Antonio de Mendonza, first viceroy of New Spain.**
Arthur Scott Aiton. New York: Russell and Russell, 1967. 240p.
maps. bibliog.
A reprint of the 1927 edition of a biography of Antonio de Mendonza, which
concentrates on the development of New Spain during his term of office from 1535 to
1550.

164 **Beyond the codices: the Nahua view of colonial Mexico.**
Edited by Arthur J. O. Anderson, Frances Berdan, James Lockhart.
Berkeley, California: University of California Press, 1976. 235p.
bibliog. (California University at Los Angeles, UCLA Latin American
Studies Series, vol. 27).
A presentation of original documents in the Nahuatl language which are important in
the study of post-Conquest and early colonial Mexico. English translations are given in
the original documents, as well as some early Spanish translations, and the differences
in viewpoint between the Indians and the Spaniards are made very clear.

165 **The idea of the devil and the problem of the Indian; the case of Mexico
in the sixteenth century.**
Francisco Cervantes. London: Institute of Latin American Studies,
1991. 28p. (Research Paper, no. 24).
A discussion of the way in which Spanish theology tackled some of the problems
arising from the conquest and colonization of Mexico.

166 **The conquest and colonization of Yucatán 1517-1550.**
Robert Stone Chamberlain. New York: Octagon Books, 1966. 365p.
maps. bibliog.
A well-documented study of the Spanish conquest and colonization of Yucatán. It was
originally published in 1948.

167 **Race and class in colonial Oaxaca.**
John K. Chance. Stanford, California: Stanford University Press,
1978. 250p. bibliog.

Conquest of the Sierra: Spaniards and Indians in Colonial Oaxaca.
John Chance. Norman, Oklahoma: University of Oklahoma Press,
1989. maps. bibliog. 233p.
Race and class is a study of the way in which the immediate post-Conquest pattern of
social stratification, based on race and culture, gradually gave way to a pattern largely
based on money. Ethnic influence remained strong, however, and the increasing
numbers of *mestizos* (of mixed Spanish and Indian blood) complicated matters further.
Conquest of the Sierra returns to this theme, but aims to provide a more general local
history of Oaxaca from Conquest to Independence.

168 **Ambivalent conquests: Maya and Spaniard in Yucatán 1517-70.**
I. Clendinnen. Cambridge, England; New York: Cambridge
University Press, 1987. 192p. (Latin American Studies Series, no. 61).

A study of the Spanish conquest of the Yucatán and early Spanish efforts to organize the province. The author also attempts to understand the Maya from Spanish documentary evidence of the time.

169 **Letters from Mexico.**
Hernán Cortés, translated from the Spanish by Anthony Pagden, with an introduction by J. H. Elliot. New Haven, New Jersey; London: Yale University Press. 449p.

By the end of his life Cortés, though Conqueror of Mexico, had lost out in the court politics of Spain. The five letters reproduced here are naturally self-interested in their interpretations of events but they are still an invaluable record of the period. Elliot's introduction is very clear and helpful.

170 **Trade, tribute and transportation. The sixteenth-century political economy of the valley of Mexico.**
Ross Hassig. Norman, Oklahoma: University of Oklahoma Press, 1985. 284p.

Hassig stresses the constraints posed by poor transportation in pre-Columbian Mexico. The Aztecs emphasized the canoe; the Spaniards brought in roads and horses. The valley was integrated economically after the Conquest, partly through coercion but partly through extended trade.

171 **The work of Bernardino de Sahagún, pioneer ethnographer of sixteenth-century Aztec Mexico.**
Edited by J. Jorge Klor de Alva, H. B. Nicholson, Eloise Quinones Keber. Albany, New York: Institute for Meso American Studies, 1988. 372p. bibliog. (Studies on Culture and Society, no. 2).

This work contains 22 articles on Bernardino de Sahagún, who was the leading chronicler of Columbian Mexico and a major source for subsequent work on the period (*see* item no. 173). Several of these essays are by well-known scholars. Most of the work deals with historical or ethnographic themes, but several articles also contain linguistic information on the Nahuatl of Sahagún's time.

172 **The broken spears: the Aztec account of the conquest of Mexico.**
Edited by Miguel León Portilla, translated from the Spanish by Lysander Kemp. Boston, Massachusetts: Beacon Press, 1962. 168p. maps. bibliog.

A collection of excerpts from manuscripts and other source materials providing accounts by native Aztec writers of the conquest of Mexico by Cortés. They were written between 1519 and 1921, and originally translated from Nahuatl into Spanish by Angel Maria Garibay K.

173 **Fray Bernardino de Sahagún 1499-1590.**
Luis Nicolau d'Oliver, translated from the Spanish by Mauricio J.
Mixto, foreword by Miguel León-Portilla. Salt Lake City, Utah:
University of Utah Press, 1987. 201p. bibliog.
Sahagún was the greatest of the early Spanish chroniclers of Mexico. Spanish-born, he
arrived in Mexico in 1529 and devoted his life to an encyclopaedia entitled 'General
History of the Things of the New Spain'. Much of this is taken up with a very detailed
account of Aztec belief systems and religious rituals. This book is a translation of a
classic biography of the historian published in 1952 with some updating, and including
some original materials.

174 **The history of the conquest of Mexico.**
William Hickling Prescott. Chicago, Illinois: University of Chicago
Press, 1966. 413p. bibliog. (Classic American Historians).
W. H. Prescott has been called America's first truly professional historian. His work on
Mexico, which was originally published in 1843, is still held in high regard by
historians. It was based on original sources, and aimed at completeness and balance
although there is some evident sympathy for Cortés and the Spanish side. The work is
written with great vividness. It has been published in no fewer than ten languages and
has been reprinted on over one hundred occasions. This is one of the more accessible
editions. An abridged edition also exists, edited by C. Harvey Gardiner.

175 **The spiritual conquest of Mexico: an essay on the apostolate and the
evangelizing methods of the mendicant orders in New Spain 1523-1572.**
Robert Ricard, translated from the French by Lesley Byrd Simpson.
Berkeley, California: University of California Press, 1966. 423p.
bibliog.
This is classic account of the conversion of the Indians and the establishment of the
Church in Mexico after the conquest by Cortés. It was originally published in French in
1933. The account focuses very much on what the Church did and how it organized
itself.

176 **Treatise on the heathen superstitions that today live among the Indians
native to this New Spain, 1629.**
Hernando Ruíz de Alarcón, translated and edited by J. Richard
Andrews, Ross Hassig. Norman, Oklahoma: University of Oklahoma
Press, 1984. 406p. bibliog. (Civilization of the American Indian Series,
no. 164).
Ruíz de Alarcón was a Mexican-born priest, concerned to promote Catholicism.
However, his lasting contribution was this account of non-Christian beliefs and belief
systems which was written a century after the Conquest. This is the definitive scholarly
translation and reproduction of the original work.

177 **Chimalpahin and the kingdoms of Chalco.**
Susan Schroeder.   Tucson, Arizona: Arizona University Press, 1991.
264p. bibliog.
The Nahuatl historian, Chimalpahin, wrote a text of the history of his home town of
Chalco. This work is an interpretation of Chimalpahin's text, and the author presents
an interesting socio-political study of Chalco and its kingdom in the years just before
and after the Spanish Conquest.

178 **Alonso de Zorita: royal judge and Christian humanist 1512-1585.**
Ralph H. Vigil.   Norman, Oklahoma: University of Oklahoma Press,
1987. 383p. map. bibliog.
A full-length study of Alonso de Zorita who was a Spanish-born judge sent to the New
Spain where he served until his retirement. In addition to his judicial duties, he was an
important chronicler of his period (*see* item no. 181). Zorita emerges as a man of
principle, concerned at the indigenous peoples under his jurisdiction, and very critical
of the way in which Spanish-born landlords and local Indian chiefs combined to exploit
them. Dr Vigil examines Zorita's years in Mexico (1548-56) and the variety of duties
which he performed.

179 **The conquest of Michoacán: the Spanish domination of the Tarascan
kingdom in western Mexico 1521-1530.**
J. Benedict Warren.   Norman, Oklahoma: University of Oklahoma
Press, 1985. 352p. map. bibliog.
The Spanish extended their conquest into Michoacán during the period 1521-30. The
Tarascans had successfully resisted the Aztecs but smallpox weakened their defences
against the Spanish. The last Tarascan king was executed by the Spaniards in 1530.
This is primarily a political and institutional history, updated from an earlier work
published in Spanish in 1977.

180 **Disease and death in early colonial Mexico: simulating Amerindian
depopulation.**
Thomas Witmore.   Boulder, Colorado; London: Westview Press,
1992. 237p. bibliog. (Dellplain Latin American Studies, no. 28).
Was there a sharp decline in the Amerindian population after the Conquest?
Simulation methodology is probabilistic rather than conclusive, but Witmore suggests
that population did indeed decline very substantially. Within the valley of Mexico,
population may have been reduced from 1.6 million in 1519 to 160,000 in 1607.

181 **Life and labor in ancient Mexico: the brief and summary relation of the
lords of New Spain.**
Alonso de Zorita, translated from the Spanish and with an introduction
by Benjamin Keen.   New Brunswick, New Jersey: Rutgers University
Press, 1963. 328p. maps. bibliog.
An English translation of the work of a Spanish judge in Mexico during the sixteenth
century who analysed the economic, political and social conditions brought upon the
Indians of Mexico by the Spanish Conquest. He compares life in Aztec Mexico before
the Conquest to life under Spanish rule. While he tends to idealize the condition of the

Indians before 1521, later scholars have generally accepted his conclusion that the Spanish Conquest brought misery to the majority of the Indian population. In addition to the translation there is a bibliographical essay on Zorita.

Colonial Mexico (1570-1820)

Comparative works

182 **The first America. The Spanish monarchy, Creole patriots and the Liberal state.**
David Brading.   Cambridge, England: Cambridge University Press, 1991. 761p. bibliog.
This work aims to trace the attempts made by Spaniards born in the New World to define their American identity. The main sources for the work are to be found in numerous works of Colonial Spanish American literature. Brading looks at the various efforts of Spanish Americans to define their social identity within the vision imposed upon them by Church and Crown. While covering the whole of Spanish America, the account includes many references to Mexico, especially in respect of the independence period and its aftermath.

183 **The economies of Mexico and Peru during the late colonial period 1760-1810.**
Edited by Nils Jacobsen, Hans Jurgen Puhle.   Berlin: Colloquium Verlag, 1986. 428p. (Bibliotheka Ibero-Americana, no. 34).
This work is the result of a symposium held at the University of Bielefeld in 1982. There are fifteen contributors. The papers cover a number of themes, of which one of the most important is population growth.

Works on Mexico

184 **The army in Bourbon Mexico 1760-1820.**
Christon I. Archer.   Albuquerque, New Mexico: University of New Mexico Press, 1978. 366p. bibliog.
A detailed and scholarly account of the army which covers a wide variety of topics. These include the relationship between the military and the Colonial administration, the merchant class, and civilian institutions. There is also material on military recruitment and discipline, which presents a wider social picture of late colonial Mexico. The key question which the author tries to understand is why the military was initially loyal to the Crown at the outbreak of the movement for independence.

185 **Bureaucracy and bureaucrats in Mexico City 1742-1835.**
Linda Arnold.   Tucson, Arizona: University of Arizona Press, 1988.
131p. bibliog.
This is a study of bureaucratic careers and bureaucratic structures in late colonial
Mexico. Its aim is to understand better the character of the state before, during and
after the transition to independence.

186 **The Mexican colonial copper industry.**
Elinore M. Barrett.   Albuquerque, New Mexico: University of New
Mexico Press, 1987. 143p. maps. bibliog.
This study of copper mining considers the economic and administrative aspects of the
industry, and the way in which these changed as the Crown became more involved.
Copper was then mainly used for weaponry, but considered far less important than
silver. The industry was largely based in Michoacán.

187 **Economic fluctuations and social unrest in Oaxaca 1701-94.**
Ulises Beltran.   In: *Riot, rebellion and revolution: rural social conflict
in Mexico*, edited by F. Katz.   Princeton, New Jersey: Princeton
University Press, 1989, p. 561–72.
Seeks to correlate the incidence of rebellion to the economic cycle and finds,
surprisingly perhaps, that rebellion was more common in good years than bad. It is
necessary to find explanations for revolt which do not rest heavily on the notion of
short-term hardship.

188 **Miners and merchants in colonial Mexico 1763-1810.**
David Brading.   Cambridge, England: Cambridge University Press,
1971. 382p. bibliog. (Cambridge Latin American Studies, no. 10).
The author looks at the structure of the mining region towns of the Bajío – notably
Guanajuato, Valenciana and San Miguel Allende. A careful and detailed study of the
late colonial period.

189 **The leverage of labor: managing the Cortés hacienda in Tehuantepec
1588-1688.**
Lolita Gutierrez Brockington.   Durham, North Carolina: Duke
University Press, 1989. 245p. maps. bibliog.
This is a study of indigenous, African and mulatto labour, both free and slave, in the
colonial *hacienda* system. The author focuses particularly upon the Marquesada del
Valle estate in the Isthmus of Tehuantepec in Oaxaca.

190 **Blacks in colonial Veracruz: race, ethnicity and regional development.**
Patrick J. Carroll.   Austin, Texas: University of Texas Press, 1991.
191p. bibliog.
Black slaves were imported into colonial Mexico, quite heavily until around 1620.
Subsequently the slave trade declined, but slavery itself only gradually. Racism in
colonial Mexico was very strong, and black people were active in the conflicts of the
independence period.

191 **The enlightened: the writings of Luis de Carvajal, el Mozo.**
Luis de Carvajal, edited and translated from the Spanish by Seymour
B. Liebman. Coral Gables, Florida: University of Miami Press, 1967.
157p. bibliog.

Luis de Carvajal was born in Spain in 1567 and executed by the Inquisition in 1596. His is the only known writing by a Jew in Spanish Mexico. The Jewish community was not especially religious but nevertheless became a target for the Inquisition when this was set up in 1571. This is a translation of the memoirs, letters and other documents of Luis de Carvajal.

192 **Social assistance and bureaucratic politics; the Montepios of colonial Mexico 1767-1821.**
D. S. Chandler. Albuquerque, New Mexico: University of New
Mexico Press, 1991. 157p. bibliog.

The rôle of the Montepios was to provide pensions for families of deceased government servants. The author has researched the archives and finds the *montes* to be 'financial nightmares'. This is a microcosm of the financial and social administration of colonial Mexico.

193 **Colonial Culhuacán: a social history of an Aztec town.**
S. L. Cline. Albuquerque, New Mexico: University of New Mexico,
1986. 258p. bibliog.

This study is based on sixty-five wills dating from 1572 to 1606; these were written in Nahuatl. They provide a considerable amount of insight into a range of social issues of the day.

194 **Bureaucrats, planters and workers: the making of the tobacco monopoly in Bourbon Mexico.**
Susan Deans-Smith. Austin, Texas: University of Texas Press, 1992.
331p. bibliog.

The author studies the interaction of colonial politics and the economic interests of tobacco planters and workers. She finds that family networks played an important part in linking the planter class to the state.

195 **Crown and clergy in colonial Mexico, 1759-1821: the crisis of ecclesiastical privilege.**
N. M. Farriss. London: Athlone Press, University of London, 1968.
288p. bibliog. (University of London Historical Series, no. 21).

A thoroughly researched work on the Spanish Crown's efforts to exert control over the Mexican clergy during the late colonial period.

196 **Prices and wages in eighteenth century Mexico.**
Richard Garner. In: *Essays on the price history of eighteenth century Latin America*, edited by Lyman L. Johnson, Enrique Tandeter.
Albuquerque, New Mexico: University of New Mexico Press. 419p.
It is still a controversial question how far economic stresses contributed towards the Mexican independence movement. Garner shows that there was an inflationary tendency during the eighteenth century which may well have caused significant social stresses.

197 **The Mexican Inquisition of the sixteenth century.**
Richard E. Greenleaf. Albuquerque, New Mexico: University of New Mexico Press, 1969. 242p. bibliog.
This is an extensively researched work, which provides details of cases taken from the Inquisition papers of the Archivo General de la Nación. The Inquisition was not used merely against religious unorthodoxy, but also to crush any signs of independence on the part of regional authorities in the New Spain.

198 **Man-gods in the Mexican highlands; Indian power and colonial society 1520-1800.**
S. Gruzinski, translated from the French by Eileen Corrigan.
Stanford, California: Stanford University Press, 1989. 191p. bibliog.
A discussion of various charismatic Indian leaders during the colonial period in an attempt to understand the nature of charisma and its rôle in political leadership. Well written if in some respects speculative. There is an afterword on Zapata.

199 **Roots of insurgency: Mexican regions.**
B. Hamnett. Cambridge, England; New York: Cambridge University Press, 1986. 276p. bibliog. (Cambridge Latin American Studies Series, no. 59).
The author is mainly interested in local and, at times, non-economic factors behind the rebellion against Spain. The book starts by looking at the independence movement before looking back at its presumed causes. It argues that the salience of many localized sources of conflict worked against the emergence of any clear-cut outcome to the independence movement.

200 **Mexico's merchant elite 1590-1660.**
Louisa Schell Hoberman. Durham, North Carolina; London: Duke University Press, 1991. 322p. bibliog.
This book looks at the rôle of the merchant capitalists in what the author refers to as a mercantile state. She analyses the operation of several sectors of the economy and shows how merchant élites during this period gained power at the expense of the Spanish Crown.

201 **Nueva Vizcaya: heartland of the Spanish frontier.**
Oakah L. Jones. Albuquerque, New Mexico: University of New Mexico Press, 1988. 342p. maps. bibliog.
Nueva Vizcaya made up what is now Durango, Chihuahua, much of Sinaloa, Sonora and part of Coahuila. The area was securely under Spanish rule by 1563. Jones has written a comprehensive and scholarly history of the region from conquest to independence.

202 *Los paisanos*: **Spanish settlers on the northern frontier of New Spain.**
Oakah L. Jones. Norman, Oklahoma: University of Oklahoma Press, 1979. 351p. bibliog.
A study of the Spanish colonists who followed the conquest into the New Spain. They were mostly ordinary country people who led a family- and community-oriented life.

203 **Remote beyond compare: letters of don Diego de Vargas to his family from the New Spain and New Mexico 1675-1706.**
Edited by John L. Kessell. Albuquerque, New Mexico: University of New Mexico Press, 1989. 596p. maps.
Diego de Vargas was a middle-ranking colonial official between 1675 and 1706. His personal letters are published here both in Spanish transcript and in translation. The volume is nicely produced, with maps and illustrations.

204 **A Jesuit *hacienda* in colonial Mexico: Santa Lucia 1576-1767.**
H. W. Konrad. Stanford, California: Stanford University Press, 1980. 332p. bibliog.
This well-researched study traces the varying fortunes of the Santa Lucia *hacienda*. The author focuses on the three-cornered conflict between the Crown, the *hacendado* and the Indian communities. Often, particularly in the eighteenth century, disputes could not be settled by legal or peaceful means and there was increasing unrest and rebellion.

205 **The making of a strike: Mexican silver workers' struggle in the Real Del Monte, 1766-1776.**
Doris M. Ladd. Omaha, Nebraska: University of Nebraska Press, 1988. 205p. maps. bibliog.
The strike considered here was the first in Mexican history. It proved successful, since the Viceroy accepted the petition of the strikers. In compiling this account, the author relies heavily upon direct quotations from the participants themselves.

206 **The Mexican nobility at independence 1780-1826.**
Doris M. Ladd. Austin, Texas: University of Texas Press, 1976. 316p. bibliog. (Latin American Monographs, no. 40).
A thorough detailed study of the Mexican nobility on the economic, social and political levels. Detailed information is provided on properties, investments, social connections and political stances.

207 **Colonial bureaucrats and the Mexican economy; growth of a patrimonial state 1763-1821.**
John S. Leiby.   New York; Berne; Frankfurt, Germany: Peter Lang, 1986. 239p. bibliog.
An analysis of the interaction between politics and the economy in late Bourbon Mexico. The author emphasizes the importance of a generally well-educated and reasonably competent bureaucracy. The bureaucracy was mostly enlightened and Mexico expanded economically during this period.

208 **The Tlaxcalan *actas*; a compendium of the records of the *cabildo* of Tlaxcala 1545-1627.**
James Lockhart, Frances Berdan, Arthur Anderson.   Salt Lake City, Utah: University of Utah Press, 1986. 156p.
This is a translation of the original Nahuatl record of the Indian municipality of Tlaxcala. It provides a rare example of evidence as to the activities of an indigenous corporation. The book includes an analysis of the institution itself.

209 **Criminal justice in eighteenth century Mexico: a study of the Tribunal of the Acordada.**
Colin M. Maclachlan.   Berkeley, California: University of California Press, 1974. 141p. bibliog.
A study of the rôle of the Tribunal, its functions and eventual decline, in terms of eighteenth-century notions of criminality and law.

210 **Rural society in colonial Morelos.**
Cheryl English Martin.   Albuquerque, New Mexico: University of New Mexico Press, 1985. 255p. bibliog.
This is a well-presented micro study of the sugar-producing era of Yautepec in Morelos, based upon archival material. It aims to present life as it was rather than offering generalizations or explanations.

211 **Water in the Hispanic southwest: a social and legal history 1550-1850.**
Michael C. Meyer.   Tucson, Arizona: Arizona University Press, 1984. 189p.
The author has studied thousands of legal cases concerning water rights in this dry climate. Meyer explores the rôle of water in the colonization of northern Mexico. He also looks at the way in which water rights influenced the character of these societies.

212 **The Apache frontier: Jacobo Ugarte and the Spanish–Indian relations in northern New Spain 1769-1791.**
Max L. Moorhead.   Norman, Oklahoma: University of Oklahoma Press, 1968. (Civilization of the American Indian Series, no. 190). 309p. maps.
Although the Spaniards quickly overcame the Aztecs, they had more difficulty in extending their control northwards. The Apache held them up until the eighteenth

century when Jacobo Ugarte became governor of Coahuila. Ugarte did push Spanish control northward; this book traces his career and analyses the success of his strategy.

213 **Irrigation in the Bajío region of colonial Mexico.**
Michael E. Murphy. Boulder, Colorado: Westview Press, 1986. 227p. bibliog. (Dellplain Latin American Studies, no. 19).
The book looks at the way in which irrigation systems and urban water supplies were installed and managed. It uses the insights gained by this to explore various aspects of economy and society in the Bajío.

214 **The *Presidio* and militia on the northern frontier of New Spain; a documentary history, volume 1; 1570-1700.**
Edited by Thomas Naylor, Charles Polzer. Tucson, Arizona: University of Arizona Press, 1986. 756p. bibliog.
The *Presidio* was generally garrisoned by regional militia with their salaries paid by the royal treasury. It played a part in moving military organization away from feudalism towards centralized control. This volume is a selection of letters, field reports, pleas from missionaries and other contemporary evidence.

215 **Slaves of the white God; blacks in Mexico, 1570-1650.**
Colin A. Palmer. Cambridge, Massachusetts: Harvard University Press, 1976. 240p. bibliog.
A study of various aspects of slavery in early colonial Mexico. These include the status of slaves in society, religious practices, and the Church's attitude towards slavery.

216 **Agrarian change in eighteenth century Yucatán.**
Robert Patch. *Hispanic American Historical Review*, vol. 65, no. 1 (1985), p. 21-49.
The article looks at the process of change in agricultural property and production during the eighteenth century. It argues that the major causes of the rise of the *hacienda* during this period were to be found internally rather than being based on any change in world markets.

217 **Pedro Moya de Contreras; Catholic reform and royal power in the New Spain 1571-1591.**
Stafford Poole. Berkeley, California: University of California Press, 1987. 309p. bibliog.
The Inquisition was active in early colonial Mexico. Pedro Moya de Contreras was an inquisitor, viceroy and archbishop. This is a thorough study of his life and times. While Contreras was a vigorous hard-liner on most issues, the author seeks to find a sympathetic angle to analyse.

218 **Soldiers, Indians and silver: North America's first frontier war.**
Philip Wayne Powell. Tempe, Arizona: Arizona State University,
1974. 317p. maps. bibliog.
An account of the Chichimeca War, which was fought between 1550 and 1590. It was
fought between the Chichimeca Indians, who were nomadic tribes in northern Mexico,
and Spanish forces.

219 **Textiles and capitalism in Mexico: an economic history of the** *obrajes*
1539-1840.
R. J. Salvucci. Princeton, New Jersey: Princeton University Press,
1986. 176p. bibliog.
A rather technical, but very thorough, study of the colonial textile industry. Working
conditions were terrible, returned value very limited and the industry found itself
unable to compete when imports were permitted after independence. At that point it
shrunk in size.

220 **Spain's colonial outpost.**
John S. Shutz. San Francisco, California: Boyd and Fraser, 1985.
126p. bibliog. (Golden State Series).
A brief but interesting account of California under Spanish rule, which began when
Cortés sent Juan Rodríguez Carillo to explore the region in 1542.

221 **Origins of Church wealth in Mexico: ecclesiastical revenues and church**
finances 1523-1600.
John Frederick Schwaller. Albuquerque, New Mexico: University of
New Mexico Press, 1985. 263p. bibliog.
This work concentrates mainly on the secular clergy rather than the monasteries. Many
of these were indeed secular since, as the author shows, they earned their livelihoods
in careers outside of the Church. It looks at the development of chantries and other
pious works. It also discusses ecclesiastical organization and finance, and issues which
arose when clergy were accused of wrongdoing.

222 **To love, honour and obey in colonial Mexico: conflicts over marriage**
choice 1574-1821.
Patricia Seed. Stanford: Stanford University Press, 1988. 320p.
bibliog.
This is a very interesting work as well as a scholarly one. The author shows that
colonial Mexican society in fact changed significantly during the seventeenth century.
She argues also that colonial Mexico had a concept of honour which was critical in
marriage, and which was significantly different from similar concepts in Europe at that
time.

223 **Puebla de los Angeles. Industry and society in a Mexican city 1700-1850.**
Guy Thompson. Boulder, Colorado; London: Westview Press, 1989.
345p. bibliog. (Dellplain Latin American Studies, no. 25).

Puebla de los Angeles was in 1630 the foremost manufacturing city in Spanish America but it thereafter underwent a slow but continued decline. Despite its manufacturing character, Puebla retained some important non-industrial characteristics. These features make the city particularly interesting, and Thompson has written the definitive regional study. The main emphasis is on the structure and evolution of the local economy, though the author also considers broader social and cultural issues.

From Independence to the Mexican Revolution (1820-1910)

224 **The Mexican empire of Iturbide.**
Timothy Anna. Lincoln, Nebraska; London: University of Nebraska Press, 1990. 286p. bibliog.

Agustín de Iturbide was briefly emperor of Mexico. He was crowned in 1822, abdicated in 1823 and was executed in 1824 following an abortive attempt at a political comeback. Iturbide was, in general, associated with conservative and religious causes. He was originally a royalist army officer but declared for the independence of Mexico in 1820 as a reaction to a liberal *coup* in Spain. Anna's book is a political history of Mexico at independence and also a study of Iturbide's career. The author attempts to rescue Iturbide's reputation from the unfavourable judgement of most historians.

225 **Los disidentes: sociedades protestantes y revolución en México 1872–1911.** (Dissidents: Protestant societies and revolution in Mexico 1872–1911.)
Jean-Pierre Bastiam. Mexico DF: Fondo de Cultura Economica and Colegio de México, 1989. 373p. bibliog.

This book traces the development of Protestant institutions. It looks at the relationship between Protestantism and other forms of dissidence, and it looks also at the locations within Mexico from which Protestants drew their strength.

226 **Mexico: from independence to the liberal republic 1821-1867.**
Jan Bazant. In: *Mexico since Independence*, edited by L. Bethell. Cambridge, England; New York: Cambridge University Press, 1991, p. 1-49. (Cambridge History of Latin America, vol. 7).

This is essentially a narrative, though a lucidly written piece. It covers the independence period, the war against the United States and the Maximilian period. This was certainly an eventful, if tragic, period of Mexican history.

227 **Judas at the Jockey Club and other episodes of Porfirian Mexico.**
William Beezley. Lincoln, Nebraska: University of Nebraska, 1987.
181p. bibliog.
The author looks at popular culture during the Porfiriato. The title refers to the transformation of ritual Judas burnings into bicycle races. The theme of this very interesting book is the clash between mass traditional culture and élite amusements.

228 **The reform in Oaxaca, 1856-76: a microhistory of the liberal revolution.**
Charles Redman Berry. Lincoln, Nebraska: University of Nebraska Press, 1980. 282p. maps. bibliog.
A discussion of the *reforma* period in the Oaxacan conflict. Here the main forces involved were the Church, the army and the landowners.

229 **Mexico views manifest destiny 1821-1846: an essay on the origins of the Mexican war.**
Gene M. Brack. Albuquerque, New Mexico: University of New Mexico Press, 1976. 194p. bibliog.
A description of the attitudes of Mexicans toward the United States prior to 1844, as shown in pamphlets, newspapers and the writings of leading Mexican figures. The emphasis is on fear and hostility towards the United States, and no mention is made of any who desired absorption into the United States.

230 **Liberal patriotism and the Mexican *reforma*.**
David A. Brading. *Journal of Latin American Studies*, vol. 20 (1988), p. 27-48.
The problem with Liberalism, Brading argues, is that Liberals both needed and distrusted a strong executive. This is a scholarly study of the thinking of several leading Liberals in the late 1850s. The issue is seen as being state building rather than nation building.

231 **Political patronage and politics at the village level in Central Mexico: continuity and change in patterns from the late colonial period to the end of the French intervention (1867).**
Raymond Buve. *Bulletin of Latin American Research*, vol. 11, no. 1 (Jan. 1992), p. 1-29.
Considers the character of patronage politics in rural Mexico. The author argues that clientelism was relatively strong in colonial Mexico and remained so in the early years of independence. The many political conflicts of the early nineteenth century, however, weakened the ability of the centre to maintain clientele links in place.

232 **The eagle: the autobiography of Santa Anna.**
Edited by Ann Fears Cranford. Austin, Texas: Pemberton Press, 1967. 299p. maps.
Santa Anna was one of the most prominent *caudillos* in post-independence Mexico. History has judged him harshly because of his lack of ideological consistency, his failure to prevent the breakaway of Texas in 1836 and his defeat by General Scott in

1847. However he was a man of his time, and his life was varied and dramatic. This is the first publication in English of his handwritten autobiography.

233 **The Mexican republic; the first decade 1823-32.**
Stanley C. Green. Pittsburgh, Pennsylvania: University of Pittsburgh, 1987. 237p. bibliog.
A general survey of Mexican politics and society around a loose, largely narrative, framework. There is some discussion of the economy, education and society. The book is lucidly written.

234 **Utmost good faith: patterns of Apache–Mexican hostilities in north Chihuahua border warfare 1821-1848.**
William B. Griffen. Albuquerque, New Mexico: University of New Mexico Press, 1988. 337p. maps. bibliog.
A careful study of the way in which differences and misunderstandings between New Spain and the Apaches made violent conflict likely. The account starts with Mexican independence and ends with the US–Mexican war.

235 **The transformation of liberalism in late nineteenth century Mexico.**
Charles Hale. Princeton, New Jersey: Princeton University Press, 1989, 263p. bibliog.
The author considers the history of ideas as these were reflected in the writings of prominent Liberals. A key element was the appearance of the doctrine of scientific politics (positivism). Hale argues that Liberals were indeed constitutionalists, but not real democrats. They were close observers of the United States and advocated rapid economic development for Mexico.

236 **Benito Juárez, early liberalism and the regional politics of Oaxaca 1828-1853.**
Brian Hamnett. *Bulletin of Latin American Research*, vol. 10, no. 1 (1991), p. 3-23.
Benito Juárez was the first full-blooded Indian to rule Mexico since the overthrow of the Aztec empire. How did he rise to power? The author sees him as a skilful politician who rose through the Oaxacan political machine.

237 **California conquered: war and peace on the Pacific 1846-1850.**
Neal Harlow. Berkeley, California: University of California Press, 1982. 499p. bibliog.
A detailed and thorough account of the conquest and assimilation of California by the United States. The Mexican government was unable, in the twenty-five years after independence, to create a strong sense of national identity in California. This was something which the United States could exploit when relations between the two countries deteriorated following the annexation of Texas in 1845.

238 **Yaqui resistance and survival; the struggle for land and autonomy 1821-1910.**
Evelyn Hu-Dehart.   Madison, Wisconsin: University of Wisconsin
1984. 222p. bibliog.

The author examines the long conflict between the Yaquis and European influences.
The Yaqui culture changed over time and by the nineteenth century featured some
Jesuit influence. By 1910, however, the Yaquis appeared on the brink of defeat as the
Mexican state strengthened, but the outbreak of Revolution changed the whole
perspective and gave Yaqui culture a new lease of life.

239 **The Liberal Republic and the Porfiriato 1867-1910.**
Friedrich Katz.   In: *Mexico since Independence*, edited by L. Bethell.
Cambridge, England; New York: Cambridge University Press, 1991,
p. 49-125. (Cambridge History of Latin America, vol. 7).

Mexican politics had become relatively tranquil by the mid-1870s. This has left Katz
sufficient opportunity to discuss rural and social conditions in addition to political ones.

240 **A Mexican elite family 1820-1980: kinship, class and culture.**
Larissa Lomnitz, Marisol Perez-Lizaur, translated from the Spanish by
Cinna Lomnitz.   Princeton, New Jersey: Princeton University Press,
1987. 294p. bibliog.

This is a historical and anthropological study of the Gómez family. Its focus on a micro
level brings out many of the themes generally considered to be features of Mexican
society. These include the importance of kinship and patronage, the high value placed
on family loyalty, the familial character of many business enterprises and the
importance of family rituals.

241 *Caudillos* **in Spanish America.**
John Lynch.   Oxford, England: Clarendon Press, 1992. 458p. bibliog.

The first part of Professor Lynch's book discusses *caudillo* [leadership] structures. The
second part considers a number of figures including Santa Anna. Lynch believes that
Mexico was not an inherently favourable environment for the emergence of successful
caudillos, but that Santa Anna bears comparison with figures such as the Argentine
Rosas and Venezuela's Paez.

242 **Life in Mexico under Santa Anna 1822-1855.**
R. R. Olivera, L. Crete.   Norman, Oklahoma: University of
Oklahoma Press, 1991. 245p. bibliog.

The author argues that Independence and its aftermath was largely irrelevant to the
lives of most Mexicans at that time. The same social hierarchy existed and in many
ways continued as before.

243 **The Mexican mining industry in the nineteenth century with special reference to Guanajuato.**
Margaret E. Rankine. *Bulletin of Latin American Research*, vol. 11, no. 1 (Jan. 1992), p. 29-49.
The wars of Independence were quite disastrous for the Mexican mining industry. However, mining made something of a recovery during the nineteenth century, despite the political turbulence of the first half-century. Margaret Rankine discusses how this was accomplished.

244 **Mexico through Russian eyes 1806-1940.**
William H. Richardson. Pittsburgh, Pennsylvania: University of Pittsburgh, 1988. 287p. bibliog.
A descriptive treatment of an unusual topic. Russian perceptions varied: some were superficial, others quite profound. Sergei Eisenstein warrants a full chapter of this volume.

245 **The view from Chapultepec: Mexican writers on the Mexican–American war 1845-48.**
Edited by Cecil Robinson. Tucson, Arizona: University of Arizona Press, 1989. 232p. bibliog.
This anthology of writings by Mexicans ranges from pieces composed at the time of the conflict to those written much later. The author starts the account with a review of the US historiography of the war.

246 **The people of Sonora and Yankee capitalists.**
Ramon Eduardo Ruiz. Tucson, Arizona: University of Arizona Press, 1988. 311p. bibliog.
The author concentrates on the development of large-scale mining in Sonora and its social implications; the key period is 1880-1910. The treatment concentrates more on 'the people of Sonora' than on the 'Yankee capitalists' who remain largely in the background. The author argues that the Americanization of Sonora dates from that time.

247 **Mexican lobby: Matias Romero in Washington 1861-1867.**
Translated from the Spanish and edited by Thomas D. Schoonover. Lexington, Kentucky: University Press of Kentucky, 1986. 184p. bibliog.
Matias Romero was a close friend of Benito Juárez, whom he represented in Washington at this time. This was clearly a critically important posting, and Romero's account is an important historical document.

248 **Dollars over dominion: the triumph of Liberalism in Mexican–United States relations 1861-1867.**
T. D. Schoonover. Baton Rouge, Louisiana: Louisiana State University Press, 1978. 285p. bibliog.

A study of how the United States Union government finally decided to support Mexican independence rather than French intervention, while the Confederates preferred Maximilian. The Union side preferred Juárez and his allies mainly for commercial reasons.

249 **The expulsion of Mexico's Spaniards 1821-1836.**
Harold Dana Sims. Pittsburgh, Pennsylvania: University of Pittsburgh Press, 1990.

Before the war of Independence, the Spanish *guachupinos* were seen as an élite although there may have been less difference between themselves and Mexicans of Spanish origin than is sometimes believed. After 1821, however, most of the Spaniards were expelled from Mexico through five separate laws. This is a well-researched account of the process and the issues involved.

250 **Origins of instability in early republican Mexico.**
Donald F. Stevens. Durham, North Carolina; London: Duke University Press, 1991. 184p. bibliog.

Why did Mexico not settle down to stability and prosperity after the war of Independence? The author argues that tensions within the revolutionaries continued and intensified; rural society was more rebellious than the cities. Political institutions were too weak to mediate the conflicts which emerged. The analysis presented here is quantitative as well as qualitative.

251 **The liberators: filibustering expeditions into Mexico, 1848-1862 and the last threat of manifest destiny.**
Joseph Allen Stout. Los Angeles, California: Westenlore, 1973. 202p. map. bibliog. (Great West and Indian Series, no. 41).

A study of the most important attempts made after the end of the war between Mexico and the United States to wrest more territory from northwestern Mexico in order to create new dukedoms or republics.

252 **Popular aspects of liberalism in Mexico 1848-1888.**
Guy Thompson. *Bulletin of Latin American Research*, vol. 10, no. 3 (1991), p. 265-93.

Thompson suggests that some other historians have underestimated the importance of popular support in explaining the triumph of Liberalism between 1848 and 1888. He argues that a more region-based and less centralist view of politics makes it clear that such support indeed existed.

253 **Disorder and progress: bandits, police and Mexican development.**
Paul J. Vanderwood. Lincoln, Nebraska: Nebraska University Press,
1981. 264p. bibliog.
The later nineteenth century was one of rapid social change. How did this affect issues
of law breaking and law enforcement? The author discusses the bandits and the rôle of
the *rurales* who (among other things) sought to combat them.

254 **Kinship, business and politics: the Martínez del Rio family in Mexico
1824-1867.**
David W. Walker. Austin, Texas: University of Texas Press, 1986.
259p. bibliog.
Walker looks at the history of the period through considering the vicissitudes of an
extended family. The Martínez del Rio family had interests in commerce, banking,
textile manufacturing and politics. The author adopts a narrative style and aims to
illustrate rather than hypothesize.

The Revolutionary period (1910-40)

255 **Shoulder to shoulder? The American Federation of Labor, the United
States and the Mexican Revolution 1910-1924.**
Greg Andrews. Berkeley, California: University of California. 272p.
bibliog.
One of the first efforts at Pan-American labour organization came with the attempt by
the American Federation of Labor (AFL) to build up a relationship with the
Confederación Regional Obrera Mexicana (CROM) during and just after the
Revolutionary years in Mexico. The AFL was both anti-Communist and opposed to
the 'big stick' approach to US diplomacy.

256 **Agrarian warlord: Saturnino Cedillo and the Mexican Revolution in San
Luis Potosí.**
Dudley Ankerson. Dekalb, Illinois: Northern Illinois University
Press, 1984. 192p. bibliog.
A well-researched narrative history of Cedillo's career; most attention is given to the
1920-39 period. The work is also a study of local political conditions in San Luis Potosí.

257 **Protestants and the Mexican Revolution; missionaries, ministers and
social change.**
Deborah Baldwin. Champaign, Illinois: University of Illinois Press,
1990. 203p. maps. bibliog.
This work looks at the connection between Mexican and United States Protestant
organizations. It asks why, given the fact that Protestants tend to favour economic
growth, Mexican Protestants should have turned against Porfirio Díaz. The answer is
found in the increasing authoritarianism of the Díaz regime.

258 **Harding and Mexico: diplomacy by economic persuasion 1920-23.**
George D. Beelen. London; New York: Garland, 1987. 173p. bibliog.
Based on a PhD thesis submitted in 1971, this is a detailed diplomatic history of the
period. It discusses the delay in US recognition of Mexico during 1921 and 1922. The
resignation of Albert Fall from the US Administration in March 1923 helped change
the US position.

259 **Provinces of the Revolution: essays on regional Mexican history 1910-
1929.**
Edited by Thomas Benjamin, Mark Wasserman. Albuquerque, New
Mexico: University of New Mexico Press, 1990. 359p. bibliog.
This collection is concerned with the progress of the Revolution in various of the states
of Mexico; it also contains more general discussions of the rôle of regionalism in the
Revolution. The main contributors are well-known historians.

260 **Edward L. Doheny: petroleum, power and politics in the United States
and Mexico.**
Dan La Botz. New York: Praeger, 1991. 202p. bibliog.
Edward Doheny was a ruthless and successful oil entrepreneur in the early years of the
present century. This book traces his career in Mexico and the United States. The
work is lucidly written and aimed as much at the general reader as the specialist.

261 *Caudillo* **and peasant in the Mexican Revolution.**
Edited by D. A. Brading. Cambridge, England; New York:
Cambridge University Press, 1980. 313p. bibliog. (Cambridge Latin
American Studies Series, no. 38).
A collection of essays by historians and sociologists reconsidering the significance of
the Mexican Revolution. This is a significant contribution to some continuing debates
about the nature of the agrarian insurgencies during the period 1910-17.

262 **Land, labor and capital in modern Yucatán: essays in regional history
and political economy.**
Edited by J. T. Brannon, Gilbert M. Joseph. Tuscaloosa, Alabama:
University of Alabama Press, 1991. 251p. bibliog.
This is an excellent synthesis of the economic history of the Yucatán. The first third of
the book deals with the nineteenth century but the rest deals with the Revolutionary
period. The focus here is to bring in regional social and economic themes which have
been neglected up to now. There are contributions from US, Mexican, Canadian and
Belizean scholars.

263 **Mexican political biographies 1884-1935.**
Roderic A. Camp. Austin, Texas: University of Texas 1991. 451p.
A hugely valuable work of reference which follows the careers of some seven hundred
people. The question of how far the Revolution transformed the pattern of élite
recruitment is obviously crucial here. The book itself is cryptic, but the career patterns
indicate the magnitude of the transformation.

264 **The Mexican Revolution in Yucatán 1915-1924.**
     James C. Carey.   Boulder, Colorado: Westview Replica Editions,
     1986. 225p. bibliog.

The Revolution in the Yucatán was also a social revolution, though it was to a large extent imposed from Mexico City. This work considers the rôle of Carillo Puerto, and the effect of the Revolution in linking the Yucatán with the rest of Mexico.

265 **Intellectual precursors of the Mexican Revolution 1900-13.**
     James D. Cockroft.   Austin, Texas: University of Texas Press for the
     Institute of Latin American Studies, 1968. 329p. maps. bibliog.
     (Institute of Latin American Studies, Latin American monographs, no.
     14).

An important study of six Mexican leaders of opinion in order to understand the intellectual climate in Mexico immediately preceding the Revolution. The work uses primary sources such as newspapers and pamphlets as well as interviews.

266 **Texas and the Mexican Revolution; a study in state and national border policy 1910-20.**
     Don M. Coerver, Linda Hall.   San Antonio, Texas: Trinity University
     Press, 1984. 167p.

Although this book is taken up largely with Texan policy, it does have some interesting insights into the course of the Mexican Revolution. The work concludes that Texas had its own Mexico policy for much of the period, and considers how far this impacted on the various Revolutionary factions in Mexico.

267 **The first *agraristas*: an oral history of a Mexican agrarian reform movement.**
     Ann Craig.   Berkeley, California; Los Angeles, California; London:
     University of California Press, 1983. 312p. bibliog.

The author looks at the rôle of the local peasantry in the municipality of Lagos de Moreño in Jalisco state during the 1920s and 1930s. She emphasizes the rôle of urban leaderships and state support in building up the reform movement.

268 **San Luis Potosí: confiscated estates – Revolutionary conquest or spoils?**
     Romana Falcón.   In: *Provinces of the Revolution*, edited by Thomas
     Benjamin, Mark Wasserman.   Albuquerque, New Mexico: University
     of New Mexico Press, 1990, p 133–62.

Romana Falcón considers how far the Revolution in San Luis Potosí represented a real social transformation, and how far a mere circulation of élites. Both factors were involved, but social change was nevertheless limited. This is a short summary of ideas developed by Romana Falcón for her PhD.

269 **The Mexican Revolution in Puebla 1908-13: the Maderista movement and the failure of liberal reform.**
David G. La France. Wilmington, Delaware: Scholarly Resources, 1989. 272p. bibliog.
This is essentially a study of the Maderista movement in Puebla and its ultimate failure. The author outlines some of the complexities of local history during the period and stresses the importance of social radicalization during the early Revolutionary years.

270 **Oaxaca: the rise and fall of state sovereignty.**
Paul Garner. In: *Provinces of the Revolution*, edited by Thomas Benjamin, Mark Wasserman. Albuquerque, New Mexico: University of New Mexico Press, 1990, p. 164–83.
Dr Garner looks at the failed effort by local establishment groups to achieve regional autonomy. He argues that the autonomy movement, supported though it was by local élites, was more than a mere alliance of reactionaries.

271 **Revolution on the border: the United States and Mexico.**
Linda Hall, Don Coerver. Albuquerque, New Mexico: University of New Mexico Press, 1988. 189p. bibliog.
This relatively short work raises several issues; these include questions of migration and trade as well as the military–political dimension. The book is succinct, well argued and concise.

272 **Counter-revolution along the border.**
Edited by Gene Z. Hanrahan. Salisbury, North Carolina: Documentary Publications, 1983. 188p. (Documents on the Mexican Revolution, vol. 8).
Disaffection in the north of Mexico during 1912 helped weaken the Madero government and thereby contributed to the brief success of Huerta. The volume is composed of original sources, mainly letters, reports and diplomatic correspondence; it covers the period from February 1912 to March 1913.

273 **The rebellion of Felix Díaz.**
Edited by Gene Z. Hanrahan. Salisbury, North Carolina: Documentary Publications 1983. 176p. (Documents on the Mexican Revolution, vol. 8).
Felix Díaz revolted against President Madero in 1912. His revolt appeared to have failed, but he subsequently reached an agreement with General Huerta which led to the initial successful conspiracy of 1913. This volume contains original documents.

274 **Anarchism and the Mexican working class.**
John M. Hart. Austin, Texas: University of Texas Press, 1978. 2nd ed., 1987. 209p. bibliog.
Hart is an important revisionist historian of the Mexican working class. This work seeks to bring out a theme which was often downplayed. Anarchism was influential at

first but, after around 1916, the labour movement was increasingly co-opted by the state and the influence of anarchism was sharply reduced.

275 **Revolutionary Mexico: the coming and process of the Mexican Revolution.**
John M. Hart. Berkeley, California; Los Angeles, California; London: University of California Press, 1987. 437p. bibliog.
Around one half of this work relates to the Porfiriato, and the other half to the Revolutionary years. The author's main question is why socially conservative élite groups and radical lower-class groups combined to overthrow the system. Hart gives the industrial working class a greater degree of prominence than do some other accounts.

276 **Presencia española en la Revolución mexicana (1910-15).** (The Spanish presence in the Mexican Revolution (1910-15).)
Carlos Illades. Mexico City: UNAM, Instituto Mora. 182p. bibliog.
Many Spaniards in Mexico migrated poor but became rich. They had a reputation for ruthlessness and were generally unpopular during the Revolution. This is an interesting study of an area which up until now has not received much attention.

277 *Ranchero* **revolt: the Mexican Revolution in Guerrero.**
Ian Jacobs. Austin, Texas: University of Texas Press, 1983. 234p. bibliog.
Jacobs argues that the Revolution in Guerrero was essentially a movement of middle-class *rancheros* attracted by the promise of political reform. They were quite different from the revolutionaries in Morelos, whose radicalism they did not support.

278 **Revolution from without; Yucatán, Mexico and the United States 1880-1924.**
Gilbert M. Joseph. Durham, North Carolina: Duke University Press, 1988. 2nd ed. 391p. bibliog.
Originally published in 1982, Gilbert Joseph's history of Yucatán during this period is a classic. The account starts during a period in which the dominant class in Yucatán appeared entrenched, and ends with the death of the socialist *cacique* [boss] Carrillo Puerto. However, as the book makes clear, the Yucatán changed principally because of the victory of the revolutionaries in Mexico City rather than because of internal factors.

279 **The Mexican Revolution.**
Alan Knight. Cambridge, England; New York: Cambridge University Press, 1986. 2 vols. bibliog.
Classic account of the Mexican Revolution, largely written from the point of view of the various Revolutionary groups and interests. The author believes that the men of action were far more important in determining the outcome than were the intellectuals who drafted the Constitution and later wrote their memoirs.

280 **US–Mexican relations 1910-40: an interpretation.**
Alan S. Knight. San Diego, California: Centre for US–Mexican Studies, University of California, 1989. 149p. (San Diego Monograph, no. 28).

The author looks at the various conflicts between Mexico and the United States during this period, but also at factors making for accommodation. He argues that the key turning point was the Calles–Morrow agreement of 1927. His account is particularly interesting in relation to the activities of US pressure groups interested in Mexico.

281 **The rise and fall of *Cardenismo* 1930-46.**
Alan S. Knight. In: *Mexico since Independence*, edited by L. Bethell. Cambridge, England; New York: Cambridge University Press, 1991, p. 241-321.

Cardenismo is a contentious subject among historians. Knight discusses the range of issues thoroughly and concludes that the conflict between Cárdenas and Calles briefly radicalized Mexican politics. The coming of war and then cold war shifted the political balance back towards a more conservative orientation.

282 **Centaur of the North: Francisco Villa, the Mexican Revolution and northern Mexico.**
Manuel Machado. Austin, Texas: Eakin Press, 1988. 195p.

A vigorous narrative of Villa's career and his period in a readable and popular style. The work deals with the man himself more than the context. There are fifteen pages of photographs.

283 **Anarchism and the Mexican Revolution: the political trials of Ricardo Flores Magon in the United States.**
Colin M. MacLachan. Berkeley, California; Los Angeles, California; Oxford, England: University of California Press, 1991. 139p. bibliog.

This work studies the career of the anarchist leader Flores Magon. Flores Magon was involved in political organization on both sides of the border. He has sometimes been seen as a radical liberal, but the author is keen to establish his anarchist identity.

284 **Revolution and reconstruction in the 1920s.**
Jean Meyer. In: *Mexico since Independence*, edited by L. Bethell. Cambridge, England; New York: Cambridge University Press, 1991, p. 201-41.

Professor Meyer offers a survey of political history, economic change and social conditions during the period. He sees the economy as being the weak link in the otherwise successful state-strengthening policies of the Sonoran dynasty.

285 **The myth of the Revolution: hero cults and the institutionalisation of the Mexican state 1920-1940.**
Irene V. O'Malley. New York; Westport, Connecticut; London: Greenwood, 1986. 179p. bibliog.
The author looks at the public images presented by the main Revolutionary leaders. She considers these as examples of political myth-making. She then looks at the way in which Revolutionary myths were used to underpin the new political order after 1920.

286 **Region, state and capitalism in Mexico: nineteenth and twentieth centuries.**
Edited by Will Pansters, Arij Ouweneel. Amsterdam, The Netherlands: Centre for Latin American Research and Documentation, 1989. 218p.
This is essentially an enquiry into the nature of regional power structures in Mexico and the way in which these withstood, or otherwise, the Revolutionary onslaught. There are chapters on Tlaxcala, Oaxaca, San Luis Potosí and other states; most of the contributors are well-known historians.

287 **Pancho Villa and John Reed; two faces of romantic revolution.**
Jim Tuck. Tucson, Arizona: University of Arizona Press, 1984. 236p. bibliog.
Villa was born poor and Reed wealthy but both became symbols of the romantic phase of the Mexican Revolution. The author is sympathetic to both figures, and provides an account of their experiences.

288 **From insurrection to revolution in Mexico: social bases of agrarian violence 1750-1940.**
John Tutino. Princeton, New Jersey: Princeton University Press, 1986. 362p. bibliog.
John Tutino's main question is why agrarian grievances, which were regionally specific in 1810, should have been the basis of a national movement by 1910. The author believes that population growth was partly responsible, as was the expansion of commercial agriculture during the Porfiriato, and also the trade cycle inherent in capitalist agriculture.

289 **The political project of Zapatismo.**
Arturo Warman. In: *Riot, rebellion and revolution: rural social conflict in Mexico*, edited by F. Katz. Princeton, New Jersey: Princeton University Press, 1989, p. 321–38.
Warman argues that Zapatismo had a coherent political plan based upon the class interests of the peasantry. He attributes the defeat of Zapatismo to tactical political errors rather than to any shortcomings in his political ideas.

290 **Zapata and the Mexican Revolution.**
John Womack. New York: Knopf, 1969. 435p. bibliog.

A definitive and full-length study of Zapata's revolt. The author provides a sympathetic, essentially narrative account of a complex process of insurgency, political negotiation and social change.

Anthropology and Ethnography

General

291 **Directions in the anthropological study of Latin America.**
Edited by Jack Rollwagen. Albany, New York: Society for Latin
American Anthropology, 1986. 219p. bibliog. (SLAA monographs,
no. 8).
A useful volume of survey articles giving an account of the state of the art in the mid-
1980s. The works include references to Mexico.

292 **Derecho indígena y derechos humanos en América Latina.** (Indigenous
law and human rights in Latin America.)
Rodolfo Stavenhagen. Mexico City: Colegio de México, 1988. 383p.
bibliog.
This work includes but is not limited to a discussion on Mexico. It looks at the impact
of state power upon indigenous groups and details human rights legislation, as well as
violations of rights. The author is a noted Mexico anthropologist.

Anthropology of Mexico

293 **Los pescadores de Tecolutla: el tiempo cotidano y el espacio doméstico en una villa de pescadores.** (The fishermen of Tecolutla: daily life and domestic space in a fishing village.)
Graciela Alcalá. Mexico City: Centro de Investigaciones y Estudios Superiores en Antropologia Social, 1985. 20p. bibliog.

This is a relatively rare anthropological study of a fishing village. Tecolutla is situated in northern Veracruz. The work studies the daily life, social structure and social conditions in this village.

294 **The state and uneven agrarian development in Mexico.**
Lourdes Arizpe. In: *Politics in Mexico*, edited by George Philip. Beckenham, England: Croom Helm, 1985, p. 54-79.

A short but important article on the way in which state policies have impacted upon households in poor rural areas. The author argues that the rôle of the state was essentially constructive until 1940, and less so thereafter.

295 **Men in a developing society: geographic and social mobility in Monterrey, Mexico.**
Jorge Balan, Harley Browning, Elizabeth Jelin. Austin, Texas: ILAS, University of Texas 1973. 383p. bibliog.

This is a detailed and well-researched discussion of class structure, social stratification and change in Monterrey. During the 1960s, however, this city was particularly dynamic and successful, and the findings are not likely to be typical across Mexico as a whole.

296 **Native ethnography: a Mexican Indian describes his culture.**
H. Russell Bernard, Jesús Salinas Pedraza. New York; London: Sage, 1989.

Salinas is a Nahua Indian from Hidalgo. Bernard has provided annotated translations from the Nahua. One problem with the Nahua culture is that it lacks written tradition. Salinas has produced this ethnography to encourage reading in his local language; the work is here produced in English. It describes the geography, flora and fauna of his native territory.

297 **Power and persuasion: fiestas and social control in rural Mexico.**
Stanley Brandes. Philadelphia, Pennsylvania: University of Pennsylvania, 1988. 212p. maps. bibliog.

The author is concerned with the social consequences of fiestas. He argues that the celebration of religious fiestas is a means of mantaining social control and transmitting shared values. The community observed is around Tzintzuntzan, which was in pre-Conquest days the capital of the Tarascan empire.

298 **The Indian Christ, the Indian King; historical substrata of Maya myth and ritual.**
Victoria Reifler Bricker. Austin, Texas: University of Texas Press, 1981. 368p. bibliog.

This work traces back a number of modern Maya rituals and argues that their origin is often to be found in colonial rather than ancient times. It analyses major events in Maya history such as the Tzeltal rebellion and the Caste War. It includes several Maya texts with the author's translations.

299 **Change and uncertainty in a peasant community: the Maya corn farmers of Zinacantan.**
Frank Cancian. Stanford, California: Stanford University Press, 1972. 208p. maps. bibliog.

A study of the response of Zinacantan corn farmers to new roads and a government corn-buying programme. Among aspects discussed are planting practices, crop yields and marketing arrangements. The key argument is that the very poor are risk averse, because any reduction in their income is life threatening, and also the relatively wealthy, because failure would threaten their status in the community. The most enterprising peasants are mainly to be found around the middle-income level.

300 **The skeleton at the feast: the Day of the Dead in Mexico.**
Elizabeth Carmichael, Chloe Sayer. London: British Museum Publications, 1991. 160p. map. bibliog.

The Days of the Dead in Mexico are 1st and 2nd November. The dead are said to be given permission to return to earth each year on these dates. This work includes an illustration of artefacts produced for the celebrations and also gives the background to the festival, which reviews pre-Hispanic religious belief and practice.

301 *Ejidos* **and regions of refuge in Northwestern Mexico.**
Edited by Ross N. Crumrine, Phil C. Weigand. Tucson, Arizona: University of Arizona Press, 1987. 113p. map. (Anthropological Papers of the University of Arizona, no. 46).

The various contributors seek to compare and explore the interaction of cultures in the northwest of Mexico. The communities discussed include the Yaqui, the Maya, the Tarascans as well as some *ejidos* [self-managed agrarian co-operatives] run by mestizos [people of mixed race].

302 **Intervillage conflict in Oaxaca.**
Philip A. Dennis. New Brunswick, New Jersey; London: Rutgers University Press, 1987. 213p. maps. bibliog.

The author argues that the Mexican state has maintained its control of rural Mexico by a policy of divide and rule. It has done this by encouraging low-level village conflict while at the same time taking care to keep it within bounds.

303 **Heaven-born Merida and its destiny: the book of Chilam Balam of Chumayel.**
Translated by Munro Edmonson. Austin, Texas: University of Texas Press, 1986. 309p. bibliog.
A new translation of this work, which is a book of Mayan prophecy and history. It was probably written at some time between 1824 and 1837, though it draws upon sources which are very much older. Edmonson provides an introduction which places the work in the context of its time.

304 **The myth of ritual: a native's ethnography of Zapotec life-crisis rituals.**
Fadiva El Gundi, Abel Hernández Jiménez. Tucson, Arizona: University of Arizona Press, 1986. 147p. maps.
This work describes the Zapotec culture from the point of view of a Zapotec Indian. The authors observe and interpret a baptism, a wedding, and funerals for married and unmarried people.

305 **Tzintzuntzan: Mexican peasants in a changing world.**
George McClelland Foster. New York: Elsevier, 1979. 392p. bibliog.
This is an updated study of fieldwork which was originally done first during 1945-46 and then between 1958 and 1965. This volume further records those changes which took place between 1966 and 1979. The focus of the research is the extent to which traditional customs and values have survived the social changes since 1945.

306 **Agrarian revolt in a Mexican village.**
Paul Friedrich. Chicago, Illinois: University of Chicago Press, 1977. 2nd ed. 162p. maps. bibliog.
An examination of the changes which took place in the village of Naranja between 1885 and 1920, and which led to Naranja's participation in the Revolutionary upheaval. The book follows two field projects undertaken in 1955-56 and 1966-68. The work was first published in 1970. This new edition contains a new preface and an updated bibliography.

307 **The Princes of Naranja: an essay in anthropological method.**
Paul Friedrich. Austin, Texas: University of Texas at Austin, 1986. 262p.
A participant-observer's study, based on interviews and observation, which was a follow-up to the author's earlier work on Naranja. This time the focus is on the political and social organization of Naranja, particularly with respect to *caciquismo* which is seen here as a natural response to troubled times. There is also a semi-autobiographical section relating to Friedrich's involvement in the earlier project.

308 **La antropología en México: panorama histórico. Tomo 1, los hechos y los dichos.** (Anthropology in Mexico: a historical panorama. Vol. 1, actions and words.)
Carlos Garcia Mora (et al.). Mexico City: INAH, 1987. 596p. bibliog.
A set of essays which cover fully and comprehensively the history of anthropological work in Mexico. There are chapters on colonial antecedents, ethnography during the national period, and the positivist approach of the Porfiriato.

309 **Blood ties; life and violence in rural Mexico.**
James Greenberg. Tucson, Arizona: University of Arizona Press, 1989. 237p.
Part one of this book is a first-person account on the part of one Don Fortino, a native of Chatino. The second part is analysis, focusing specifically on the question of violent homicide – of which there is a great deal. Alcohol and fear seem to play the major parts. However, the incidence of violence fell after 1977 due, in part, to an increasingly active women's movement.

310 **Anthropological perspectives on rural Mexico.**
Cynthia Hewitt de Alcantara. London; Boston, Massachusetts; Melbourne, Australia; Henley, England: Routledge and Kegan Paul, 1984. 192p. bibliog.
The author, one of Mexico's foremost anthropologists, considers various conceptual approaches to rural Mexico. The work is rather theoretical but will be important to those interested in conceptual issues.

311 **Modernizing Mexican agriculture; socio-economic implications of technological change 1940-70.**
Cynthia Hewitt de Alcantara. Geneva, Switzerland: United Nations Research Institute for Social Development, 1976. 350p. bibliog.
(UNRISD Studies on the Green Revolution, no. 11. Report, 76.5).
This is a well-documented study of agricultural change in Mexico, from the viewpoint of a prominent anthropologist. The work contains a considerable amount of data on agricultural production, the value and distribution of crops. The author is critical of the authorities for neglecting agriculture during the 1960s.

312 **Irrigation and the Cuicatec ecosystem: a study of agriculture and civilization in north central Oaxaca.**
Joseph W. Hopkins 3rd. Ann Arbor, Michigan: University of Michigan Press, 1984. 148p. bibliog. (Memoirs of the Museum of Anthropology, no 17. Studies in Latin American ethnohistory and archaeology, no. 2).
This is a discussion of both historical and contemporary forms of agriculture of the Cuicatec people in the La Canada region of Mexico.

313 **The Mexican Kikapoo Indians.**
Felipe A. Latorre, Dolores L. Latorre. Austin, Texas: University of Texas Press, 1976. 401p. bibliog. (Texas Pan-American Series).

An anthropological study of a tribe of Indians which had its origin in the United States but which moved in the nineteenth century to just south of the US–Mexican border at Coahuila. The tribe is conservative in outlook, and the authors were among the first to win permission to visit and study them.

314 **Pedro Martinez: a Mexican peasant and his family.**
Oscar Lewis. New York: Random House, 1964. 507p.

Oscar Lewis's approach was to encourage individuals or several members of the same family to participate in lengthy, relatively unstructured interviews with little editing. This is a good example of such a work, with the story being told by means of tape-recorded interviews over a period of twenty years.

315 **Life in a Mexican village: Tepoztlán restudied.**
Oscar Lewis. Urbana, Illinois: University of Illinois Press, 1963. 512p. maps. bibliog.

Tepoztlán is in Morelos and was near the centre of the Zapatista Revolutionary movement. In the 1940s the village was studied by the anthropologist Robert Redfield. Oscar Lewis returned to the village twenty years later, to chronicle the effect of changes since then.

316 **Politics and ethnicity in the Rio Yaqui: Potam revisited.**
Thomas R. McGuire. Tucson, Arizona: University of Arizona Press, 1986. 165p. bibliog.

The author is interested in the fact that the Yaquis have been able to retain an essentially separate identity within overall Mexican society. They are frequently involved in conflict with the authorities. McGuire discusses the ability of Yaqui culture to maintain the allegiance of its young people despite rapid social change.

317 **Harmony ideology: justice and control in a Zapotec mountain village.**
Laura Nader. Stanford, California: Stanford University Press, 1990. 343p. bibliog.

Harmony ideology is based essentially on compromise, conciliation and consensus. It is central to the legal system and social organization of the Zapotec mountain villages studied. The author argues that it has been developed under colonial rule as a survival strategy; conflict is likely to bring in the unwelcome involvement of outsiders. The author studies the way in which the local court system works.

318 **The structure and historical development of the** *compadrazgo* **system in rural Tlaxcala.**
Hugo Nutini, Betty Bell.   Princeton, New Jersey: Princeton University Press, 1980. 494p. bibliog.

Ideological and structural integration of the *compadrazgo* **system in rural Tlaxcala.**
Hugo Nutini, Betty Bell.   Princeton, New Jersey: Princeton University Press, 1984. 503p. bibliog.

Todos Santos in rural Tlaxcala: a syncretic, expressive and symbolic analysis of the cult of the dead.
Hugo G. Nutini.   Princeton, New Jersey: Princeton University Press, 1988. 471p. maps. bibliog.
These three volumes comprise a major study of social institutions in Tlaxcala, which is a relatively underdeveloped state in central Mexico. The first volume studies the institution of *compradrazgo* [artificial kinship] in historical context. It argues that the original meaning was largely religious, but that it has become increasingly secular. This opens the way to great inequality within the relationship, which can now amount to a form of clientelism. The second volume is based on the structure and function of *compadrazgo*, while the third volume is concerned with the well-known cult of the dead. The author shows how the cult continued from pre-Columbian days with the toleration of the Church.

319 **Escalating disputes: social participation and change in the Oaxacan highlands.**
Philip C. Parnell.   Tucson, Arizona: University of Arizona Press, 1988. 175p.
Philip Parnell here focuses on the 25 *municipios* of the Villa Alta judicial district of the Sierra de Juárez. The inhabitants speak both Zapotec and Spanish. The author looks at the interaction between local law and custom, village politics, the Oaxacan state government and its legal system. An interesting and valuable account.

320 **El impacto de la industrialización en las comunidades rurales; el caso de Atequiza, Jalisco 1920-80.** (The impact of industrialization on rural communities: the example of Atequiza, Jalisco 1920-80.)
Fernando Pozos Ponce.   Guadalajara, Jalisco: Universidad de Guadalajara, 1987. 64p. bibliog. (Cuadernos de Difusión Científica, no. 9).
This is a study of the increasing complexity of social and economic life in a traditional agricultural community in the state of Jalisco. Recent industrial developments have had a major transforming effect. There is also a short historical section.

321 **Conflict, violence and morality in a Mexican village.**
Lola Romanucci-Ross. Chicago, Illinois: University of Chicago, 1986.
2nd ed. 222p. bibliog.

An anthropological study of a village in Morelos since the Revolution of 1910, which aims to show the way in which social and moral codes have evolved. Examples include concepts of *machismo*, bonds of kinship, and patronage. The main focus of the study is on the use of force and violence. The author shows that this has complex causes which, however, have much to do with feelings of powerlessness.

322 **Ethnicity and class conflict in rural Mexico.**
Frans Schryer. Princeton, New Jersey: Princeton University Press, 1990. 363p. bibliog.

This work looks at the interaction between ethnicity and class conflict. It focuses on the Huasteca region of Hidalgo. The period covered is from around 1880 to 1950. This is a complex, multidimensional analysis.

323 **Where the dove calls: the political ecology of a peasant corporate community in northwestern Mexico.**
Thomas E. Sheridan. Tucson, Arizona: University of Arizona Press, 1988. 237p. bibliog. (Arizona Studies in Human Ecology, no. 1).

A specifically focused study of two communities in northern Sonora. 'Political ecology' is a somewhat rarified name for conflicts around water and land issues. The account is rather narrow but nevertheless insightful.

324 **Class and society in central Chiapas.**
Robert Wasserstrom. Berkeley, California: University of California Press, 1984. 357p. bibliog.

The author adopts a regional rather than village framework for this study. He plays down the rôle of the Maya heritage and emphasizes instead the colonial and post-colonial period as shaping forces for contemporary society.

325 **Medical choice in a Mexican village.**
James Clay Young. New Brunswick, New Jersey: Rutgers University Press, 1981. 233p. bibliog.

The people of Pichataro, a Tarascan Indian village in the highlands of west central Mexico, use both orthodox medicine and traditional folk medicines. Dr Young here identifies the factors that influence the patient's choice, and constructs a formal model of the decision-making process employed. In general the key consideration is the severity of the illness. Patients suffering from life-threatening illnesses pay for the service of physicians, while minor ailments are treated with folk remedies.

Language and Linguistics

326 Tzotzil clause structure.
Judith L. Aissen.   Dordrecht, The Netherlands: D. Riedel, 1987.
290p.
Tzotzil is a Mayan language spoken by some 120,000 people, mostly living in Chiapas.
This work explores the natural language syntax through analysing the grammar.

327 Studies in the syntax of Mixtecan languages.
Edited by Charles Henry Bradley, Barbara E. Hollenbach.   Dallas,
Texas: Academic Book Center, Summer Institute of Linguistics, 1989.
449p. bibliog. (Summer Institute of Linguistics Publications in
Linguistics, no. 83).
This work contains syntactic sketches of three varieties of Mixtec. Each provides
information about the location and number of speakers of the language, a statement of
the phonological structures, a core grammar and bibliography.

328 Some aspects of the lexical structure of a Mazatec historical text.
George M. Cowan.   Norman, Oklahoma: University of Oklahoma,
Summer Institute of Linguistics, 1965. 146p. bibliog. (Summer Institute
of Linguistics Publications, no. 11).
The title is largely self-explanatory. This is a study of the structure of the Mazatec
language.

329 Generative syntax of Penoles Mixtec.
John P. Daly.   Dallas, Texas: Summer Institute of Linguistics, 1973.
90p. bibliog. (Publications in Linguistics Series, no. 42).
An analysis of Mixtec grammar, originally presented as a doctoral thesis and revised
for publication.

330 **The Jacaltec language.**
Christopher Day.   Bloomington, Indiana: Indiana University Press,
1973. 135p. (Language Science Monographs, vol. 12).
A grammar of the Mayan language of Jacaltec, which is spoken in parts of Guatemala
and in the Mexican state of Chiapas.

331 **Tzutujil grammar.**
John Philip Dayley.   Berkeley, California: University of California
Press, 1985. 412p. bibliog. (Publications in Linguistics, no. 107).
Tzutujil is a Mayan language. This is a thorough and detailed work with a full
bibliography.

332 **A grammar of Mam, a Mayan language.**
Nora C. English.   Austin, Texas: University of Texas Press, 1983.
353p. bilbliog. (Texas Linguistics Series).
Mam is one of the most complicated of the Mayan languages. This work includes
phonology, roots and words, sentence formations, complex structures and other aids to
understanding the language. It will be a standard reference book.

333 **Speaking Mexicano: dynamics of syncretic language in Central Mexico.**
Jane H. Hill, Kenneth C. Hill.   Tucson, Arizona: University of
Arizona Press, 1986. 493p.
Mexicano is an ancient language spoken by the Toltecs and the Aztecs which has
adapted by incorporating some Spanish. Most Mexicano speakers in fact speak
Spanish, which is necessary for economic participation, but there are social pressures
toward bilingualism. This is both a sociological and linguistic analysis of Mexicano
speakers who live mainly around the Malinche volcano in the states of Puebla and
Tlaxcala.

334 **The foreign impact on lowland Mayan language and script.**
John S. Justeson, William Norman, Lyle Campbell, Terence
Kaufman.   New Orleans, Louisiana: University of Tulane, Middle
America Research Institute, 1985. 97p. bibliog.
This work studies the way in which the Mayan language has borrowed from others
within the same linguistic area.

335 **Nahuatl in the middle years: language control phenomena in texts of the
colonial period.**
Frances Karttunen, James Lockhart.   Berkeley, California: University
of California Press, 1976. 146p. bibliog. (Publications in Linguistics
Series, vol. 85).
A study of the language of central Mexican Indian communities during the colonial
period. The book also examines the influence of Spanish on the language.

336 **Maya; the completed catalog of glyph readings.**
Edited by Kornelia Kurbjulin. Kassel, Germany: Schneider and
Weber, 1989. 239p. bibliog.
This is a catalogue of proposed readings of Maya script with material from 28 leading
scholars. As a result, the whole range of possible interpretations is presented in the
same volume, with full data on the differences between the various approaches.

337 **The great Tzotzil dictionary and Santo Domingo, Zinacantan; with
grammatical analysis and historical commentary. v.1 Tzotzil–English.
v.2 English–Tzotzil. v.3 Spanish–Tzotzil.**
Robert M. Laughlin, John Beard Haviland. Washington, DC:
Smithsonian Institution Press, 1988. 3 vols (1119p.). bibliog.
(Smithsonian Contributions to Anthropology, no. 31).
An anonymous Dominican friar produced a Tzotzil dictionary towards the end of the
sixteenth century. This new edition is a definitive work. It has added two volumes
translating into and out of English. There is also a thesaurus and a comparative
grammatical sketch of colonial Tzotzil.

338 **Yaqui syntax.**
Jacqueline Lindenfield. Berkeley, California: University of California
Press, 1974. 162p. bibliog. (University of California Publications in
Linguistics, vol. 76).
A study of the syntactic structure of the Yaqui language. The Yaqui-speaking
community is located in Sonora, and is mostly bilingual.

339 **Chatino syntax.**
Kitty Price. Norman, Oklahoma: University of Oklahoma, Summer
Institute of Linguistics, 1965. 248p. bibliog. (Publications in Linguistics
and Related Fields Series, no. 12).
A grammar dealing with the Yaitepec dialect of the Indian language of Chatino,
spoken by an Indian community living in the southwest of Oaxaca.

340 **Papago and Pima to English, English to Papago and Pima dictionary.**
Dean Saxton, Lucille Saxton. Tucson, Arizona: University of Arizona
Press, 1969. 191p. bibliog.
A useful reference manual for the Papago–Pima language which is used by the desert
people of northern Sonora.

341 **Maya hieroglyphs without tears.**
J. Eric Thompson. London: British Museum, Department of
Ethnography, 1972. 84p. maps.
An updated version of the author's earlier *Maya hieroglyphic writing*. The work is well
illustrated and emphasizes the use of the calendar and ritual.

Religion

342 **Alienation of Church wealth in Mexico: social and economic aspects of the liberal revolution, 1856-1875.**
Jan Bazant, edited and translated from the Spanish by Michael P. Costeloe. Cambridge, England: Cambridge University Press, 1971. 332p. bibliog. (Cambridge Latin America Series, no. 11).
The most noteworthy feature of Mexican liberalism in the mid-nineteenth century was its anticlericalism. The Church was divested of much of its wealth between 1856 and 1875. Bazant has written a classic account of this process.

343 **Prophecy and myth in Mexican history.**
D. A. Brading. Cambridge, England: Centre for Latin American Studies, University of Cambridge, 1984. 96p.
Mexico is officially a secular state, but with a religious tradition involving both Catholicism and pre-Columbian myths. The result has often been tension and conflict. Brading's short collection of essays, lucid and scholarly in presentation, are markedly sympathetic to the Catholic tradition in Mexico.

344 **Book of the gods and rites and the ancient calendar.**
Diego Durán, edited and translated from the Spanish by Fernando Horcasitas, Doris Heyden. Norman, Oklahoma: University of Oklahoma Press, 1971. 502p. bibliog. (Civilization of the American Indian Series, no. 102).
A translation of one of the classic studies of the Aztec religion and calendrical system. It includes a biographical study of Durán taken from his own writings.

345 **Mary, Michael and Lucifer: folk Catholicism in central Mexico.**
John M. Ingham. Austin, Texas: Institute of Latin American Studies,
University of Texas, 1986. 216p. bibliog. (Latin American Monographs,
no. 69).
A study of folk Catholicism in a village of Spanish-speaking inhabitants of Morelos.
The author argues that Catholic myth and symbolism remains very pervasive and
culturally important.

346 **Quetzalcoatl and Guadalupe: the formation of Mexican national
consciousness, 1531-1812.**
Jacques Lafae, translated from the French by Benjamin Keen.
Chicago, Illinois: University of Chicago Press, 1976. 336p.
A study of the character and importance of religious beliefs in colonial Mexico, with
discussion of the pre-Columbian legacy as well as the doctrines brought to Mexico by
the Spanish religious orders.

347 **Native Mesoamerican spirituality.**
Edited by Miguel León Portilla. New York; Toronto, Canada: Paulist
Press, 1980. 279p.
Apart from the introduction, most of this work consists of ancient myths, stories,
poems and other insights into the religious culture of the main pre-Columbian
Mesoamericans. This volume is mainly for the student or general reader.

348 **The Cristero rebellion: the Mexican people between Church and state,
1926-1929.**
Jean Meyer. Cambridge, England; New York: Cambridge University
Press, 1976. 260p. bibliog. (Cambridge Latin American Studies Series,
no. 24).
A translation of the three-volume work published in 1974 in Spanish under the title *La
cristiada*. Meyer's account is generally regarded as the definitive study of the Cristero
revolt, which the author regards with considerable sympathy. The English-language
version is much shorter, but nevertheless intellectually formidable.

349 **Mexican churches.**
Eliot Porter, Ellen Auerbach. Albuquerque, New Mexico: University
of New Mexico Press, 1987. 20p.
This work has a short text but 89 illustrated plates; many of the churches photographed
have since been altered through being modernized. The churches are heavily adorned,
and the influence of Indian culture can be seen in much of the décor.

350 **The Mexican revolution and the Catholic Church 1910-1929.**
Robert E. Quirk. Bloomington, Indiana: Indiana University Press,
1973. 276p.
A study of the confrontation between the Mexican revolutionary nationalists and the
Catholic Church. There is also material on the earlier history of the Church.

Religion

351 **Spanish Jesuit churches in Mexico's Tarahumara.**
Paul M. Roca. Tucson, Arizona: University of Arizona Press, 1979.
369p. bibliog.
This book is useful both for its architectural details, including many photographs, and for the religious history of the Tarahumara Indians. It is concerned mainly with Jesuit churches built in Western Chihuahua between 1611 and 1767.

352 **Traditional papermaking and paper cult figures of Mexico.**
Alan R. Sandstrom, Pamela Effrein Sandstrom. Norman, Oklahoma: University of Oklahoma Press, 1986. 327p. bibliog.
A discussion of the use of paper images by shaman of the Huasteca region, and their rôle in religious symbolism. There is also an historical introduction.

353 **Mexico mystique: the coming sixth world of consciousness.**
Frank Waters. Chicago, Illinois: Sage, 1975. 326p. bibliog.
A study of the religious and spiritual background of Mexico, as seen in its mythology and symbolism. The concepts of time found in the Mayan calendar and astronomical calculation are also discussed.

Social Services, Health and Welfare

354 The political economy of income distribution in Mexico.
Edited by Pedro Aspe, Paul Sigmund. New York: Holmes and Meier, 1984. 543p.

This is a collection of sixteen chapters covering education, health, housing, food subsidies, taxation, foreign investment and many other issues. The editors' introduction states that the distribution of income in Mexico has remained essentially unchanged since 1950 despite many efforts by policy-makers to improve it. If there has been a trend, it has been one of slow deterioration. A key element in poverty is non-completion of primary school education.

355 Distribution of education and health opportunities and services.
Pedro Aspe, Jorge Berinstain. In: *The political economy of income distribution in Mexico*, edited by Pedro Aspe, Paul Sigmund. New York; London: Holmes and Meier, 1984, p. 265-327.

This study shows that the level of education correlates closely with the distribution of income in Mexico. Geographical factors are important both in addition to and as a predictor of educational achievement. There is, broadly speaking, a north–south division in Mexico with the northern states providing more thorough education. However, the Federal District remains important as a location for secondary and university education.

356 Economic crisis and the decentralisation of health services in Mexico.
M. A. Gonzalez Block. In: *Social responses to Mexico's economic crisis of the 1980s*, edited by M. Gonzalez de la Rocha, A. Escobar Latapí. San Diego, California: Center for US–Mexican Studies, University of California, 1991, p. 67-91.

The author examines the promised decentralization of health provision in Mexico. He finds that it is taking place, but that it has been slowed down by local opposition and lack of funds. The results of the decentralization are uneven.

357 **Mexico City: the supply of a primary health care service.**
Margaret Harrison. *Bulletin of Latin American Research*, vol. 10, no. 2 (1991), p. 239-59.

The article is critical of government health care policies, which the author sees as heavily constrained by lack of funds. The few resources which are available are devoted to the bureaucratically run contributory system rather than to community health care.

358 **Health and social security in Mexico.**
Emilio Lozoya Thalmann. In: *The political economy of income distribution in Mexico*, edited by Pedro Aspe, Paul Sigmund. New York; London: Holmes and Meier, 1984, p. 397-439.

A historical survey of the plurality of institutions involved with provision of health care and social security in Mexico. The system is contributory and mostly benefits people in government employment. There has, however, been increased coverage within this sector.

359 **Production and participation in rural areas; some political considerations.**
Carlos Salinas de Gortari. In: *The political economy of income distribution in Mexico*, edited by Pedro Aspe, Paul Sigmund. New York; London: Holmes and Meier, 1984, p. 523-43.

An important piece by the future President of Mexico. Here he looks critically at rural development programmes. He argues that their outcome did little to improve either income distribution or political support for the system, though they did have some positive impact on economic growth. Salinas thinks that there should be more careful targeting of these programmes.

360 **U.S.–Mexican border public health; a policy analysis.**
Reuel Stallones, Lorann Stallones. In: *United States relations with Mexico: context and content*, edited by Richard Erb, Stanley Ross. Washington, DC; London: American Enterprise Institute for Public Policy Research, [n.d.], p. 89-96.

The article looks at cross-border cooperation in controlling the transmission of infectious disease. It compares comparative morbidity ratios in Mexico and the United States.

361 **Re-thinking the circle of poison: the politics of pesticide poisoning among Mexican farm workers.**
Angus Wright. *Latin American Perspectives*, vol. 13, no. 4 (1986), p. 26-59.

Wright relates the issue of the article to a larger environmental and community health concern, and also to the policies of transnational corporations and the Mexican state.

Society

Social conditions

362 **Law and market society in Mexico.**
George Armstrong. New York: Praeger, 1989. 155p. bibliog.
This is a study of Mexico's legal and economic development. Armstrong argues that Mexico lacks an adequate legal concept of private property, and that development has therefore been held back by excessive state control of the legal system.

363 **A rich land, a poor people: politics and society in modern Chiapas.**
Thomas Benjamin. Albuquerque, New Mexico: University of New Mexico, 1989. 350p. bibliog.
Chiapas is one of the poorest states of Mexico, whose social structure resembles that of Guatemala more than that of some other parts of Mexico. Benjamin's study aims to demonstrate that Chiapas is governed by a power élite, based on property, which is committed above all to keeping the poor in their place.

364 **Los migrantes de la crisis: the changing profile of Mexican migration to the United States.**
Wayne Cornelius. In: *Social responses to Mexico's economic crisis of the 1980s*, edited by M. Gonzalez de la Rocha and A. Escobar Latapí. San Diego, California: Center for US–Mexican Studies, University of California, 1991, p. 155-95.
Professor Cornelius traces out the ways in which the 1980s economic crisis changed the pattern of migration to the United States. There was migration from a greater diversity of states; the Federal District sent more migrants; there was increased female migration; and there was a growing tendency to seek urban destinations within the United States.

365 **Politics and the migrant poor in Mexico City.**
Wayne Cornelius.   Stanford, California: Stanford University Press,
1975. 319p. bibliog.

Cornelius uses a variety of techniques – interviews, questionnaires, and general surveys –
to study the life of the migrant poor in Mexico City. His study includes discussion of
community leadership and leadership rôles, political attitudes and involvement, the
making of political demands and the response of the political system. He finds that
recent migrants are relatively conservative, their demands upon the system moderate
and their manner deferential. As a result they are more likely to be a source of support
for the system than a threat to it.

366 **The poverty of revolution: the state and the urban poor in Mexico.**
Susan Eckstein.   Princeton, New Jersey: Princeton University Press,
1977. 300p. maps. bibliog.

This work analyses a city slum, a semi-rural area and a government-financed planned
community. It is very much concerned with the means by which the poor are
incorporated into the political system. Eckstein sees this incorporation as a bad bargain
because the poor give up their capacity to exert power in an independent manner in
return for a few benefits which do not seriously alter the pattern of inequality within
Mexican society.

367 **Being Indian in Hueyapan: a study of forced identity in contemporary
Mexico.**
Judith Friedlander.   New York: St Martin's Press, 1975. 205p. bibliog.

A description of life in Hueyapan which is a Nahuatl-speaking community. Being
Indian, as the author shows, is to be poor and oppressed. What little Indian culture
survives contains much European influence.

368 **Landlord and tenant: housing the poor in urban Mexico.**
Alan Gilbert, Ann Varley.   London: Routledge, 1991. 201p. bibliog.

Most Mexicans have traditionally lived in rented accommodation though there is now a
move in the direction of self-help housing. Renting remains important, however, and
may even have been increasing after the economic crisis of the 1980s. The authors
discuss the cases of Guadalajara and Puebla in some detail, from the historical and
economic viewpoints, and present a range of policy options for discussion.

369 **State and peasantry in Mexico: a case study of rural credit in
La Laguna.**
Fernando Rello.   Geneva, Switzerland: UNIDO, 1987. 113p. (Report
no. 85).

The author is very critical of the self-perpetuating character of the state-owned rural
development bank's loans to poor peasants. These reinforce dependency, add to
inefficiency and reinforce the lack of democracy within the *ejidos*.

370 **Land reform in Mexico 1910-80.**
Susan Walsh Sanderson.   Orlando, Florida: Academic Press, 1984.
186p. bibliog. (Studies in Social Discontinuity).
This work is a survey of land reform in Mexico, bringing the account up to the end of
the 1970s. The book focuses mainly on political concerns, but it also sees a conflict
between the political and the economic objectives of reform.

371 **Urbanization and agrarian law; the case of Mexico City.**
Ann Varley.   *Bulletin of Latin American Research*, vol. 4, no. 1
(1985), p. 1-17.
The *ejido* land tenure system was intended to apply to agriculture. With the spread of
urbanization, however, *ejido* territory was in some cases converted into valuable real
estate. This article shows how the Constitution's intention that collective interests
should be protected has been systematically undermined by the powerful who have
used or subverted the system in order to make fortunes.

Social change

372 **Population and development in Mexico since 1940: an interpretation.**
Francisco Alba, Joseph Potter.   *Population Development Review*, vol.
12, no. 1 (March 1986), p. 47-76.
This article examines government population policies and considers how far official
action was responsible for the slow decline in the Mexican birth rate which started
around 1970. The article also looks at the relevance of the Mexican experience for
other less developed countries (LDCs).

373 **The population of Mexico: trends, issues and policies.**
Francisco Alba, translated from the Spanish by Marjory Mattingly
Urquidi.   New Brunswick, New Jersey: Translation Books, 1982.
127p. bibliog.
A short but excellent introduction to an important topic. Subjects discussed include the
growth of population, migration, the age distribution of the population, and
employment prospects. The author also discusses social problems and policy issues.
The book was originally published in Spanish in 1979.

374 **Political conflict and land tenure in the Mexican isthmus of Tehuantepec.**
Leigh Binford.   *Journal of Latin American Studies*, vol. 17, no. 1 (May
1985), p. 179-200.
The author is concerned to explain the outbreak of political militancy in a previously
quiet area of rural Mexico. He finds a link to disappointment felt among the peasants
who did not benefit from access to the new land made available for colonization after
the opening of the Benito Juárez dam.

375 **Rhetoric, reality and self-sufficiency: recent initiatives in Mexican rural development.**
Merilee S. Grindle. *Journal of Developing Areas*, vol. 19, no. 2 (1985), p. 171-84.
Grindle looks mainly at attempts made during the oil boom years to improve the position of the Mexican rural population. Progress was very mixed.

376 **Como somos los mexicanos.** (Mexicans as we are.)
Edited by Alberto Hernández Medina, Luis Narro Rodríguez.
Mexico City: Centro de Estudios Educativos, 1987. 299p. bibliog.
A study of Mexican social attitudes to a variety of issues. Chapters cover Mexican political values, religion and morality, attitudes towards work, education and so forth. Sophisticated sampling data is used and efforts are made to separate out the attitudes of different genders, age groups, social classes and so on.

377 **Social inequality in Oaxaca: a history of resistance and change.**
Arthur D. Murphy, Alex Stepick. Philadelphia, Pennsylvania: Temple University Press, 1991. 282p. bibliog.
This is a study which covers a period of more than 2,000 years. The authors argue that although Oaxaca is poor, it is more equally poor than other parts of Mexico. This is a controversial thesis. The main data used by this book are from 1977. Much information is included about the social and political structure of present-day Oaxaca.

378 **La industria en los magueyales: trabajo y sindicatos en Ciudad Sahagún.**
(Industry in the rural areas: work and trade unions in Ciudad Sahagún.)
Victoria Novelo, Augusto Urteaga. Mexico City: Nuevo Imagen, 1979. 229p. bibliog.
A classic study of the development and transformation of Mexican working-class society at Ciudad Sahagún in Hidalgo. This was a rural site as recently as the 1960s but it industrialized heavily in the 1970s and many of the workers brought in were of rural origin.

379 **Nutritional strategies and agricultural change in a Mexican community.**
Kathleen M. De Walt. Ann Arbor, Michigan: University of Michigan Research Press, 1983. 211p. bibliog. (Studies in Cultural Anthropology).
This work examines the relationship between several factors in a mixed *mestizo/Mazuhua municipio* in Central Mexico. These factors include diet, nutritional status and the availability of food. De Walt finds that household economic status strongly influences diet and nutrition, while agricultural strategies are much less important.

The rôle of women

380 **The women of Mexico City 1790-1857.**
Silvia Marina Arrom. Stanford, California: Stanford University Press, 1985. 384p. bibliog.

The author considers the impact of independence upon the status of women. She examines their legal position, demographic patterns, employment, marital relations and divorce. She considers also the way in which international trends and ideas shaped the behaviour of women during the period.

381 **Women and survival in Mexican cities: perspectives on gender, labour markets and low-income households.**
Sylvia Chant. Manchester, England: Manchester University Press, 1991. 270p. bibliog.

This is an important study based on fieldwork carried out in three cities with different types of economy. These are Puerta Vallarta, León and Queretaro. The theme of the book is the way in which women's employment, household structure and economic circumstances interrelate. The work includes material from a household and an employer survey.

382 **The Isthmus Zapotecs: women's roles in cultural context.**
Beverly Chinas. New York: Holt, Rinehart and Winston, 1973. 122p. map. bibliog. (Cast Studies in Cultural Anthropology).

An account of the social positions of women in the locality, with reference to marriage, mourning behaviour, the rôle of women in mediating conflicts, and as market salespeople.

383 **Plotting women: gender and representation in Mexico.**
Jean Franco. London: Verso, 1989. 235p. bibliog. (Critical Studies in Latin American Culture).

A discussion of the efforts by Mexican women to express their own identity in pre-feminist days. This was no easy matter, and a good deal of moral courage was often necessary.

384 **Economic crisis, domestic reorganisation and women's work in Guadalajara, Mexico.**
Mercedes Gonzalez de la Rocha. *Bulletin of Latin American Research*, vol. 7, no. 2 (1988), p. 207-25.

As a result of the economic crisis of the early 1980s, an increasing proportion of women went out to work; so, indeed, did older children. If this strategy failed, then households had no choice but to curtail already limited consumption.

385 **The Mexican *corrido*: a feminist analysis.**
Maria Herrera Sobek. Bloomington, Indiana: Indiana University
Press, 1990. 151p. bibliog.
The *corrido* is a popular form of folk song in Mexico. The author examines over 3,000
songs and analyses several typical rôles. These include the good mother, the bad
mother, the lover, the soldier and the goddess. The author is influenced by Jungian
concepts of archetype.

386 **Development strategies and the status of women: a comparative study of
the United States, Mexico, the Soviet Union and Cuba.**
Margaret E. Leahy. London; Boulder, Colorado: Lynne Rienner
Publishers; London: Francis Pinter Publishers, 1986. 167p. bibliog.
The aim of the book is to consider the status of women in two Communist countries
and two capitalist ones. There is a case-study chapter of women in Mexico.

387 **Women on the US–Mexican border: responses to change.**
Edited by Vicki Ruiz, Susan Tiano. Hemel Hempstead, England:
Allen and Unwin, 1987. 247p. bibliog.
This book challenges the stereotyped image of Mexican women as passive, and shows
that they often migrate either alone or with their children. The essays cover a range of
aspects of women as migrants, wage earners and contributors to the culture of the
border region.

388 **Two boys, a girl and enough! Reproductive and economic decision
making on the Mexican periphery.**
Jeanne M. Simonelli. Boulder, Colorado: Westview Press, 1991.
231p. bibliog. (Studies in Cross-Cultural Perspective Series).
This book considers the impact of modernization upon child-rearing practices in
various Sonoran *mestizo* peasant households. It predicts a decline in family size as
women become more influential in making decisions on reproduction.

389 **Emergence of the modern Mexican woman: her participation in
Revolution and struggle for equality 1910-40.**
Shirlene S. Soto. Denver, Colorado: Arden Press, 1990. 145p.
This is essentially a political history which is concerned with the ways in which female
workers were organized. The author discusses their participation in the Revolution and
in subsequent political life. The author states that female successes have been only
limited, and believes that attitudes derived from Catholicism have presented problems.

390 **From Calpixqui to *corregidor*: appropriation of women's cotton textile
production in early colonial Mexico.**
Margaret Villanueva. *Latin American Perspectives*, vol. 12, no. 1
(Winter 1985), p. 17-40.
Villanueva adopts a broadly Marxist orientation to examine the appropriation of
surplus value from women in the form of cotton textile products. The period refers to
the pre-*obraje* [colonial factory] days.

391 **Sweaters: gender, class and workshop based industry in Mexico.**
Fiona Wilson. London: Macmillan, 1991. 212p. bibliog. (International
Political Economy Series).
This is a local study of Santiago Tangamunchapio, in Michoacán. It discusses the
spread of workshop textile industry to a previously rural area in the 1960s. The main
focus is on gender rôles, unionization and conflict.

Migration and related issues

392 **Campesinado y migración.** (Peasants and migration.)
Lourdes Arizpe. Mexico City: SEP, 1985. 153p. bibliog.
Arizpe provides a general survey of the dynamics of Mexican peasant migration. She is
interested in both migration within Mexico itself and migration to the USA. The work
focuses on the period since the late 1940s and pays particular attention to the position
of women and indigenous peoples.

393 **Mexican migration to the United States: de facto rules.**
Jorge A. Bustamante. In: *Mexico and the United States; studies in
economic interaction,* edited by Peggy Musgrove. Boulder, Colorado:
Westview Press, 1985, p. 185-207.
The author reviews the history of Mexican–US diplomatic discussions over the
migration issue. He is sceptical that changes in law or regulations will have very much
effect.

394 **Regional and sectoral development in Mexico as alternatives to
migration.**
Edited by S. Díaz Briquets, S. Weintraub. Boulder, Colorado:
Westview Press, 1991. 389p. bibliog. (Series on Development and
International Migration in Mexico, Central America and the Caribbean
Basin, Vol. 2).
These authors have compiled a series of papers which look at various aspects of the
problem. It does seem that the pressures to migrate are very strong, and the kinds of
development considered here are likely to have only limited impact.

395 **The effects of receiving-country policies on migration flows.**
Edited by S. Díaz Briquets, S. Weintraub. Boulder, Colorado:
Westview Press, 1991. 298p. bibliog. (Series on Development and
International Migration in Mexico, Central America and the Caribbean
Basin, Vol. 6).
Most migrants are motivated primarily by economic considerations. This volume
discusses the wisdom of attempts to promote development in Mexico in order to
reduce the flow of migrants. The volume features considerable statistical analysis of
migration and its response to policy changes.

396 **Mexican migration to the United States; a critical review.**
Jorge Durand, Douglas Massey. *Latin American Research Review*,
vol. 27, no. 2 (1992), p. 3-42.
This is a general survey article which discusses a whole range of issues relating to migration. Who migrates? Why? With what effect? What migrant strategies are adopted and why? The approach adopted by the authors is cautious but informative.

397 **The Mexican–American border region. Issues and trends.**
Raul A. Fernández. Notre Dame, Indiana: University of Notre Dame
Press, 1989. 147p.
Fernández includes chapters on water issues, migrants, industrial and economic policy. It is written mainly for the general reader.

398 **Mexican immigration to the United States: a study of human migration
and adjustment.**
Manuel Gamio. New York: Dover, 1971. 262p. bibliog.
Mexican migration to the United States is not a new phenomenon. This is the reprint of a work which was researched during 1926 and 1927 and covered the migration during and just after the First World War.

399 **The Immigration Reform and Control Act of 1986: its implications and
prospects.**
Walter Greene, Jerry Prock. In: *US–Mexican economic relations:
prospects and problems*, edited by Khoscow Fatemi. New York;
London: Praeger, 1988, p. 65-75.
The authors are sceptical as to whether the latest immigration control law enacted in the United States will be any more effective than its predecessors. The United States economy needs undocumented migrants.

400 **Undocumented Mexicans in the United States.**
David Heer. Cambridge, England: Cambridge University Press, 1990.
229p. bibliog.
The author, a demographer, aims to provide a comprehensive statistical profile of a range of issues dealing with undocumented Mexican migration. Under the 1986 Immigration Control and Reform Act, some 3,100,000 Mexicans applied for legalization in the United States. Over 1 million per year are still deported as illegal.

401 **Changing boundaries in the Americas: new perspectives on the
U.S.–Mexican, Central American and South American borders.**
Edited by Lawrence A. Herzog. San Diego, California: Center for
US–Mexican Studies, 1992. 247p.
This work includes chapters on issues relating to the economy, the environment, migration and development. The US–Mexican border receives coverage in several chapters. Two of these are reviewed separately below (*see* items 405, 408). There is also one article on the Mexico–Guatemala border.

402 **Explaining origin patterns of undocumented migration to south Texas in recent years.**
Richard C. Jones. In: *The U.S. and Mexico: borderland development and the national economies*, edited by Lay James Gibson, Alfonso Corona Renteria. Boulder, Colorado; London: Westview Press, 1985, p. 203-20.
This is a study of who migrates from Mexico, to where and why. The author finds that those *municipios* sending most migrants to south Texas are wealthier, more urbanized and with a more equal income distribution than the others. Those who migrate to the United States are not generally the poorest.

403 **Migration and adaptation: Tzintzuntzan peasants in Mexico City.**
Robert V. Kemper. Beverly Hills, California: Sage Publications, 1977. 223p. maps. bibliog. (Sage Library of Social Research, vol. 43).
Fieldwork for this book was conducted between 1969 and 1976. This was the time when Mexico was just becoming a predominantly urban society. Kemper studies both the migration and the adaptation within Mexico itself.

404 **The welfare economics of labor migration from Mexico to the United States.**
John M. McDowell. In: *The U.S. and Mexico: borderland development and the national economies*, edited by Lay James Gibson, Alfonso Corona Renteria. Boulder, Colorado; London: Westview Press, 1985, p. 189-203.
Who benefits from migration? The migrants themselves presumably, but what about the receiving and sending communities? The author considers these points, and argues that the skill level of the migrants is a crucial factor.

405 **Urbanization and development of the United States–Mexico border.**
Rebecca Morales, Jesús Tamayo-Sanchez. In: *Changing boundaries in the Americas: new perspectives on the U.S.–Mexican, Central American and South American borders*, edited by Lawrence A. Herzog. San Diego, California: Center for US–Mexican Studies, 1992, p. 49-69.
This chapter provides a concise historical account of what the authors regard as the progressive integration of the two economies resulting from socio-economic change in the border region.

406 **Foreign immigrants in early Bourbon Mexico 1700-60.**
Charles F. Nunn. Cambridge, England: Cambridge University Press, 1979. 243p. bibliog. (Cambridge Latin American Studies, no. 31).
A study of the composition of foreign migrants to colonial Mexico (soldiers, sailors, merchants, prisoners of war who stayed on, churchmen, and others), the official attitudes of the government to them, laws that evolved, and the hurdles to acceptance which they faced.

407 **U.S. immigration in the 1980s: reappraisal and reform.**
Edited by David Simcox.   Boulder, Colorado: Westview Press, 1988.
308p.

This edited collection features a large number of articles.   Only three of these, by Richard Estrada, David Simcox, and the Urban Institute are specifically about Hispanic or Mexican migrants but several other presentations consider general issues raised by migration.

408 **The *maquila* industry and the creation of a transnational capitalist class in the United States–Mexico border region.**
Leslie Sklair.   In: *Changing boundaries in the Americas: new perspectives on the U.S.–Mexican, Central American and South American borders*, edited by Lawrence A. Herzog.   San Diego, California: Center for US–Mexican Studies, 1992, p. 69-87.

Sklair seeks to relate the rapid growth of the *maquila* industry to the development of what he calls a transnational capitalist class. There is an empirical study of the rôle of local business élites.

409 **Guatemalan refugees in Mexico 1980-84.**
Elicecer Valencia.   New York: America's Watch Committee, 1984.
104p. bibliog.

There may be as many 400,000 migrants into Mexico, many of whom are political refugees. Perhaps as many as 150,000 of these are Guatemalans. The Mexican government decided in the early 1980s to relocate refugees away from the border despite the fact that the move is resisted by the refugees themselves.

Government and Politics

The political system

410 **Electoral patterns and perspectives in Mexico.**
Edited by Arturo Alvarado. San Diego, California: Center for
US–Mexican Studies, 1987. 287p.

A collection of studies on regional and local electoral politics in Mexico up to, and
including, the 1985 elections. There is a wealth of detail on political geography and
voting behaviour.

411 **Governing Mexico: the statecraft of crisis management.**
John J. Bailey. Basingstoke, England: Macmillan Press, 1988. 238p.
bibliog.

A good general account of politics and policy-making in Mexico, dating from the mid-
1980s. A good deal has happened since then, but Bailey's account of interest-group
politics and government–business relations remains very relevant.

412 **Elections and political culture in Mexico.**
Miguel Basáñez. In: *Mexican politics in transition*, edited by Judith
Gentleman. Boulder, Colorado; London: Westview Press, 1987,
p. 181-201.

Basáñez is one of the first political scientists to have worked with electoral survey
material in Mexico. This is a study of public opinion in the early and mid-1980s. It is
clear that the Institutional Revolutionary Party (PRI) was still by far the most popular
party at that time.

413 **El pulso de los sexenios: 20 años de crisis en México.** (The rhythm of the presidential terms [each of 6 years]: twenty years of crisis in Mexico.) Miguel Basáñez. Mexico City: Siglo XXI, 1990. 411p. bibliog.

This is a very empirical study of trends in Mexican society and politics during the period 1968-88. The work includes material on public opinion. It is essentially a reference book for those interested in politics and recent political history.

414 **Mexico: auge, crisis y ajuste.** (Mexico: power, crisis and adjustment.) Edited by Carlos Bazdresch, Nisso Bucay, Soledad Loaeza, Nora Lustig. Mexico City: Fondo de Cultura Económica, 1991. 460p.

A collection of articles relating to the Mexican political system, Mexican foreign policy, and the policies of President de la Madrid. The contributors are both Mexican and foreign. There is a considerable amount of electoral survey material, introduced here for the first time.

415 **The political culture of authoritarianism in Mexico, a re-examination.** John Booth, Mitchell Seligson. *Latin American Research Review*, vol. 19, no. 1 (1984), p. 106-25.

An award-winning article which discusses the question of authoritarianism within Mexican political culture. After surveying the literature, the article provides new survey evidence which suggests that the supposed authoritarianism in Mexican political culture is a myth.

416 **Sucesión presidencial: the 1988 Mexican presidential election.** Edited by Edgar W. Butler, Jorge A. Bustamante. Boulder, Colorado; San Francisco, California; Oxford, England: Westview Press, 1991. 264p.

The essays in this volume are mostly short. There are some interesting insights. There is a tendency to sympathize with the political opposition.

417 **Mexican political biographies 1935-75.** Roderick A. Camp. Tucson, Arizona: University of Arizona Press, 1976. 468p. bibliog.

Camp is well known as the foremost exponent of political biography in Mexico. This is a relatively early volume which includes biographies of people prominent in Mexican political life between 1935 and early 1974. There are a number of appendices with lists of office-holders.

418 **Mexico's leaders: their education and recruitment.** Roderick A. Camp. Tucson, Arizona: University of Arizona Press, 1980. 259p. bibliog.

This is a study of the relationship between education and other cultural factors and the recruitment of Mexico's political leaders between 1911 and the 1950s. The book is well documented, well written and important. However, the pattern of recruitment would seem to have changed considerably since the early 1980s, and a new volume would be necessary to reflect this.

419 **Generals in the Palacio: the military in modern Mexico.**
Roderick A. Camp. Oxford, England: Oxford University Press, 1992.
263p. bibliog.

An analysis of military career structures and career paths. The author shows that the rôle of the military was very limited between the late 1940s and the early 1990s but the author believes that the military may now come to enjoy increasing influence over the policy-making process.

420 **The Mexican Left, the popular movements and the politics of austerity.**
Edited by Barry Carr, Ricardo Anzaldúa. San Diego, California: University of San Diego, Center for Mexican Studies, 1986. 96p.
(Monograph, no. 18).

The contributors consider the way in which the Left responded to the economic crisis of 1982 and after. At the time when the book went to press, the Left had not yet achieved the breakthrough which it was to enjoy in 1988.

421 **Marxism and communism in twentieth century Mexico.**
Barry Carr. Lincoln, Nebraska; London: University of Nebraska Press, 1992. 437p. bibliog.

A well-researched and well-written account of the organized Left in Mexico. Carr concerns himself mainly with the far Left rather than the populist Left which has in recent years posed a far stronger challenge to the régime.

422 **Professions and the state: the Mexican case.**
Peter S. Cleaves. Tucson, Arizona: University of Arizona Press, 1987. 147p. bibliog.

Cleaves studies the character and political orientations of a number of professions including petroleum engineering, agronomy, economics and medicine. All of these are involved, to some degree, in the making of public policy. Despite its tentative tone, the work itself is path-breaking.

423 **The Mexican political system in transition.**
Wayne Cornelius, Ann Craig. San Diego, California: Center for US–Mexican Studies, University of California, 1989. 125p. bibliog.
(Monograph Series, no. 35).

This is essentially a political sociology of Mexico. It covers the rôle of élites, labour, the military, culture, political structure and political institutions. An ideal book for the student or general reader.

424 **Mexico's alternative political futures.**
Edited by Wayne Cornelius, Judith Gentleman, Peter Smith.
San Diego, California: University of California Press, 1989. 445p.
(San Diego Monograph, no. 30).

A lengthy multi-contributor volume written during the political crisis year of 1988. Given the range and heterogeneity of the contributions, several are reviewed separately in this volume.

425 **Political liberalisation in an authoritarian regime: Mexico 1976-85.**
Wayne Cornelius. In: *Mexican politics in transition*, edited by Judith
Gentleman. Boulder, Colorado; London: Westview Press, 1987,
p. 41-63.
A good empirical study of political change during the period reviewed. The story
begins with political reform, and ends with the notorious rigging of governorship
elections in several northern states of Mexico in 1985.

426 **El sistema político mexicano: las posibilidades de cambio.** (The Mexican
political system: possibilities for change.)
Daniel Cosio Villegas. Mexico City: Joaquin Mortiz, 1972. 116p.
Although Cosio Villegas is primarily recognized as an historian, his books on Mexican
politics are very interesting and well worth reading. This is part of a path-breaking
trilogy which appeared in the early 1970s.

427 **Changes in the Mexican political system.**
Norman Cox. In: *Politics in Mexico*, edited by George Philip.
Beckenham, England: Croom Helm, 1985, p. 15-54.
This is above all a study of local and regional politics in Mexico in the early years of de
la Madrid. The author explains the difficulties in reforming the PRI, and the problems
faced by challengers from rival political parties.

428 **Popular movements and political change in Mexico.**
Edited by Joe Foweraker, Ann Craig. Boulder, Colorado; London:
Lynne Rienner, 1990. 314p. bibliog.
This is a collection of sixteen essays which discuss a range of social movements and
their consequences. Women's movements, peasant movements and various kinds of
middle-class movement are discussed. The editors believe that popular movements
have become stronger and more pervasive since 1968 on account of increased middle-
class militancy and the greater difficulties of organizing repression. The state has not
found it easy to respond to the new situation.

429 **Un partido sin militantes.** (A party without militants.)
Luis Javier Garrido. In: *La vida política mexicana en la crisis*, edited
by Soledad Loaeza, Rafael Segovia. Mexico City: Colegio de México,
1987, p. 61-77.
A study of the PRI as it had become by the early 1980s. It was essentially a party
without active supporters or members, though it had few difficulties in declaring itself
the winner in contested elections.

430 **Hope and frustration: interviews with leaders of Mexico's political
opposition.**
Carlos Gil. Wilmington, Delaware: SR Books, 1991. 356p. bibliog.
The book features interviews with six opposition figures. There are two from the
National Action Party (PAN), two from the Party of the Democratic Revolution
(PRD), and two from the Marxist Left. The interviews were conducted during 1986

and 1987, which is before the partial breakthrough achieved by the opposition parties in 1988. However, the introduction to the volume carries the story forward to 1991.

431 **Entrepreneurs and politics: businessmen in electoral contests in Sonora and Nuevo León, July 1985.**
Graciela Guaderrama S. In: *Electoral patterns and perspectives in Mexico*, edited by Arturo Alvarado. San Diego, California: Center for US–Mexican Studies, 1987, p. 81-111.
This important article is not just an electoral study, but a contribution to our understanding of local politics in the north of Mexico. The author has carried out significant research into the politics of small and big businessmen in this area.

432 **Mexican politics in transition.**
Edited by Judith Gentleman. Boulder Colorado; London: Westview Press, 1987. 320p. (Westview Special Studies on Latin America and the Caribbean).
The year 1980 saw a significant change in Mexican politics in that the electoral dimension became increasingly significant. This edited collection is overwhelmingly centred on political reform and party competition.

433 **Modern Mexico: state, economy and social conflict.**
Edited by Nora Hamilton, Timothy Harding. Beverly Hills, California; London: Sage, 1986. 312p.
This is a volume of articles reproduced from *Latin American Perspectives*. The orientation is broadly Marxist but independent of any specific political line. The articles cover 'the state' (which is defined rather broadly), the economy, the working class and popular mobilization.

434 **Mexico: dilemmas of transition.**
Edited by Neil Harvey. London: ILAS, University of London and British Academic Press, 1993. 381p. bibliog.
This work contains a number of chapters, most of which are clearly political in focus although there are also discussions of broader topics such as women's rights, social questions, the rôle of intellectuals, the character of Mexico's foreign policy, and some discussion of the economy.

435 **Mexico in crisis.**
Judith Adler Hellman. New York: Holmes and Meier, 1983. 2nd ed. 345p. bibliog.
Hellman is a critic of the Mexican system from a Left-wing standpoint. She believes that the system is in crisis because it has failed to meet the aspirations of most Mexicans, despite the promises of social reform made in the country's Constitution.

436 **Mexican democracy; a critical view.**
Kenneth F. Johnson. New York: Praeger, 1984. 3rd ed. 279p. bibliog.
Johnson's account focuses on the authoritarian characteristics of Mexican politics. He is sympathetic toward the PAN and provides detailed material on some of the campaigns fought by that political party.

437 **La contienda presidencial, 1988. Los candidatos y sus partidos.**
(The presidential election, 1988. The candidates and the parties.)
Adrian Lajous. Mexico City: Diana, 1988. 126p.
A brief but very perceptive account of the personalities involved in the electoral competition of 1988. Lajous was the first major Mexican commentator to identify the political promise of Carlos Salinas de Gortari.

438 **University and government in Mexico: autonomy in an authoritarian system.**
Daniel Levy. New York: Praeger, 1980. 173p. bibliog. (Praeger Special Studies in Comparative Education).
Levy argues that the universities in Mexico, particularly the National Autonomous University, have retained a high degree of control over their own affairs despite the authoritarian characteristics of Mexican politics. The author looks at issues such as the selection of the Rector of the university, the recruitment of students, financial organization and tuition.

439 **Clases medias y política en México: la querella escolar, 1959-1963.**
(The middle classes and politics in Mexico: the school books controversy, 1959-1963.)
Soledad Loaeza. Mexico City: Colegio de México, 1988. 427p. bibliog.
This work is an adaptation of a doctoral thesis about the Mexican school books controversy, which involved Church and state at around the time of the Cuban Revolution. Despite the ostensible narrowness of the topic, the author has much of value to say about the character and political rôle of the Mexican middle class.

440 **La vida política mexicana en la crisis.** (Mexican political life in crisis.)
Edited by Soledad Loaeza, Rafael Segovia. Mexico City: Colegio de México, 1987. 184p.
A group of distinguished Mexican political scientists discuss various aspects of the political situation in the mid-1980s. Chapters include regional studies, studies of the opposition PAN, the electoral reform law, the relationship between the state and business, and the PRI itself.

441 **The emergence and legitimation of the modern Right 1970-1988.**
Soledad Loaeza. In: *Mexico's alternative political futures*, edited by Wayne Cornelius, Judith Gentleman, Peter Smith. San Diego, California: University of California Press, 1989, p. 351–67.
This chapter is important because it deals with a topic which has not been much covered in English, although the author has written about it in Spanish to a

considerable extent. Loaeza looks at the rôle of the middle class in politics and at its fragmenting political identity. There is a brief study of Manuel Clouthier, the late leader of the National Action Party.

442 **Political anachronisms: the *navista* movement and political processes in San Luis Potosí 1958-1985.**
Enrique Marquez. In: *Electoral patterns and perspectives in Mexico*, edited by Arturo Alvarado. San Diego, California: Center for US–Mexican Studies, 1987, p. 111-27.
The *Navista* movement in San Luis Potosí is of considerable local political importance, though Nava has never succeeded in establishing a rôle in national politics. This is a good and useful study.

443 **Corruption and politics in contemporary Mexico.**
Stephen D. Morris. Tuscaloosa, Alabama: University of Alabama Press, 1991. 143p. bibliog.
Corruption is undoubtedly a problem in Mexico. This work seeks to quantify the extent of it and considers proposals for reform. The work is ambitious and the theme important, but the book lacks a clear conclusion.

444 **Mexican politics; the containment of conflict.**
Martin C. Needler. New York; Westport, Connecticut; London: Praeger, 1990. 2nd ed. 154p. bibliog.
Martin Needler is one of the most eminent and experienced US-based commentators on Mexican affairs. This is a new edition of a standard textbook on Mexican politics and society. There are chapters on the historical background, the workings of the political system, key interest groups, the nature of economic policy, foreign policy, and the press and political parties.

445 **Politics in Mexico.**
Edited by George Philip. Beckenham, England: Croom Helm, 1985. 223p.
This volume is based on the proceedings at a conference held in London in the summer of 1984. It took place at a time when observers of Mexico were just beginning to understand that the crisis of 1982 was likely to lead to some profound changes, but it was not yet clear what these were likely to be.

446 **The presidency in Mexican politics.**
George Philip. Basingstoke, England: Macmillan, 1992. 213p. bibliog.
This work provides a discussion of the evolution of Mexican politics since the early 1960s in terms of what it has to say about the nature of the presidential political institution. It seeks to relate presidential power to conflict and consensus between élite groups within Mexican political society.

447 **Mexico in transition; implications for US policy.**
Edited by Susan Kaufman Purcell. New York: Council on Foreign
Relations, 1988. 147p.
Purcell looks at the political situation in the late 1980s. Themes discussed include the
changing state of the Mexican economy, immigration, and diplomatic relations with the
United States.

448 **The Mexican profit-sharing decision: politics in an authoritarian regime.**
Susan Kaufmann Purcell. Berkeley, California: University of
California Press, 1975. 216p. bibliog.
This book is a minor classic. It played a major part in shifting scholarly perspectives
away from a perception that Mexican politics was essentially pluralist towards the idea
that it was fundamentally authoritarian. It argues that the Mexican profit-sharing
decision in 1962 was merely a consolation for organized labour after the far more
important defeat of union militancy during the period 1959-60. The work was based on
interviews, and for that reason some of the findings remain controversial.

449 **Opposition politics, power and public administration in urban Mexico.**
Victoria Rodríguez, Peter Ward. *Bulletin of Latin American
Research*, vol. 10, no. 1 (1991), p. 23-37.
Since the early 1980s, opposition parties – mainly the PAN – have started to win local
and regional elections. They therefore control a significant number of administrations,
but still have to deal with the central government. The authors raise questions as to
how the new system will develop.

450 **The modern Mexican military: a reassessment.**
Edited by David Ronfeldt. San Diego, California: Center for
US–Mexican Studies, University of California at San Diego, 1984.
218p.
A varied set of articles around the same theme. Some of the authors are historians,
others political scientists and others military officers. There was agreement that the
military played a part in the policy-making process, but that a military takeover of
power was far from imminent.

451 **State policies, leftist oppositions, and municipal elections: the case of the
COCEI in Juchitán.**
Jerry Rubin. In: *Electoral patterns and perspectives in Mexico*, edited
by Arturo Alvarado. San Diego, California: Center for US–Mexican
Studies, 1987, p. 127-61.
Although the conservative PAN has won control of a significant number of
municipalities, electoral victory by the Marxist Left has been rare. However, a Left-
wing coalition did briefly win control of the significant municipality of Juchitán in 1981,
but the experiment came to an end when the central government intervened in 1985.
Rubin provides a good account of the matter.

452 **Tamaulipas: mafias, *caciques* and civic-political culture.**
Carlos F. Salinas Dominguez. In: *Electoral patterns and perspectives in Mexico*, edited by Arturo Alvarado. San Diego, California: Center for US–Mexican Studies, 1987, p. 161-81.

Tamaulipas is an electorally lively state which has not received much scholarly attention. Perhaps this is because of the significant rôle of the 'inside Left' parties which have not been as interesting as the formal opposition. This is a valuable and informative study.

453 **Los presidentes.** (The presidents.)
Julio Scherer Garcia. Mexico City: Grijabo, 1986. 259p.

At times impressionistic but nevertheless important political reminiscences of Julio Scherer Garcia. Scherer is a prominent Mexican journalist who worked on Mexico's leading daily, *Excelsiór*, before moving on to *Proceso* in 1977.

454 **Modernization and political restoration.**
Rafael Segovia. In: *Sucesión presidencial: the 1988 Mexican presidential election*, edited by Edgar Butler, Jorge Bustamante. Boulder, Colorado; San Francisco, California; Oxford, England: Westview Press, 1991, p. 65-79.

A general commentary on the 1988 presidential election. The author is a leading Mexican academic and political observer who is on the whole sceptical of claims that there have been major changes to Mexican politics in recent years.

455 **Protest and response in Mexico.**
Evelyn Paniagua Stevens. Cambridge, Massachusetts: MIT Press, 1974. 372p. bibliog.

This is another of the works which, appearing in the mid-1970s, stressed the authoritarian characteristics of the Mexican system. The author is very good on the subject of the repression of the student movement of 1968. She also has interesting things to say about the railway workers' strike of the early 1960s and the doctors' strike of 1965.

456 **The Mexican ruling party: stability and authority.**
Dale Story. New York; Westport, Connecticut; London: Praeger, 1986. Co-published with the Hoover Institution Press, 1986. 151p. bibliog.

A good, broadly structured, introduction to the nature and character of the PRI as it appeared in the mid-1980s. The author is mostly sympathetic to the Mexican system.

457 **The PAN, the private sector and the future of the Mexican opposition.**
Dale Story. In: *Mexican politics in transition*, edited by Judith Gentleman. Boulder, Colorado; London: Westview Press, 1987, p. 261-81.

After languishing during the 1950s and early 1960s, the PAN has increasingly emerged as a significant regional party even though it is not yet in a position to challenge effectively for national power. Nevertheless, it remains more of a conservative Catholic party than a secular pro-business party. Story looks at the relations between the PAN, the government and the business community in the early 1980s.

458 **Democracy and power in Mexico: the meaning of conflict in the 1979, 1982 and 1985 federal elections.**
Silvia Gómez Tagle. In: *Mexican politics in transition*, edited by Judith Gentleman. Boulder, Colorado; London: Westview Press, 1987, p. 41-63.

A general study of the importance of elections in recent Mexican history. The author believes that the 1977 political reform, limited though it was, was a critical move because it opened space for electoral competition. Although the short-term result of this was an increase in electoral fraud and fraud-related controversies, the longer-term result may have been to increase greatly the importance of electoral competition in Mexico.

459 **Policymaking in Mexico; from boom to crisis.**
Judith Teichman. Boston, Massachusetts: Allen and Unwin, 1988. 158p. bibliog.

Teichman has written a detailed and convincing account of economic policy-making under President López Portillo. The author has interviewed several high officials and provides significant new information. The account is tied in with a theoretical discussion about the nature of the Mexican state and political system.

Constitution, legal system and local government

460 **Judicial review in Mexico: a study of the *amparo* suit.**
Richard Don Baker. Austin, Texas: University of Texas Press for the Institute of Latin American Studies, 1971. 304p. bibliog. (Latin American Monographs, no. 22).

The *amparo* suit is one of the few legal instruments in Mexico which gives the right of individual representation against the state. In fact, *amparos* are rarely given without some tacit political agreement in advance. Baker has written a study of the rôle of *amparo* in theory and practice, and to do so he examines cases, established procedures and relevant laws.

461 **La composición del poder; Oaxaca 1968-1984.** (The composition of power; Oaxaca 1968-1984.)
Edited by Miguel Basáñez. Mexico City: INAP, 1987. 183p. bibliog.

A careful study of regional politics, based broadly on an attempt to understand the nature and operation of power élites in Oaxaca. The rôle of Mexico City is generally to arbitrate between conflicting local political forces.

Government and Politics. Constitution, legal system and local government

462 **El poder presidencial.** (Presidential power.)
Jorge Carpizo. Mexico City: Siglo XXI, 1988. 6th ed. 240p. bibliog.
The author, a prominent Mexican jurist and lawyer, sets out the legal arrangements surrounding presidential power. He concludes that there are in practice extremely few constraints on presidential power.

463 **Politics and privilege in a Mexican city.**
Richard R. Fagan, William S. Tuohy. Stanford, California: Stanford University Press, 1971. 208p.
This work looks at local politics in the state capital city of Jalapa, Veracruz. The authors find that the city is run in an authoritarian manner which rewards the privileged and those with educational attainments. Local rule is less brutal than it once was, but is far from democratic. The authors see this pattern of rule as stemming from an economic model which requires considerable inequality.

464 **Confesiones de un gobernador.** (Confessions of a governor.)
Carlos Loret de Mola. Mexico City: Grijalbo, 1978. 306p.
Loret de Mola was governor in the Yucatán in the early 1970s. This first-person account seeks to settle some scores, but also gives an interesting perspective on regional politics and government in Mexico.

465 **El poder de los gobernadores.** (The power of the governors.)
Carlos Martínez Assad, Alvaro Arreola Ayala. In: *La vida política en la crisis*, edited by S. Loaeza, R. Segovia. Mexico City: Colegio de México, 1987, p. 107-31.
This important study of regional political organization in Mexico concentrates more on facts than on constitutional theories, but it is instructive about the real distribution of power within the Mexican system.

466 **Estadistas, caciques and caudillos.**
Edited by Carlos Martínez Assad. Mexico City: UNAM, Instituto de Investigaciones Sociales, 1988. 403p.
This study adopts a historical perspective, to understand how the structures of regional power came to be formed. There are twenty-three contributions, most of which focus on a particular region or locality. The title defies translation but refers to three types of leadership based on forms of power in provincial Mexico.

467 **Política y gestión municipal en México.** (Politics and municipal government in Mexico.)
Carlos Martínez Assad, Alicia Ziccardi. Mexico City: UNAM, Instituto de Investigaciones Sociales, 1988. 92p. bibliog. (Cuadernos de Investigación Social, no. 18).
A discussion of how far municipal government is truly independent of more central sources of power. The authors judge the weak link to lie in the lack of financial resources available to local government.

468 **Atencingo: the politics of agrarian struggle in a Mexican *ejido*.**
David F. Ronfeldt. Stanford, California: Stanford University Press, 1973. 283p. bibliog.
The study of agrarian conflict in Atencingo. The author questions the idea that the state easily dominates the Mexican peasantry. On the contrary, conflicts have been endemic in Atencingo and protesting groups have often been able to bring about changes in local power structures and politics.

469 **Power and conflict in a Mexican community: a study of political integration.**
Antonio Ugalde. Albuquerque, New Mexico: University of New Mexico Press, 1970. 193p. maps. bibliog.
A pioneering study of local government in Mexico. It studies Enseñada, Baja California. The author considers the local power groups, and also their relationship with the central administration.

Interest groups and pressure groups

470 **Coparmex and Mexican politics.**
Luis Felipe Bravo Mena. In: *Government and private sector in contemporary Mexico*, edited by Silvia Maxfield, Ricardo Anzaldúa Montoya. San Diego, California: Center for US–Mexican Studies, 1987, p. 89-105.
Coparmex is the most independent and aggressive of the Mexican business associations. This is a historical and institutional study which sees Coparmex as the ideological conscience of the private sector. It exists to articulate concerns rather than to represent interests.

471 **Entrepreneurs and politics in twentieth century Mexico.**
R. A. Camp. Oxford, England; New York: Oxford University Press, 1989. 285p. bibliog.
A good, detailed analysis of the private sector in Mexico. There are chapters on social origins, relations with the public sector, interest groups within the private sector and details of the main family business empires. The focus is mainly historical, but there is also discussion of the present-day situation.

472 **Intellectuals and the state in twentieth century Mexico.**
R. A. Camp. Austin, Texas: University of Texas Press, 1985. 285p. bibliog.
This work discusses the social origins, family affiliations and social and political rôle of Mexican intellectuals. Camp discusses the characteristics of the Mexican media and cultural establishments. The work covers the effects of the 1968 student movement.

473 **The new agrarian movement in Mexico 1979-1990.**
Neil Harvey. London: Institute of Latin American Studies, 1990.
bibliog. (Research paper no. 23).
Harvey provides a study of two recent autonomous peasant movements which fight for
the right to land. The author follows the story of two peasant league movements, the
CNPA and the UNORCA, from early success to subsequent difficulties.

474 **Government and private sector in contemporary Mexico.**
Edited by Silvia Maxfield, Ricardo Anzaldúa Montoya. San Diego,
California: Center for US–Mexican Studies, University of California,
1987. 145p. (Monograph Series, no. 20).
The contributors are mainly concerned with the causes and consequences of the
breakdown in relations between the public and private sector following the bank
nationalization. These included a closer relationship between some businessmen and
the National Action Party (PAN), and also far greater assertiveness on the part of
some important business pressure groups.

475 **Union locals in Mexico: the 'new unionism' in steel and automobiles.**
Ian Roxborough, Ilan Bizberg. *Journal of Latin American Studies*,
vol. 15, no. 1 (May 1983), p. 117-35.
This article discusses increased trade union militancy in Mexico in the late 1970s, as
well as the growth of independent unionization. It explores the implications of these
changes, and focuses on the car and steel industries.

476 **The Monterrey elite and the Mexican state, 1880-1940.**
Alex M. Saragoza. Austin, Texas: University of Texas Press, 1988.
249p. bibliog.
The so-called 'Monterrey group' were the leading members of the Mexican bourgeoisie
prior to the crisis of 1981-82. This work discusses the 1880-1940 period as one in which
a self-conscious national capitalist class was created around leadership in Monterrey.
The confrontation of 1934-40 reflected both a strengthened state and a strengthened
capitalist class. This is a sophisticated and well-researched analysis.

477 **Industry, the state and public policy in Mexico.**
Dale Story. Austin, Texas: University of Texas Press, 1986. 265p.
bibliog. (Latin American Monographs, no. 66).
A well-researched discussion of Mexican industry and industrialists, though it suffers
from the fact that most of the research was conducted during the oil boom years and is
therefore somewhat dated. However, it is still of value as a picture of business–
government relations at the beginning of the 1980s.

478 **Crónica del sindicalismo en México 1976-88.** (The history of trade
    unionism in Mexico 1976-88.)
    Raul Trejo Delarbe.   Mexico City: Siglo XXI and UNAM, 1990.
    420p.

This is a good, detailed account of a number of issues relating to the politics of
organized labour. The author supports the idea of some kind of corporatism, believing
that the unions are too weak and divided to win many concessions by collective
bargaining.

479 **State, class and the nationalization of the Mexican banks.**
    Russell N. White.   New York: Taylor and Francis, 1992. 157p. bibliog.

The author considers the political rôle of finance and banking in Mexico from the
standpoint of owners and employees. The work effectively ends with a study of the
nationalization of 1982.

Historical interpretations of politics

480 **Pensar el 68.** (Thinking about 1968.)
    Edited by Cal y Arena.   Mexico City: Cal y Arena, 1988. 273p.

A number of people who had been active in the student movement of 1968 reminisce
and also evaluate the extent to which this movement had a lasting impact upon
Mexican politics.

481 **Después del Milagro.** (After the Miracle.)
    Hector Aguilar Camín.   Mexico City: Cal y Arena, 1988. 296p.
    bibliog.

Aguilar Camín is a prominent Mexican historian and novelist. Here he shows how
Mexico has changed over the last generation and expresses his confidence that these
changes will lead to increasingly democratic forms of government.

482 **La lucha por la hegemonía en México 1968-90.** (The struggle for
    hegemony in Mexico 1968-90.)
    Miguel Basáñez.   Mexico City: Siglo XXI, 1990. 8th ed. 305p.

The author discusses the major crises and power conflicts in Mexico during the last
generation within a broad power élite approach. An extensive review of the literature
on the rôle of the state is followed by a series of discussions of Mexican power élites
and the conflicts between them.

483 **La ideología de la revolución mexicana: la formación del nuevo regimen.**
(The ideology of the Mexican revolution: the formation of the new
régime.)
Arnaldo Cordova. Mexico DF: Era, 1973. 508p. bibliog.

This important work is the result of an attempt to understand why a country which
adopted a Revolutionary Constitution in 1917 should have so little to show by way of
social reform. Cordova argues that the Revolutionaries were in reality more interested
in controlling the people than in empowering them.

484 **The Mexican state 1915-73: a historical interpretation.**
Juan Felipe Leal. In: *Modern Mexico: state, economy and social
conflict*, edited by Nora Hamilton, Timothy Harding. Beverly Hills,
California; London: Sage, 1986, p. 21-43.

The author argues that the Mexican system is fundamentally governed by the logic of
dependent capitalism and, for that reason, has become corporatist and authoritarian.

485 **El llamado de las urnas.** (The appeal of the voting booth.)
Soledad Loaeza. Mexico City: Cal y Arena 1989. 319p.

A collection of essays from a distinguished Mexican political scientist. Topics relate to
a variety of themes, but many of them cover issues relating to recent history, chosen
for their impact in shaping contemporary Mexico.

486 **The crisis of Cardenismo.**
Albert L. Michaels. *Journal of Latin American Studies*, vol. 2, no. 1
(May 1970), p. 51-79.

This is an important article which seeks to demystify the Cárdenas presidency by
pointing out that it ended in economic crisis and amid strong dissatisfaction from the
middle class. The author believes it inevitable that politics would take a more
moderate course after 1940.

487 **Echeverría en el sexenio de López Portillo.** (Echevarría during the six
years of López Portillo.)
Luis Suarez. Mexico City: Grijalbo, 1988. 7th ed. 320p.

A volume of Echeverría's political reminiscences. Suarez is the interviewer and editor
of the volume. Echeverría has some interesting, if not fully convincing, things to say
about several controversial incidents during the course of his own presidency.

Foreign relations

488 **The challenge of interdependence: Mexico and the United States.**
Lanham, Maryland; New York; London: University Press of America,
1989. 235p. bibliog. (Report of the Bilateral Commission on the Future
of United States–Mexican Relations).

The issues examined in this report include debt, trade and investment, migration and
drugs, and foreign policy generally. The report argues for a new and better relationship
between the United States and Mexico.

489 **The Mexican Revolution, 1910-14: the diplomacy of Anglo-American
conflict.**
Peter Calvert. Cambridge, England: Cambridge University Press,
1968. 331p. maps. bibliog. (Cambridge Latin American Studies, no. 3).

Although there has subsequently been significant scholarship on external aspects of the
Mexican Revolution, this was a path-breaking work when it appeared. Calvert
demonstrates that much of the apparent Anglo-American conflict in the early stages of
the Revolution was due to misunderstanding and misperception.

490 **Images of Mexico in the United States.**
John Coatsworth, Carlos Rico. San Diego, California: University of
California, Center for US–Mexican Studies, 1989. 135p. (Dimensions of
US–Mexican Relations, Vol. 1).

This volume looks at the US media, Hollywood and the way in which subjects
involving Mexico are taught in the schools. It suggests that popular images do have an
impact on US policies toward Mexico. The authors see a slow change from unflattering
stereotypes about Mexico in the direction of a more balanced view.

491 **The United States versus Porfirio Díaz.**
Daniel Cosio Villegas. Lincoln, Nebraska: University of Nebraska
Press, 1963. 259p. bibliog.

This is a famous book, though in some respects now overtaken by more recent
scholarship. The author emphasizes the extent to which Porfirio Díaz sought to attract
support and investment from Europe in order to counterbalance excessive dependency
on the United States, though relations were never quite as antagonistic as the title of
this book suggests.

492 **Mexico's relations with Central America: changing priorities, persisting
interest.**
Cheryl Eschbach. In: *Mexico's external relations in the 1990s*, edited
by Riordan Roett. Boulder, Colorado: Lynne Rienner, 1991, p. 171-95.

The 1980s saw a retreat from the very activist Mexican foreign policy in Central
America which had been the norm during the 1970s. In any event the easing of Cold
War tensions has made foreign policy activism less necessary. However, Mexico
continues to have major security and political interests in Central America, which will
probably now be pursued by quieter means.

493   **U.S.–Mexican economic relations: prospects and problems.**
Edited by Khoscow Fatemi.   New York; London: Praeger, 1988. 223p.
bibliog.
The issues discussed in this survey include Mexico's external debt, migration and
related issues, the narcotics trade, *maquiladoras*, transfers of technology and energy
relationships.

494   **Oil and Mexican foreign policy.**
George Grayson.   Pittsburgh, Pennsylvania: University of Pittsburgh
Press, 1988. 207p. bibliog.
A well-researched and informative discussion of Mexico's foreign policy during the
1980s. The oil theme is evidently given priority but the book's coverage is much
broader than the title suggests.

495   **The secret war in Mexico: Europe, the United States, and the Mexican
Revolution.**
Friedrich Katz.   Chicago, Illinois: University of Chicago Press, 1981.
659p. bibliog.
This is an important and very thoroughly researched account of the international
conflicts surrounding Mexico at the time of the Revolution. There is no other study
which covers the relations between Mexico and the powers of Continental Europe, and
Katz also discusses US and British policies. Some judgements in this book may over-
emphasize the foreign aspect of developments within Mexico during this period.

496   **Mexico's foreign policy as a middle power: the Nicaragua connection.**
David Mares.   *Latin American Research Review*, vol. 23, no. 3 (1988),
p. 81-107.
When the Sandinistas came to power, they were strongly supported and materially
aided by Mexico. By the mid-1980s there was some degree of distancing and Mexican
help declined as a result of that country's economic difficulties and also because of
frustration with some of the policies of the Sandinistas.

497   **Relations between Mexico and Canada.**
Edited by O. Martínez Logorreta.   Mexico City: Colegio de México,
1990. 379p.
This is a collection of essays based on a conference with both Mexican and Canadian
participants. The essays are often detailed, and cover economic and diplomatic issues.
A range of viewpoints is presented.

498   **Mexico and the United States in the oil controversy, 1917-1942.**
Lorenzo Meyer, translated from the Spanish by Muriel Vasconcillos.
Austin, Texas: University of Texas Press, 1977. 367p. bibliog.
Meyer was the first Mexican historian to use US documents for a study of the oil
conflict and its aftermath. It is excellent as a diplomatic history, and highlights the
tensions in the US–Mexican relationship during 1919 and 1926-27. In contrast, the
actual expropriation was handled by Washington in a very restrained way.

499 **Su majestad británica contra la revolución Mexicana, 1900-1950: el fin de un imperio informal.** (His Britannic Majesty versus the Mexican Revolution, 1900-1950: the end of an informal empire.) Lorenzo Meyer. Mexico City: Colegio de México, 1991. 579p. bibliog.

Extremely full, well-judged and nicely told story of the turbulent course of British–Mexican relations during and after the Revolution. The British clearly backed the authoritarian régimes of Porfirio Díaz and Victoriano Huerta and found themselves at a disadvantage when these lost.

500 **Apportioning groundwater beneath the US–Mexican border. Obstacles and alteratives.** Stephen Mumme. San Diego, California: University of California, Center for US–Mexican Studies, 1988. 45p. (Research Report Series, no. 45).

A detailed discussion of both the legal and the hydrological issues involved. The author calls for a case-by-case analysis of the matters outstanding.

501 **Mexico and the United States; studies in economic interaction.** Edited by Peggy Musgrove. Boulder, Colorado: Westview Press, 1985. 261p. bibliog. (Westview Special Studies in International Economics).

The articles in this volume discuss four main issues. These are: capital flow and the foreign dependence resulting; US–Mexican trade issues; the effect of economic fluctuations in one country upon the neighbouring economy; and the impact of Mexican macroeconomic policies upon its foreign relations with the US.

502 **Limits to friendship: United States and Mexico.** Robert C. Pastor, Jorge G. Castañeda. Boulder, Colorado: Westview Press, 1988. 415p.

A general, thought-provoking, work written in two parts. Each author discusses the theme at length and each is clear about their disagreements as well as about the ideas which they have in common. Some of the concerns expressed will have changed as a result of negotiations about the North American Free Trade Area (NAFTA).

503 **La expropriación petrolera y el contexto internacional.** (Oil expropriation and the international context.) Maria Emilia Paz Salinas. *Revista Mexicana de Sociología*, vol. 50, no. 3 (July-Sept. 1988), p. 75-97.

The author wrote her PhD in London on the international politics of the Cárdenas period. This article, taken from the research, concerns the way in which Britain and the United States responded to the oil expropriation of 1938.

504 **La política exterior de México: desafíos en los ochenta.** (Mexico's foreign policy: the challenges of the 1980s.)
Edited by Olga Pellicier. Mexico City: CIDE, 1983. 303p.

Olga Pellicier is one of Mexico's leading commentators on foreign affairs. This collection, which appeared just after the financial crisis of 1982, features Mexican writers. Topics include Mexican–US trade, negotiations between the two countries over water rights, oil-related issues, and Mexican economic co-operation with Central America.

505 **The vicissitudes of the Mexican economy and their impact on Mexican–American political relations.**
Olga Pellicier de Brody. In: *The U.S. and Mexico: borderland development and the national economies*, edited by Lay James Gibson, Alfonso Corona Renteria. Boulder, Colorado; London: Westview Press, 1985, p. 177-89.

This article looks at the oil boom years, and considers the way in which Mexico had to move quickly to mend fences with the United States following the deterioration of the Mexican economy in 1982.

506 **Mexico and the Spanish Civil War.**
Thomas G. Powell. Albuquerque, New Mexico: University of New Mexico Press, 1981. 210p. bibliog.

An important study of this period, which is well researched from a variety of sources. The Mexican government supported the Republican side in the Civil War, but to only a limited degree, in order to avoid becoming excessively involved in controversy.

507 **Policy and political implications of foreign indebtedness in Mexico.**
Rogelio Ramirez de la O. *Journal of Interamerican Studies and World Affairs*, vol. 29, no. 4 (1987-88), p. 147-56.

The author, a distinguished Mexican economist, concludes by arguing that Mexico should aim to reduce its debt gradually without suspending its debt payments. Such a policy would set the course for other Latin American countries as well.

508 **Mexico and the United States: managing the relationship.**
Edited by Riordan Roett. Boulder, Colorado: Westview Press, 1988. 226p. bibliog. (Westview Special Studies on Latin America and the Caribbean).

A comprehensive and well-organized collection. Among the topics covered are trade and private investment in the Mexican economy, narcotics-related issues, migration and related questions, and the debt question.

509 **Mexico's external relations in the 1990s.**
Edited by Riordan Roett. Boulder, Colorado: Lynne Rienner, 1991.
277p.
This is a well-edited collection of essays which cover the main aspects of Mexico's
international concerns. Many of the essays are taken up with discussion of particular
geographical areas, though there are also some general analyses.

510 **The United States and revolutionary nationalism in Mexico, 1916-32.**
Robert Freeman Smith. Chicago, Illinois: Unversity of Chicago Press,
1972. 288p. bibliog.
Smith is sympathetic toward the economic nationalist policies adopted sporadically
rather than consistently during the period under review, and unsympathetic to the
'dollar diplomacy' of the United States. The book is well researched, though it perhaps
exaggerates the degree of antagonism between Washington and Mexico City during the
period.

511 **The United States and Mexico.**
Josefina Vázquez, Lorenzo Meyer. Chicago, Illinois; London:
University of Chicago Press, 1985. 220p. bibliog. (United States in the
World. Foreign Perspectives Series).
This is a survey, mainly for the general reader, by two prominent Mexican historians.
The story begins in 1821 when Mexico emerged into independence poor, under-
developed and weighed down with debt. It ends in 1985 when these problems had by
no means been fully overcome.

512 **A marriage of convenience; relations between Mexico and the United
States.**
Sydney Weintraub. New York; Oxford, England: Oxford University
Press, 1990. 238p. bibliog. (A Twentieth Century Fund Report).
A broad and general discussion of a range of issues affecting the United States and
Mexico. This include trade, industry, energy, debt, the border and migration. The
author presents a good deal of empirical data. He is critical of US governmments of
the past for a lack of co-operation toward Mexico.

The Economy

General and recent history

513 **Distorted development: Mexico in the world economy.**
David Barkin. Boulder, Colorado: Westview Press, 1990. 162p.
(Studies in Political Economy and Economic Development in Latin
America).
The 'distortion' referred to in the title refers to Mexico's need to import food, its
environmental problems, its unequal income distribution and the stagnation of the
1980s. Barkin calls for a more self-sufficiency-based alternative. However, this is
evidently not the way in which things are going.

514 **Mexico's political economy; challenges at home and abroad.**
Edited by Jorge Dominguez. Beverly Hills, California; London; New
Delhi: Sage 1982. 238p.
This work contains chapters on petroleum, agricultural trade, the automobile industry,
and discusses some international features of Mexico's political economy.

515 **Mexico's 1986 financial rescue: palliative or cure?**
Esperanza Duran. In: *The Mexican economy*, edited by George
Philip. London: Routledge, 1988, p. 95-110.
The collapse in world oil prices at the beginning of 1982 finally convinced many
international financial experts than the Mexican economy could not recover without
some help. There followed the Baker Plan in 1986. The author of this article discusses
the background to the plan and analyses the plan itself.

516 **The rise and collapse of Stabilising Development.**
Rosario Enríquez. In: *The Mexican economy*, edited by George
Philip. London: Routledge, 1988, p. 41-78.
An important study of the reasons for the switch in Mexican policy-making from the
market-oriented Stabilising Development of the 1960s to the far more statist pattern of

economic policy-making after 1970. The author is sympathetic toward Stabilising Development and regards the main reasons for the switch as being political.

517   **The financial constraint on relative autonomy: the state and capital accumulation in Mexico, 1940-82.**
E. V. K. Fitzgerald.   In: *The state and capital accumulation in Latin America*, edited by Christian Anglade, Carlos Fortin.   London; Basingstoke, England: Macmillan, 1985, p. 210-41.

Fitzgerald identifies the main problem facing the Mexican economy during 1970-82 as an increased volume of state investment with insufficient backing by domestic savings. One of the author's key arguments, which is important but controversial, is that this increased public investment was actually required to maintain the momentum of Mexican capitalism rather than representing a departure from it.

518   **Causas y efectos de la crisis económica en México.** (Causes and effects of the economic crisis in Mexico.)
Pascual Garcia Alba, Jaime Serra Puche.   Mexico City: Colegio de México, 1984. 124p. bibliog. (Jornadas, no. 104).

The two authors of this work are market-oriented economists. Serra Puche later served as Commerce Secretary in the cabinet of Carlos Salinas de Gortari. Here they seek to understand the causes and impact of the 1982 financial disaster.

519   **Mexican oil and dependent development.**
Judith Gentleman.   New York: P. Lang, 1984. 260p. bibliog. (American University Studies Series X, Political Science, no. 2).

This work examines the impact of oil on the rôle of the state, local and foreign capital, income distribution, social welfare and other factors. The main period covered is 1970-82.

520   **The U.S. and Mexico: borderland development and the national economies.**
Edited by Lay James Gibson, Alfonso Corona Renteria.   Boulder, Colorado; London: Westview Press, 1985. 261p.

A collection of essays related to the economic development of the US–Mexican border region. Sixteen different contributions cover a range of related issues.

521   **Socio-economic groups and income distribution in Mexico.**
Wouter van Ginnekin.   New York: St Martin's Press, 1980. 237p. bibliog.

This study was carried out between 1974 and 1978 by the Income Distribution and Employment Project of the International Labour Office World Employment Programme. It finds that the two factors most involved in income inequality in Mexico are the very high returns available on capital, and the fact that many of the Mexican poor are unorganized.

522 **The politics of Mexican development.**
Roger D. Hansen. Baltimore, Maryland: Johns Hopkins University
Press, 1971. 298p. bibliog.
Hanson explores the relationship between political authoritarianism and economic
progress in Mexico since 1940. He may have exaggerated the extent to which income
distribution worsened under Stabilising Development, but he poses the question of how
far an essentially inegalitarian development strategy made political authoritarianism
necessary.

523 **Empresarios, banca y estado: el conflicto durante el gobierno de José
López Portillo.** (Entrepreneurs, banking and the state: the conflict
during the government of José López Portillo.)
Rogelio Hernández Rodríguez. Mexico City: Miguel Angel Porrua,
1988. 302p. bibliog.
This is an important study of the complex relations between entrepreneurs and the
state during the 1976-82 period. These relations began very well and ended in complete
breakdown, following the bank nationalization of 1982. This book is well researched
and dispassionate.

524 **The political economy of revolutionary Mexico.**
Alan Knight. In: *Latin America: economic imperialism and the state*,
edited by C. Abel, C. Lewis. London: Athlone Press, 1985, p. 288-318.
Knight asks why Mexican agriculture proved so dynamic during the 1930-60 period,
and argues that the key factors were land reform and public policy commitment to
raising agricultural output. Knight argues that this economic pattern was the direct
result of revolution.

525 **The Mexican rescue.**
Joseph Kraft. New York: Group of Thirty, 1984. 65p.
A well-researched account of how the Mexican economic crisis of 1981-82 developed
and how policy-makers responded to it. We now know that the Mexican economy was
not really 'rescued' until 1989, but outright default was avoided by some urgent action
by US and Mexican central bankers during the summer and early autumn of 1982.

526 **Economic policymaking in Mexico: factors underlying the 1982 crisis.**
Robert E. Looney. Durham, North Carolina: Duke University Press,
1985. 309p. bibliog.
The first part of this volume is a survey of the behaviour of the Mexican economy
during the 1970-82 period and its responsiveness to policy. The second part of the book
is more technical and principally of interest to professional economists. There are a
considerable number of data about the Mexican economy during the period surveyed.

527 **Debt and oil-led development: the economy under López Portillo.**
Paul Luke. In: *The Mexican economy*, edited by George Philip.
London: Routledge, 1988, p. 41-78.
A concise and balanced account of the López Portillo period (1976-82) from an economic viewpoint. The period started with an economic crisis, was followed by a huge boom, and ended with renewed crisis.

528 **Mexico; the remaking of an economy.**
Nora Lustig. Washington, DC: Brookings Institution, 1992. 186p.
bibliog.
A full discussion of the thorough re-organization of the Mexican economy which took place during the 1980s. The book discusses the policies themselves, the social costs which followed, and the character of institutional reform. There is abundant documentation.

529 **Mexico's dilemma: the political origins of economic crisis.**
Roberto Newell, Luis Rubio. Boulder, Colorado: Westview Press, 1984. 319p. bibliog. (Westview Special Studies on Latin America and the Caribbean).
This is an important study of the political constraints which influenced the management of the Mexican economy up until the 1982 crisis. The authors argue that the authorities responded to the 1968 crisis, not by making Mexico more democratic but rather by seeking to become more popular by increasing public spending. The result was growing debt and crisis.

530 **Mexico 1991-1992.**
Paris: OECD, 1992. 265p. bibliog. (OECD Report).
A very thorough and extremely detailed discussion of the Mexican economy. There is abundant statistical information relating to trade, investment, the balance of payments, the activities of central government and the performance of particular sectors. This should become a standard reference for the period.

531 **Crisis and social change in Mexico's political economy.**
Wayne Olson. *Latin American Perspectives*, vol. 12, no. 3 (Summer 1985), p. 7-28.
The author was one of the first to conclude that the Mexican economic crisis of 1982 marked a definite turning-point in the direction of economic change. He argues that the policy of industrialization based on home markets had come up against its natural limits, and that attempts to pursue it led to crisis. Olson predicted a move towards a more market-oriented pattern of growth.

532 **The Mexican economy.**
Edited by George Philip. London: Routledge, 1988. 345p. bibliog.
A collection of eleven essays surveying the state of the Mexican economy in the late 1980s. Some of these adopt a broad macro approach while others focus on particular sectors or regions. At this time Mexico had just begun to recover from the debt crisis, but recovery was still very precarious.

533 **The Mexican economy: twentieth century structure and growth.**
Clark Winston Reynolds. New Haven, Connecticut: Yale University
Press, 1970. 468p. map. bibliog.
A classic, if slightly dated, account of Mexico's twentieth-century economic history. It
takes the story up to the late 1960s.

534 **Mexico from the oil boom to the debt crisis: an analysis of policy
responses to external shocks 1978-85.**
Jaime Ros. In: *Latin American debt and the adjustment crisis*, edited
by Rosemary Thorp, Laurence Whitehead. Basingstoke, England:
Macmillan, 1987, p. 68-117.
A detailed macroeconomic study of the evolution of the Mexican economy between
1978 and 1985. The author is broadly sympathetic to a structuralist economic approach,
but nevertheless recognizes some merit in the policies adopted after 1983.

535 **The dilemma of Mexico's development: the roles of the private and
public sectors.**
Raymond Vernon. Cambridge, Massachusetts: Harvard University
Press, 1963. 226p.
Vernon's discussion of Stabilising Development in Mexico is a classic. It poses the
question of how far economic development led by the private sector is compatible with
effective government control over the economy. The solutions which Vernon offers
have dated, but the question itself remains very much alive.

536 **Mexico from bust to boom: a political evaluation of the 1976-79
stabilisation programme.**
Laurence Whitehead. *World Development*, vol. 8 (1980), p. 843-64.
This is an account of the political economy of economic stabilization in Mexico in the
mid-1970s. Some of the conclusions in the article have not stood the test of time, but
the article is nevertheless well researched and covers an important period in Mexican
economic history.

537 **La economía presidencial.** (The presidential economy.)
Gabriel Zaid. Mexico City: Vuelta, 1987. 244p.
A series of essays published in *Vuelta* by Gabriel Zaid. The title essay, which is backed
up by the themes of several others, is that the Mexican economy has been damaged by
an excessive concentration of presidential power. The best presidents were those who
left significant power in the hands of their cabinet secretaries rather than seeking to
influence economic policy directly.

recent balance of payments experience and prospects for

Zedillo Ponce de León. *World Development*, vol. 14, no. 8
. 963-92.

One of Mexico's leading economists examines the evolution of the country's balance of payments since 1973. Prospects have in fact improved considerably since the article was written.

Trade

539 Trade and employment in Mexico.
Jaime Behar. Stockholm: Swedish Institute for Social Research, 1989. 295p. bibliog.

This is a study of the links between industrial employment and foreign trade. A part of the work is conducted at macro level, while there is also a study of Monterrey, in Nuevo León. The author shows that diversification and growth are linked to capital intensity. This is not good news for those who hoped that industrial growth would bring a corresponding increase in employment.

540 Mexico's trade policy: the US, GATT and the future of economic relations.
Edited by Pamela Falk, Blanca Torres. Boulder, Colorado: Westview Press, 1989.

Topics considered in this volume include the General Agreement on Tariffs and Trade (GATT), Mexican trade with the United States, and Mexico's political economy. However, the book went to press before Mexico's participation in the North American Free Trade Area was actively negotiated.

541 Internationalization of industry: U.S.–Mexican linkages.
Joseph Grunwald. In: *The U.S. and Mexico: borderland development and the national economies*, edited by Lay James Gibson, Alfonso Corona Renteria. Boulder, Colorado; London: Westview Press, 1985, p. 97-110.

Grunwald concludes that assembling for export has brought about positive changes within Mexico, and that the cost of labour is so much lower than in the United States that continued rapid growth of manufacturing for export in Mexico is likely.

542 **Mexico in the global economy: high technology and work organisation in export industries.**
Harley Shaiken. San Diego, California: University of California, Center for US–Mexican Studies, 1985. 125p. (Monograph Series, no. 33).
This work examines high-technology plants in Mexico. Why should these have been set up? Should plants of this kind ever be set up in a developing country? Shaiken concludes that 'the diverse plants visited . . . all performed extremely well'.

543 **Mexico's *maquiladora* programme: a critical evaluation.**
Leslie Sklair. In: *The Mexican economy*, edited by George Philip. London: Routledge, 1988, p. 286-328.
Despite the title, Sklair's evaluation is ultimately agnostic rather than negative. There is much empirical information, which makes clear how rapidly the sector has grown during the 1980s. The author nevertheless points out that the sector is well short of providing the basis for sustained economic development within Mexico.

544 **Assembling for development; the *maquila* industry in Mexico and the United States.**
Leslie Sklair. Boston, Massachusetts: Unwin Hyman, 1989. 240p. bibliog.
The work contains a great deal of interesting detail. The author shows that the *maquila* sector is no longer just a phenomenon of the border area; it has growth rapidly across the whole of Mexico. He stresses the importance of women workers in this sector. He is concerned at the sociological implications of this transformation.

545 **The United States and Mexico: face to face with the new technology.**
Catherine Thorup (et al.). New Brunswick, New Jersey; Oxford, England: Transaction Books for Overseas Development Council, 1987. 210p.
Contains articles on motor vehicles; the employment of women; the rôle of biotechnology; pharmachemicals and pharmaceuticals; and Mexico's industrial development strategy.

546 **Mexican trade policy and the North American community.**
Sidney Weintraub. Washington, DC: Center for Strategic and International Studies, 1988. 55p.
At the time when this was written, the North American free trade agreement was scheduled to include only the United States and Canada. This work considers the way in which the creation of a North America Free Trade Area would impact on the Mexican economy.

547 **US–Mexican industrial integration: the road to free trade.**
Sidney Weintraub, Luis Rubio, Alan Jones. Boulder, Colorado:
Westview Press, 1991. 337p.
This work contains sectoral analyses of automobiles, petrochemicals, pharmaceuticals, textiles, computers, food and the environment. Each section features one Mexican and one US perspective. There is a wealth of detail.

Industry and commerce

548 **Transnational corporations versus the state; the political economy of the Mexican auto industry.**
Douglas C. Bennett, Kenneth E. Sharpe. Princeton, New Jersey:
Princeton University Press, 1985. 300p. bibliog.
A discussion of negotiations between the Mexican state and the large US automobile companies, mainly during the 1960s. There is abundant information, though the treatment of the company perspective is more satisfying than either the Mexican state or the policy-making aspect.

549 **Multinationals and market structure in Mexico.**
Magnus Blomstrom. *World Development*, vol. 14, no. 4 (1986),
p. 523-30.
This article analyses how foreign investment influences market concentration in Mexican manufacturing industry. The author's results suggest that the presence of transnational corporations is positively related to the degree of concentration irrespective of other industrial variables which are commonly thought to be of determining importance.

550 **Agrarian reform and public enterprise in Mexico: the political economy of Yucatán's henequen industry.**
J. Brannon, E. Baklanoff. Tuscaloosa, Alabama: University of
Alabama, 1987. 237p. bibliog.
An account of the state's rôle in the Yucatán henequen industry. It is historical in approach and concentrates mainly on the drawbacks of the system of policy-making, which the authors believe to be mainly motivated by political considerations.

551 **Changing networks: Mexico's telecommunications options.**
Edited by P. F. Cowhey, J. D. Aronson, G. Szekely. San Diego,
California: University of California, Center for US–Mexican Studies,
1989. 127p. (Monograph series, no. 32).
A very specialized and detailed topic. The book is based on a conference held in November 1987. The first half deals mainly with global issues and the second part mainly with Mexico. There are abundant statistics. The sector has in fact been privatized since the conference was held.

552 **Demand, supply and politics in the Mexican salt industry 1560-1980: a study in change.**
Ursula Ewald. Stuttgart, Germany; New York: Gustav Fischer Verlag, 1985. 480p. bibliog.
An extremely well-researched study around the theme of economic change. Mexico exhibits the widest range of methods in the world in the recovery of salt. It was the first country to use salt on a large scale for industrial purposes. It is still the world's largest exporter of sun-dried salt.

553 **The pharmaceutical industry and dependency in the Third World.**
Gary Geroffi. Princeton, New Jersey: Princeton University Press, 1983. 291p. bibliog.
This work includes a case-study of the hormone industry in Mexico. The author documents the displacement of national firms by transnationals, and considers the way in which transnationalization has altered pricing policy.

554 **Las Truchas; historia de una empresa.** (Las Truchas; the history of a firm.)
Nelson Minello. Mexico City: Colegio de México, 1982. 317p. bibliog.
The steel plant at Las Truchas was one of the showpiece public investments of the 1970s. Minello defends the essential rationality of the decision to invest there, and explains subsequent difficulties in terms of changing conditions. Minello also argues that the project was, despite problems, of positive value for Mexican development.

555 **Foreign direct investment and industrial development in Mexico.**
Wilson Pérez Nuñez. Paris: OECD, 1990. 164p. bibliog.
Pérez Nuñez, although a native Uruguayan, is a leading authority on the Mexican industrial economy. This study is divided into two parts. The first looks at the macroeconomics of foreign investment in Mexican industry. The second part is a study of three specific industries – electronics, automotive and pharmaceuticals.

556 **Development banking in Mexico: the case of the Nacional Financiera S.A.**
Miguel Ramirez. New York: Praeger, 1986. 228p. bibliog.
Nacional Financiera (Nafinsa) was founded in 1934 as a state development bank. The author discusses its history, and particularly its rôle in the growth and development of the financial sector.

557 **El futuro de la política industrial en México.** (The future of industrial policy in Mexico.)
Saul Trejo Reyes. Mexico City: Colegio de México, 1987. 318p. bibliog.
This is a definitive study of the pattern of Mexican industrialization. There are chapters on industrial policy and the structure of production; employment and the distribution of income; the evolution of relative prices; the process of urbanization; macroeconomic policies; and many other topics.

Mining, Oil and Energy

558 **Laguna Verde nuclear? No gracias!** (A nuclear power station in Laguna
Verde? No thanks!)
Edited by Jose Arias, Luis Barquera. Mexico City: Claves
Latinoamericanos, 1988. 367p. bibliog.
Laguna Verde is the site of Mexico's first and so far only major nuclear power station.
Construction of this plant has been fraught with problems. This is a collection of
articles which are critical of nuclear power in general and Laguna Verde in particular.

559 **The Mexican national petroleum industry: a case study in
nationalization.**
Antonio J. Bermúdez. Stanford, California: Stanford University
Press, 1963. 269p. map.
This is a classic account of the early years of Pemex, written by the man who was
Director-General from 1946 to 1958. He strongly defends the state company from its
critics, arguing that its achievements in supplying a rapidly growing market more than
compensate for its financial weaknesses.

560 **The Mexican petroleum industry in the twentieth century.**
Edited by Jonathan Brown, Alan Knight. Austin, Texas: University
of Texas Press, 1992. 310p.
A broadly historical discussion which is largely focused around the oil expropriation of
1938, but which also includes several chapters looking at the evolution of Mexican oil
after the expropriation. A particular strength of the volume is its concentration on
issues relating to labour.

561 **Pemex: the trajectory of a national oil policy.**
Esperanza Duran. In: *Latin American oil companies and the politics of energy*, edited by John Wirth. Lincoln, Nebraska: University of Nebraska, 1985, p. 145-89.

A historical discussion of Mexican oil policy during the course of the century. The author argues that the political events which led up to the nationalization of oil were of decisive importance in tracing the subsequent history of the organization.

562 **Petroleum and political development: the cases of Mexico and Norway.**
Ragaci El Mallakh, Oystein Noreng, Barry Poulson. New York: D. C. Heath, 1984. 197p.

Mexico and Norway are in some ways a strange match. They are, however, both oil exporters in the context of an otherwise fairly well-diversified economy. In both cases oil has to some extent proved a destabilizing influence and brought about growing indebtedness.

563 **Firewood versus alternatives – domestic fuel in Mexico.**
Margaret Evans. Oxford, England: University of Oxford, Department of Forestry Institute, 1984. 70p. bibliog.

Wood is five times more expensive than liquified petroleum gas in Mexico, and less productive in terms of energy, but it still remains the subsistence fuel of many poor families. Shortages of both fuels are common and this causes hardships.

564 **Mining and the state in twentieth century Mexico.**
William E. French. *Journal of the West*, vol. 27, no. 4 (Oct. 1988), p. 85-94.

A general historical account of the development of mining during the century. Most attention is paid to labour disputes and labour politics during the period 1906-40. In fact government policy tended to ignore mining between 1940 and 1982, though increasing attention has been paid to it subsequently.

565 **Energy efficiency and conservation in Mexico.**
Oscar Guzman, Antonio Yuñez-Naude, Miguel S. Wionczek, translated by Glenn Gardner, Rodney Williamson. Boulder, Colorado: Westview Press, 1987. 354p. bibliog. (Westview Special Studies on Latin America and the Caribbean).

This work studies trends in Mexican energy consumption. It analyses sectoral problems within the Mexican energy sector. It offers a quantitatively based diagnosis of energy trends. Finally it considers various policy proposals. All of this work highlights the essential fact that Mexico is very dependent on hydrocarbons for its energy consumption.

566   **La formación de la política petrolera en México 1970-86.** (The formation of an oil policy in Mexico 1970-86.)
Isidro Morales (et al.).   Mexico City: Colegio de México, 1988. 277p. bibliog.

A detailed account of oil policy and policy-making during the oil boom period. The authors sometimes tend to accept official pronouncements at face value, though they do provide some significant new insights into Echeverría's policies during 1975-76.

567   **PEMEX: la caída de Díaz Serrano.** (PEMEX: the fall of Díaz Serrano.)
Mexico City: Proceso, 1981. 214p.

A sensational but historically important volume. The key article reflects the leaking to the journal of an internal report commissioned within the Planning and Budgetary Ministry which was radically critical of the conduct of Pemex under the Directorship of Díaz Serrano. The mismanagement of Pemex is detailed in the report.

568   **The political economy of Mexican oil.**
Laura Randall.   New York: Praeger, 1989. 228p. bibliog.

This is essentially a study of the state oil company, Pemex, and its relationship with the rest of Mexican industry and with national policy-making. There is also a history of successive governments' oil and energy policies, and a discussion of the effect of oil on the economy as a whole.

569   **La industria de refinación en México 1970-85.** (The refining industry in Mexico 1970-85.)
Michele Snoeck.   Mexico City: Colegio de México, 1989. 242p. maps. bibliog.

A very thorough empirical study of a particular sector. There are abundant tables, maps, appendices and so forth. The author is at home with the considerable technicalities involved in this area.

570   **Exploración, reservas y producción de petróleo en México, 1970-85.** (Exploration, oil reserves and petroleum production in Mexico, 1970-85.)
Ana Maria Sordo, Carlos Roberto López.   Mexico City: Colegio de México, 1988. 281p. bibliog.

Another of the Colegio's series of well-researched studies of oil. This one looks at oil exploration, the extent of national oil reserves and oil production from 1970 to 1985. This was a very important period in Mexican oil history. Issues relating to Mexican oil reserves tend to be controversial, and a dispassionate study is welcome.

571   **Energy use in Mexican industry.**
Thomas Sterner.   Gothenburg, Sweden: University of Gothenburg, 1985. 185p. bibliog.

A detailed econometric study which shows that the effect of cheap energy prices during the 1970s was to increase the energy consumption of industry without necessarily adding either to its rate of growth or its efficiency.

572 **La economía política del petróleo en México 1976-1982.** (The political economy of oil in Mexico 1976-82.)
Gabriel Szekely. Mexico City: Colegio de México, 1983. 203p. bibliog.

The author has produced a careful and balanced study of the controversial oil boom period in Mexico. The rôle of Pemex is examined in detail. There is a considerable amount of statistical material.

573 **Petróleo y ecodesarrollo en el sureste de México.** (Oil and ecodevelopment in south-east Mexico.)
Alejandro Toledo (et al.). Mexico City: Centro de Ecodesarrollo, 1982. 254p. maps. bibliog.

Given the economic importance of oil to the Mexican economy, ecological questions involving Pemex are too often ignored. This is a valuable corrective, at macro as well as micro level.

574 **Mexico's energy resources: towards a policy of diversification.**
Miguel Wionczek, Ragaci El Mallakh. Boulder, Colorado: Westview Press, 1985. 176p.

While Mexico has abundant supplies of hydrocarbons, there is long-run vulnerability in the fact that it has few other sources of energy. Nuclear energy development has not been a success either. The authors here discuss in detail Mexico's oil potential, oil policies and energy prospects generally.

Agriculture

575 **Food policy in Mexico: the search for self-sufficiency.**
Edited by James Austin, Gustavo Esteva. Ithaca, New York: Cornell
University Press, 1987. 383p. bibliog.
This collection includes contributions on food strategies, the implementation of
agricultural policies, policy impacts and general issues relating to self-sufficiency.

576 **Sorghum and the Mexican food crisis.**
David Barkin, Billie R. De Walt. *Latin American Research Review*,
vol. 23, no. 3 (1988), p. 30-59.
This article argues that technology, modernization and the application of market
principles to Mexican agriculture have done little to improve the lot of the majority.

577 **Agrarian struggle and political power in Mexico.**
Roger Batra, translated by Stephen Ault. Baltimore, Maryland;
London: Johns Hopkins University Press, 1993. 219p. bibliog.
A detailed and theoretically sophisticated account of the evolution of the Mexican
peasantry and of Mexican agriculture since the early 1940s. The work uses both
sociological and political economy angles. It ends on a pessimistic note, concluding that
the peasantry is now a declining force in Mexico.

578 **Rural industry, social differentiation and the contradictions of provincial
Mexican capitalism.**
Scott Cook. *Latin American Perspectives*, vol. 11, no. 4 (Fall 1980),
p. 60-85.
A survey of industrial commodity production and related mercantile activity in 23
towns and villages in the Oaxaca valley.

579 **The state and henequen production in Yucatán 1955-80.**
Roberto Escalante. London: ILAS, 1988. 44p. (ILAS Occasional
Paper, no. 18).
The author argues that the state has played an essentially constructive rôle in
protecting and investing in the henequen industry in Yucatán. He traces out changes in
policy and approach during the period under review.

580 **Intensification of peasant agriculture in Yucatán.**
Peter T. Ewell. Ithaca, New York: Department of Agricultural
Economics, New York State College of Agriculture and Life Sciences,
Cornell, 1984. 233p. bibliog.
This is a study of the Puuc region of southern Yucatán where peasants have moved
successfully to a more intensive system of production, shifting from subsistence farming
to the cultivation and marketing of fruits and vegetables.

581 **Contradictions in Mexican food policy.**
John Heath. In: *Politics in Mexico*, edited by George Philip. London:
Routledge, 1985, p. 97-137.
A discussion of changes in Mexican food policy during the 1970s and early 1980s.
Mexican agriculture performed extremely well until around the mid-1960s when it took
a sharp turn for the worse. Policies attempting to reverse this deterioration were not
successful.

582 **An overview of the Mexican agricultural crisis.**
John Heath. In: *The Mexican economy*, edited by George Philip.
London: Routledge, 1988, p. 129-64.
A general and detailed discussion of the reasons for the relatively poor performance of
agriculture in recent years, following on from the rapid growth of the 1950s and early
1960s. The author blames price controls and a reduction in state investment in
agriculture.

583 **Foundations of international agricultural research: science and politics
in Mexican agriculture.**
Bruce H. Jennings. Boulder, Colorado: Westview Press, 1988. 196p.
(Westview Special Studies in Agriculture Science and Policy).
This is a study of the Rockefeller Foundation in Mexico up to the formation of
International Maize and Wheat Improvement Centre in 1966. The author discusses the
relationship between national and social sciences, and looks at the social and political
impact of the research itself.

584 **The route to self-sufficiency in Mexico. Interactions with the U.S. Food System.**
Casio Luiselli Fernández. San Diego, California: University of California, Center for US–Mexican Studies, 1985. 64p. bibliog. (Monograph Series, no. 17).
This work was written when the Mexican economy was deep in crisis. It argues for a selective approach to agricultural policy rather than either free trade or pure protectionism. The author was one of the principal economic advisers of President López Portillo, 1976-82.

585 **Penetrating the international market: theoretical considerations and a Mexican case study.**
David R. Mares. New York: Columbia University Press, 1987. 294p. bibliog.
This work focuses to a considerable extent on export agriculture in Mexico. Mares sees the development of export agriculture fairly positively, which is not a universally shared view, and provides a wealth of detail on farming in Sinaloa.

586 **Agrarian populism and the Mexican state: the struggle for land in Sonora.**
Steven E. Sanderson. Berkeley, California: University of California Press, 1981. 290p. bibliog.
Using the state of Sonora as his case-study, Sanderson argues that the Mexican state has moved from a pro-peasant orientation in the 1930s to a policy which is increasingly supportive of agrarian capitalism. He examines the agrarian redistributions of Echeverría, and argues that these are no answer to the changing situation.

587 **The transformation of Mexican agriculture: international structure and the politics of rural change.**
Steven E. Sanderson. Princeton, New Jersey: Princeton University Press, 1986. 314p. bibliog.
Sanderson believes that Mexican peasants have on the whole suffered from the opening of Mexican agriculture to international trade. He argues that this makes for greater capital intensity, the expulsion of labour and the growing of crops which do not meet Mexico's overriding need for food.

588 **Good farmers: traditional agricultural resource management in Mexico and Central America.**
Gene C. Wilkens. Berkeley, California: University of California, 1987. 302p. bibliog.
The author has over thirty years' experience with traditional agriculture in Mesoamerica. Here he lists a number of good farming practices associated with traditional agriculture. This is an important study.

589 **Mexico's agricultural dilemma.**
P. Lamartine Yates. Tucson, Arizona: University of Arizona Press, 1981. 291p. maps. bibliog.
The dilemma discussed in this book is whether Mexico should adopt a growth-maximizing and capital-intensive agricultural policy or one which accepts some inefficiencies in return for greater social justice. This work was originally published in Spanish in 1978 under the title *El campo Mexicano*.

Labour and Trade Unions

590 **El movimiento ferrocarrilero en México 1958-59.** (The railway workers'
movement in Mexico 1958-59.)
Antonio Alonso. Mexico City: Era, 1986. 7th ed. 196p.
This is a famous, if in some respects controversial, account of the rise and defeat of the
railway workers during 1958-59. The author emphasizes the repressive and authoritarian
character of the official response to the movement.

591 **Outcasts in their own land: Mexican industrial workers 1906-11.**
Rodney D. Anderson. De Kalb, Illinois: Northern Illinois University
Press, 1976. 407p. maps. bibliog.
A well-researched and amply documented book which is sympathetic to labour and its
rôle in the political upheavals after 1910.

592 **Organised labor and the Mexican revolution under Lázaro Cárdenas.**
Joe C. Ashby. Chapel Hill, North Carolina: University of North
Carolina Press, 1967. 350p. bibliog.
Although this work predates the opening of some of the main British and American
archives on Mexico, it is still a useful guide to the politics of labour under Lázaro
Cárdenas. Topics covered include changes in the organization of labour and a
discussion of the various disputes of the period – notably those relating to oil and the
railways.

593 **Estado y sindicalismo en México.** (The state and trade unionism in
Mexico.)
Ilan Bizberg. Mexico City: Colegio de México, 1990. 390p. bibliog.
An important and comprehensive study of Mexican labour by one of Mexico's leading
sociologists. It looks at the character of the Mexican working class, trade unionism and
the politics of trade union activism.

594 **The myth of market failure; employment and the labor market in Mexico.**

Peter Gregory. Baltimore, Maryland: Johns Hopkins Press for the World Bank, 1986. 299p. bibliog.

Gregory argues that the post-war period was one of rising real wages in Mexico despite the potentially negative influence of rapid migration from rural to urban areas. He believes that the labour market worked relatively well during this period.

595 **Unions, workers and the state in Mexico.**

Edited by Kevin Middlebrook. San Diego, California: Center for US–Mexican Studies, University of California at San Diego, 1991. 247p.

An edited collection of nine articles covering a range of aspects involving labour, such as the effect of the Mexican legal system, trade union relations with the political Left, the nature of independent trade unionism, the continuing rôle of the Confederation of Mexican Workers, and the impact of recent social and economic change.

596 **Unions and politics in Mexico; the case of the automobile industry.**

Ian Roxborough. Cambridge, England: Cambridge University Press, 1984. 205p. bibliog.

A detailed study of trade union organization and behaviour in the automobile industry in Mexico. The author is careful not to draw too many conclusions about national politics in view of the diversity of some of the local situations discussed.

The Environment

597 **Environmental problems of the borderland.**
Howard G. Applegate.   El Paso, Texas: Texas Western Press, 1979.
124p. bibliog. (Inter-American Studies, no. 2).
Increasing attention is being given to the environmental problems of border areas. The
study focuses on issues arising from the US–Mexican border.

598 **The emerging environmental crisis along the United States–Mexico**
border.
C. Richard Bath.   In: *Changing boundaries in the Americas*, edited by
Lawrence Herzog.   San Diego, California: Center for US–Mexican
Studies, 1992, p. 113-29.
Bath looks at issues of water pollution, air quality and policies on hazardous wastes.
He shows how these are increasingly becoming political issues in Mexican–United
States relations.

599 **Fields of the Tzotzil: the ecological bases of tradition in highland**
Chiapas.
George Allen Collier.   Austin, Texas: University of Texas Press, 1975.
255p. maps. bibliog. (Texas Pan-American Series).
An analysis of the lifestyle of the Tzotzil, who inhabit highland Chiapas. The emphasis
is on the relationship between the society and the environment.

600 **Political development and environmental policy in Mexico.**
Stephen Mumme, R. Ball, V. Assetti.   *Latin American Research*
Review, vol. 23, no. 1 (1988), p. 7–24.
This work considers the development of an environmental policy after around 1970. It
discusses policy formulation, decision-making and policy implementation.

601 **Agriculture and the environment: the Mexican experience.**
Michael Redclift. In: *The Mexican economy*, edited by George Philip.
London: Routledge, 1988, p. 164-83.
This article discusses the way in which the physical environment of Mexico has deteriorated in recent years, and looks at the proposals of the Green Party in Mexico for environmental renovation.

602 **Prehistoric coastal adaptations: the economy and ecology of maritime middle America.**
Edited by Barbara Stark, Barbara Voorhies. New York: Academic Press, 1978. 313p. bibliog. (Studies in Archaeology).
This volume covers the ecology and economy of pre-Columbian Mesoamerican coastal peoples. There are chapters on Chiapas, the southern isthmus of Tehuantepec and southern Veracruz.

Education and Science

603 **El Colegio de México: una hazaña cultural 1940-62.** (The Colegio de México: a cultural achievement 1940-62.)
     Clara E. Lida, Jose A. Matesanz. Mexico City: Colegio de México, 1990. 395p. bibliog.

The Colegio de México was founded in 1938 as a kind of half-way house to welcome Spanish Republican exiles. In 1940 it was re-founded as an institution devoted to higher education. It is now one of the leading higher education institutions in Mexico. The authors, in this work published as part of the fiftieth anniversary celebrations, show how the emphasis of the Colegio has shifted from historical studies to social sciences.

604 **Education and national development in Mexico.**
     Charles Nash Myers. Princeton, New Jersey: Princeton University Press, Department of Economics, 1965. 147p. (Princeton University, Industrial Relations Section. Research Report Series, no. 106).

This is intended to be the Mexican dimension of a comparative study of the relationship between education and economic growth. The author shows that there is such a relationship, though its character changes from region to region.

605 **Mexico: the challenge of poverty and illiteracy.**
     Ramon Eduardo Ruiz. San Marino, California: Huntington Library, 1963. 234p. bibliog. (Huntington Library Publications).

A general history of education in Mexico, covering the period from 1910 to the early 1960s. The author believes that rural education is of crucial importance to Mexico.

128

606 **Medicine in Mexico, from Aztec herbs to betatrons.**
Gordon Schendel. Austin, Texas: University of Texas Press, 1968.
329p. bibliog. (Texas Pan-American Series).
An interesting survey of medicine in Mexico, including material on Aztec medicine,
Spanish Colonial medicine and modern medicine.

607 **The state, education and social class in Mexico 1880-1928.**
Mary Kay Vaughan. De Kalb, Illinois: Northern Illinois University
Press, 1982. 316p. bibliog.
The author argues that the Mexican Revolutionaries, like their predecessors, saw the
rôle of education primarily as a means of social control. The period covered by the
book was one of both social mobilization and increased bureaucratic control of
education.

608 **El Colegio de México; años de expansión e institucionalización 1961-
1990.** (The Colegio de México: the years of expansion and
institutionalization, 1961-90.)
Josefina Vázquez. Mexico City: Colegio de México, 1990. 401p.
bibliog.
This is sequel to the history of the first generation of the Colegio de México. It covers
the expansion of the Colegio and its move from the centre of Mexico City to its present
purpose-built campus to the south west. Josefina Vazquez is a prominent historian
connected with the Colegio.

609 **On the viability of a policy for science and technology in Mexico.**
Miguel S. Wionczek. *Latin American Research Review*, vol. 26, no. 1
(1981), p. 57-78.
Wionczek argues that Mexico had at the end of the 1970s no national scientific or
technological policy. He argues that such a policy cannot easily be formulated in
Mexico, given the multiplicity of bureacratic interests involved. He considers the effect
of the 1976 National Plan for Science and Technology.

610 **Literacy and basic needs satisfaction in Mexico.**
Richard Wood. *World Development*, vol. 16, no. 3 (March 1988),
p. 405-17. bibliog.
This is an important article which argues that variations in literacy rates explain
statistically a significant part of the variation in child mortality rates, whether as cause
or as a proxy variable. The author believes that there is indeed a causal effect.

Sport

611 **Men and horses of Mexico. History and practice of** *Charreria.*
Jose Alvarez del Villar, translated by Margaret Fischer de Nicolin.
Mexico DF: Ediciones Lara, 1979. 115p.
A general survey of the Mexican *charro* [horseman] and equestrian sports generally.
The book discusses the breeding of horses, bull riding, equipment, costumes, racing,
hunting and fiestas. Although Alvarez del Villar has written technical books about
equestian sports in Spanish, this translated volume is aimed more at the general
reader.

612 **My life as a matador. The autobiography of Carlos Arruza.**
Carlos Arruza, with Barnaby Conrad. Boston, Massachusetts:
Houghton-Mifflin, 1956. 246p.
Arruza was born in Mexico City in 1920. He began to train as a bullfighter at the age of
13. He retired in 1953 after having killed some 1260 bulls and become a millionaire.
Since retiring he has raised bulls on his own ranch.

613 **A Mexican popular image of the United States through the baseball
hero, Fernando Valenzuela.**
David G. LaFrance. *Studies in Latin American Popular Culture*, vol.
4 (1985), p. 14-23.
Valenzuela is a Mexican who became a hero with the Dodgers. He is admired in his
own country, but with a touch of ambiguity. Some Mexicans believe that the North
Americans do not appreciate him sufficiently; others regret that he had to go to the
United States.

614   **The sporting scene. Mundial notebook: Ariel vs Caliban.**
      Alastair Reid.   *The New Yorker*, vol. LXII, no. 32 (29 Sept. 1986),
      p. 45-60.

A discussion of the 1986 World Cup which was held in Mexico City. It discusses the deep pessimism in Mexico over the economic situation, considers the quality of the actual football, and criticizes the commercialization of the event.

615   **La fiesta del alarido y las Copas del Mundo.** (The festival of cheering
      and the World Cup.)
      Manuel Seyde.   Mexico DF: Litografia Cultural, 1984. 253p.

The author was, between 1935 and 1983, head of the sports section of the Mexican daily *Excelsiór*. He published a kind of memoir in 1970, and this is a revised and expanded edition of that same work. It is mainly about Mexican soccer, and has much to say about the World Cup competition held in Mexico in 1970.

616   **Casa llena, bola roja. La lucha de los peloteros de la ANABE.**
      (Full house, red ball. The struggle of the ANABE baseball players.)
      Benito Terrazas.   Mexico City: Información Obrera-Leega, 1984.
      108p.

There has been considerable industrial unrest in Mexican baseball. In 1980 the players formed their own union, ANABE, and later went on strike. Eventually ANABE decided in 1981 to found its own Liga Nacional. This account is sympathetic to the position of the workers.

Literature

617 **Morir en el Golfo.** (Death in the Gulf.)
Héctor Aguilar Camín. Mexico City: Oceano, 1985. 245p.

This is a lightly fictionalized account of a corrupt and violent trade union structure in Veracruz during the oil boom years. The villain is a trade union Godfather figure. A few years after the book was published, the head of the oilworkers union was arrested on charges which included multiple murder.

618 **The sky in Mayan literature.**
Edited by Anthony Aveni. Oxford, England; New York: Oxford University Press, 1992. 296p.

This work is a collection of articles focused around the problem of trying to understand the rôle of time and time-keeping in Maya culture. A considerable number of texts, both ancient and modern, are analysed. The book came out of a conference held in 1989.

619 **Octavio Paz: homage to the poet.**
Edited by Kosrof Chantikan. San Francisco, California: Kosmos, 1981. 248p. bibliog.

The title is largely self-explanatory. Octavio Paz is Mexico's foremost poet and literary theorist. This is mainly a collection of literary criticism of his work. Some of Paz' own work is included, including several poems and a translation of a 1956 play *Rappaccini's daughter*.

620 **Voices, visions and a new reality; Mexican fiction since 1970.**
Ann J. Duncan. Pittsburgh, Pennsylvania: University of Pittsburgh Press, 1986. 263p. bibliog.

A discussion of the fiction of six young Mexican writers who became prominent in the 1970s. These are José Emilio Pacheco, Carlos Montemayor, Humberto Guzman, Ester Seligson, Antonio Delgado and Jesús Gardea.

621 **Where the air is clear.**
Carlos Fuentes, translated by Sam Hileman. London: André
Deutsch, 1986, 376p.
Carlos Fuentes' first novel was originally published in 1958 under the title *La región
mas transparente*. It portrays a cross-section of society in Mexico City during the post-
revolutionary period.

622 **The old gringo.**
Carlos Fuentes, translated by Margaret Sayers Peden, Carlos
Fuentes. London: André Deutsch, 1986. 148p.
Ambrose Bierce, an elderly American journalist and humourist, rode into Mexico at
the time of the Revolution and disappeared. This historical fact evidently gave Fuentes
the idea for this interesting novel, though here 'the old gringo' is never actually
identified. Fuentes is able to explore themes relating to the association between
Mexico and the United States.

623 **History of Mexican literature.**
Carlos Gonzalez Peña, translated from the Spanish by Gusta Barfield
Nance, Florence Johnson Dunstan. Dallas, Texas: Southern
Methodist University Press, 1968. 3rd ed. 540p.
An authoritative work on the subject, with critical evaluations of poets, dramatists and
novelists from the sixteenth to the twentieth centuries.

624 **Efrén Hernández: a poet rediscovered.**
Mary Harmon. Jackson, Mississippi: University Press of Mississippi,
1972. 128p. bibliog.
A critical study of the works of Hernández, presented through biographical
information together with statements from the writer and examples from his works
(poetry, novels and short stories).

625 **The transformation of the Hummingbird: cultural roots of a
Zinacantecan mythical poem.**
Eva Hunt. Ithaca, New York: Cornell University Press, 1977. 312p.
bibliog. (Symbol, Myth and Ritual Series).
The author provides us with an analysis of the mythical symbolism found in the poem
'The Hummingbird' and uses the historical record to relate it to the culture in which it
originated.

626 **Pre-Columbian literature of Mexico.**
Miguel León-Portilla, translated from the Spanish by Grace Labanov,
Miguel León-Portilla. Norman, Oklahoma: University of Oklahoma
Press, 1969. 191p. bibliog. (Civilization of the American Indian Series,
no. 92).
A work which presents many examples of pre-Columbian literature (myths, lyric
poetry, early drama, and prose) together with a commentary. The author attempts to

bring out the character of the symbolism found in the early literature, which includes examples from the Nahuatl, Maya, Mextec, Zapotec, Tarascan and Otomi literature.

627 **Escenas de pudor y livianidad.** (Scenes of shame and levity.) Carlos Monsivais. Mexico DF: Grijalbo, 1988. 354p.

This is a lightly fictionalized reflection on the sports and entertainments open to Mexicans since the beginning of the century. These include cinema, comedy, fiestas, radio and TV. The account touches on some historical events and mentions some real personalities.

628 **New poetry of Mexico.** Compiled by Octavio Paz, edited by Mark Strand. New York: Dutton, 1970. 224p.

Octavio Paz is Mexico's foremost poet. Here he introduces his selection of other Mexican poets' work. The collection is of seventy-one poems based on *Poesia en Movimiento, México 1915-1966*, published in Mexico in 1966. The selection includes the work of twenty-four poets, with translations and brief biographical notes useful for the English-speaking reader.

629 **On poets and others.** Octavio Paz, translated by Michael Schmidt. London: Carcanet Press, 1987. 219p.

This is a collection of essays written at various times between 1945 and 1980 about various literary figures, interspersed with reflections on his own individual growth and views, and in particular his aversion to dictatorship of all kinds.

630 **Emilio Carballido.** Margaret Sayers Peden. Boston, Massachusetts: Twayne, 1980. 192p. bibliog. (Twayne's World Authors Series, no. 561; Mexico).

This volume is part of a series aimed at making world literature available to the English-speaking reader. Emilio Carballido is one of Mexico's leading dramatists. Here his work is analysed, some biographical information provided and some of his quotations are translated into English.

631 **The Mexican historical novel 1826-1910.** John Lloyd Read. New York: Russell and Russell, 1973. 337p. bibliog.

A reprint of the 1929 edition. The author examines the early Romantic novels dealing with the Conquest period and that immediately following, and he also discusses works concerned with the nineteenth century which were written as contemporary history by authors of that time.

632 **Mexican society during the Revolution; a literary approach.** John David Rutherford. Oxford, England: Clarendon Press, 1971. 347p. bibliog.

This is a combination of literary criticism and social history. The author uses the novel as his main source of information as to the social dimensions of the Mexican

Revolution. The work is organized according to the social sector discussed. There are chapters on the intellectuals, the leadership of the Revolution, the 'fighting masses' and the anti-Revolutionaries. The author emphasizes the often haphazard and amorphous nature of the Revolution and sees only the Zapatista movement as being truly Revolutionary.

633   **B. Traven; life and work.**
Edited by Enid Schurer, Philip Jenkins.   Pittsburgh, Pennsylvania: Pennsylvania University Press, 1987. 368p. bibliog.
The majority of the contributions to this volume are concerned with Traven's work rather than his life. It is increasingly recognized that Traven's works on Mexico are valuable in their own right and not merely as expressions of a political viewpoint.

634   **After the storm: landmarks of the modern Mexican novel.**
Joseph Sommers.   Albuquerque, New Mexico: University of New Mexico Press. 1968. 208p. bibliog.
This is a work of literary criticism which discusses the novels of Agustín Yáñez, Juan Rulfo and Carlos Fuentes. The works under study were written between 1947 and 1962.

635   **Octavio Paz.**
Jason Wilson.   Basingstoke, England: Macmillan, 1986. 165p. bibliog.
This is a literary and intellectual study of Mexico's most eminent poet. It stresses the essential moral honesty of the author during the whole of his long and changing career.

636   **B. Traven: a vision of Mexico.**
Heidi Zogbaum.   Wilmington, Virginia: Scholarly Resources, 1992. 255p. bibliog.
Traven is best known for his *Treasures of the Sierra Madre* and for other novels which illustrate his concern for the underprivileged Indians of Mexico. This study is part biography and part history. Traven was an anarchist who fled Germany in 1919 and arrived in Mexico in 1924. He began writing optimistically about the Mexican Revolution but eventually became disillusioned.

The Arts

Painting

637 **Art of the Huichol Indians.**
Edited by Kathleen Berrin. New York: Abrams, for the Fine Arts
Museums of San Francisco, 1978. maps. bibliog.

A series of articles on Huichol art forms, written by anthropologists and psychologists,
attempting to show these forms from differing points of view. Some present
psychological analyses and others discuss the cultural context of the works.

638 **Mexican art and the Academy of San Carlos 1785-1915.**
Jean Charlot. Austin, Texas: University of Texas Press, 1961. 177p.
(Texas Pan-American Series).

An attempt to understand the period of neo-classicism in Mexico which was dominated
by the Royal Academy of San Carlos, founded in 1785 by the king of Spain. The
period studied is mostly post-colonial and decidedly pre-modern.

639 **Indian art of Mexico and Central America.**
Miguel Covarrubias. New York: Knopf, 1957. 360p. maps. bibliog.

A richly illustrated volume on pre-Columbian art. The author presents the theories of
many schools of archaeology as well as his own interpretations. Some of these theories
may now be dated, but Covarrubias himself is an important figure in Mexican
intellectual history.

640 **Indian art in Middle America.**
Frederick J. Dockstader. Greenwich, Connecticut: New York
Graphic Society, 1964. 221p. maps. bibliog.

This is essentially an illustrated volume, which includes Mexican works as well as
works from further south. The illustrations are accompanied by descriptive captions.

641 **Diego Rivera: the Cubist years.**
Ramon Favela.   Phoenix, Arizona: Phoenix Art Museum, 1984. 176p.
bibliog.

Before achieving international fame as a muralist, Diego Rivera was already a considerable artist. He was influenced by the Cubist style. This work is a condensed version of Favela's PhD dissertation and is likely to become the definitive interpretation of this phase of Rivera's career.

642 **A guide to Mexican art, from its beginnings to the present.**
Justino Fernández, translated from the Spanish by Joshua C. Taylor.
Chicago, Illinois: University of Chicago Press, 1969. 398p. bibliog.

This is an illustrated survey of Mexican art and architecture. The periods covered divide into pre-Columbian, Colonial, modern, and contemporary. The work is aimed mainly at the non-specialist.

643 **Modern Mexican artists: critical notes.**
Carlos Merida.   Freeport, New York: Books for Libraries Press, 1968.
202p. (Essay Index Reprint Series).

The original work was published in 1937 and therefore refers to the post-Revolutionary period in Mexico. It presents a series of biographical sketches with illustrations of the works of the artists included.

644 **The art of Mesoamerica; from Olmec to Aztec.**
Mary Ellen Miller.   New York; London: Thames and Hudson, 1986.
240p.

This is a survey which is aimed at the non-specialist. The work is clearly written and takes some of the latest scholarly thinking into account.

645 **Mexican painting in our time.**
Bernard S. Myers.   Oxford, England: Oxford University Press, 1956.
283p. bibliog.

As can be seen from the date of publication, this work focuses mainly on the first half of the present century. It is heavily illustrated. The author relates the artists' works to the historical period out of which they grew.

646 **Arts of ancient Mexico.**
Jacques Soustelle, translated from the French by Elizabeth
Carmichael.   New York: Viking Press, 1967. 160p. maps. bibliog.
(Studio Book).

A view of the arts of early Mexico, including sculpture, pottery, painting and architecture. The volume includes 206 photographs taken by Claude Arthaud and F. Hebert-Stevens.

647 **Colonial art in Mexico.**
Manuel Toussaint, edited and translated from the Spanish by Elizabeth
Wilder Weismann. Austin, Texas: University of Texas Press, 1967.
493p. bibliog. (Texas Pan-American Series).
A classic work on Mexican arts and architecture, available to the English-speaking
reader through this translation. The book is illustrated by many excellent plates.

648 **Olmec: an early art style of pre-Columbian Mexico.**
Charles R. Wicke. Tucson, Arizona: University of Arizona Press,
1971. 188p. bibliog.
A scholarly work on the Olmec culture, which seeks to undertand the art style in terms
of both the social and the psychological points of view.

Architecture, sculpture and other visual arts

649 **Pre-Columbian Mexican miniatures: the Josef and Anni Albers
collection.**
Anni Albers. New York: Praeger, 1970. 84p. bibliog.
A well-illustrated catalogue of Mesoamerican figurines and other miniature objects,
with introductory text and informative captions.

650 **Style in Mexican architecture.**
Richard Aldrich. Coral Gables, Florida: University of Miami Press,
1968. 110p.
A critical text, accompanied by sixty-four very good black-and-white photographs
illustrating Mexican architecture from pre-Columbian to modern. Many colonial
examples are given, including numerous churches.

651 **Ancient sculpture from western Mexico: the evolution of artistic form.**
John L. Alsberg, Rodolfo Petshek. Berkeley, California: Nicole
Gallery, 1968. 135p. bibliog.
This is an appraisal of sculptures from Nayarit, Colima and Jalisco, illustrated by some
very good black-and-white photographs.

652 **Edzna, Campeche, Mexico: settlement patterns and monumental
architecture.**
George F. Andrews (et al.). Eugene, Oregon: University of Oregon,
Department of Architecture, 1969. 149p. maps.
Much of this work consists of maps, analyses of buildings, site plans and photographs
of stelae and glyph panels.

653 **El edificio del Hospital de Jesús: historia y documentación sobre su construcción.** (The Hospital of Jesus: its history and some documentation on its construction.) Eduardo Baez Macias. Mexico City: UNAM, 1982. 164p. (Monografias de Arte, no. 6).
The building which is the subject of this work has been used as a hospital since it was founded in 1528. This is a well-documented study which includes 42 pages of plates. There is one chapter per century from the foundation to the present day.

654 **The churches of Mexico, 1530-1810.** Joseph Armstrong Baird. Berkeley, California: University of California Press, 1962. 126p. maps. bibliog.
This volume is well illustrated with photographs and line drawings and is a valuable addition to collections on Colonial art and architecture. Many of the churches covered here are not discussed in other works. The author illustrates variations in regional architecture.

655 **Builders in the sun.** Clive Bamford-Smith. New York: Architectural Book Publishing Co., 1957. 224p.
A fully illustrated volume on the work of Juan O'Gorman, Luis Barragan, Felix Candelar, Mathias Goeritz and Mario Pani.

656 **The architecture of Mexico yesterday and today.** Hans Beacham. New York: Architectural Book Publishing Co., 1969. 255p.
A collection of interesting black-and-white photographs of Mexican architecture. Many building details are included. The record provided here is all the more important as new construction and earthquake damage have so altered the physical landscape since the book was published.

657 **Colossal heads of the Olmec culture.** C. William Clewlow, Richard A. Cowan, James F. O'Connell, Carlos Bennemann. Berkeley, California: University of California, 1967. 170p. maps. bibliog. (Archaeological Research Facility Contributions, no. 4).
One of the most striking images in the whole of pre-Columbian visual art is the Olmec sculpture of very large heads. A number of these were found at San Lorenzo. This volume is a well-illustrated, detailed volume about twelve stone sculptures in the round. Information is given on style, the sculpting techniques employed and the condition of the works.

658 **A stylistic and chronological study of Olmec monumental sculpture.**
Carl William Clewlow Jr.   Berkeley, California: University of
California, Department of Anthropology, 1974. bibliog. (University of
California Archaeological Research Facility, Contributions, no. 19).
A heavily documented monograph based upon a PhD thesis. There is abundant
material on the sculpting techniques employed and attempts are made to date the
works studied.

659 **An early stone pectoral from southeastern Mexico.**
Michael D. Coe.   Washington, DC: Dumbarton Oaks Trustees for
Harvard University. 1966. 18p. bibliog. (Studies in Pre-Columbian Art
and Archaeology, no. 1).
An examination of a pectoral in the Robert Wood Bliss collection of pre-Columbian
art at Dumbarton Oaks.

660 **Lords of the underworld: masterpieces of classic Maya ceramics.**
Michael D. Coe.   Princeton, New Jersey: Art Museum, Princeton
University, distributed by Princeton University Press, 1978. 142p.
bibliog.
A heavily illustrated catalogue of Mayan ceramics; a detailed descriptive text
accompanies each photograph.

661 **Mexican masks.**
Donald Cordry.   Austin, Texas: University of Texas Press, 1980. 280p.
maps. bibliog.
Writers such as Octavio Paz have suggested that masks play an important rôle in
Mexican culture. This volume, which includes many illustrations, covers the subject
from the points of view of art, symbolism, history, and psychology of use.

662 **The ceramic history of the central highlands of Chiapas, Mexico.**
T. Patrick Culbert.   Provo, Utah: Brigham Young University, 1915.
91p. maps. (New World Archaeological Foundation Paper 19,
Publication no. 14).
A description of ceramic types and forms found, together with the site date, from nine
prehistoric Chiapas sites. The period covered ranges from 300 BC to AD 1524.

663 **Mexican folk art.**
Gerd Dorner, translated from the German by Gladys Wheelhouse.
Munich, Germany; Vienna: W. Andermann Verlag, 1962. 67p. bibliog.
A short history of Mexican folk art with many coloured photographs showing examples
of pottery, weaving and beadwork.

664 **Design motifs of ancient Mexico.**
Jorge Enciso. New York: Dover, 1953. 153p.
A collection of primitive designs derived from carved stamps made by early Mexican peoples. These are now used by artists and designers. The work was originally published in Spanish under the title *Sellos del antiguo México*.

665 **Designs from pre-Columbian Mexico.**
Jorge Enciso. New York: Dover, 1971. 105p. (Dover Pictorial Archives).
An illustrated collection of three hundred original motifs created by pre-Columbian Mexican peoples such as the Aztecs, Toltecs and others. These designs were found in archaeological digs on malacates, objects of baked clay.

666 **So far from heaven: David Alfaro Siqueiros. The march of humanity and Mexican revolutionary politics.**
Leonard Folgarait. Cambridge, England: Cambridge University Press, 1987. 140p. bibliog. (Cambridge Iberian and Latin American Studies).
Siquieros was one of Mexico's leading muralists and also an active promoter of Left-wing political causes. The title refers to *The March of Humanity on Earth*, Siquieros' more important work which was begun in 1954 and completed in 1971. This is a definitive study.

667 **Mezcala stone sculpture: the human figure.**
Carlos T. E. Gay. Greenwich, Connecticut: New York Graphic Society, 1967. 39p. maps. bibliog. (Museum of Primitive Art Studies, no. 5).
A study of pre-Columbian stone sculpture found in the state of Guerrero.

668 **Rock art of Baja California.**
Campbell Grant. Los Angeles, California: Dawson's Book Shop, 1974. 146p. maps. bibliog. (Baja California Travels Series, no. 33).
The author originally translated Leon Diguet's article of 1895 on the rock art of Baja California Sur. He then became interested in pursuing the matter further, and updated and expanded the original work. The volume is heavily illustrated.

669 **Crafts of Mexico.**
Marian Harvey. New York: Macmillan, 1973. 243p.
An illustrated volume which contains descriptive sections on weaving, reeds, metals, clay, wood and paper.

670 **Diego Rivera; a retrospective.**
Edited by Cynthia Newman Helms. New York: W. W. Norton, 1986. 372p. bibliog.
This book contains ten essays on various aspects of Rivera's life and work. There is also an extensive bibliography. The murals themselves are well photographed.

671 **Pre-Columbian architecture of Meso America.**
Doris Heyden, Paul Gendrop. New York: Abrams, 1976. 340p.
(History of World Architecture Series).

A well-illustrated survey of pre-Columbian styles, which focuses on key archaeological sites and discusses the culture of the period. The work is aimed principally at the non-specialist reader.

672 **Mexican landscape architecture: from the street and from within.**
Rosina Greene Kirby. Tucson, Arizona: Arizona University Press, 1972. 163p. bibliog.

The author makes good use of some excellent photographs to illustrate Mexican landscape design. Material on plazas, parks, patios and gardens is included.

673 **M. Alvarez Bravo.**
Jane Livingston. Boston, Massachusetts: David R. Godine, 1978. 45p.

A collection of photographs which illustrate the work of one of Mexico's best-known photographers. The author provides a text describing Alvarez Bravo's fifty-year career.

674 **The open-air churches of sixteenth-century Mexico: *atrios*, *posas*, open chapels and other studies.**
John McAndrew. Cambridge, Massachusetts: Harvard University Press, 1965. 755p. bibliog.

A beautiful work of architectural history, which includes the line drawings of the structures discussed, and provides an overview of sixteenth-century Mexican life.

675 **Ceramics.**
Richard S. MacNeish, Frederick A. Peterson, Kent V. Flannery.
Austin, Texas: University of Texas Press, 1970. map. bibliog.
(Prehistory of the Tehuacán Valley, vol. 3).

An important work on the development and distribution of Mesoamerican ceramics. Included in the study are the Valleys of Mexico and Oaxaca, the Gulf Coast and the Maya area.

676 **The murals of Bonampak.**
M. E. Miller. Princeton, New Jersey: Princeton University Press, 1986. 176p. bibliog.

In 1948 there was discovered an impressive set of murals at Bonampak, which is located on a tributary of the Usumacinta in the Yucatán. The architectural structure where the murals was discovered was much less impressive. The images depicted in the murals were violent and warlike. The author summarizes various interpretations but does not seek to go beyond them. The work is lavishly illustrated.

677 **Some hypotheses regarding the petroglyphs of West Mexico.**
Joseph B. Mountjoy.   Carbondale, Illinois: University Museum,
Southern Illinois University at Carbondale, 1974. 36p. maps. bibliog.
(Mesoamerican Studies, no. 9).

A brief study of an art form which had previously received little attention, and which is
compared here to designs found in ceramics, textiles, plastered walls, etc.

678 **Dominican architecture in sixteenth century Oaxaca.**
Robert J. Mullen.   Phoenix, Arizona: Arizona State University,
Center for Latin American Studies, 1975. 260p. bibliog.

A study of over seventy church–convent complexes founded by the Dominicans, giving
case-histories, architectural styles, foundation dates, and so forth.

679 **The Puuc: an architectural survey of the hill country of Yucatán and
northern Campeche, Mexico.**
Harry Evelyn Dorr Pollock.   Cambridge, Massachusetts: Peabody
Museum of Archaeology and Ethnology, Harvard University, 1980.
600p. map. bibliog. (Memoirs of the Peabody Museum, vol. 19).

The Puuc are a series of low hills extending from western Campeche into the state of
Yucatán. They were the focal point for much of the artistic and intellectual culture of
the Maya. Uxmal is the most important site within the region. Mayan art was as much
influenced by painting as by sculpture, but most of it may have perished with the
passage of time. This is a detailed architectural study with photographs, architectural
renderings, plans, etc.

680 **Stonework of the Maya.**
Edward Ranney.   Albuquerque, New Mexico: University of New
Mexico Press, 1974. 119p. bibliog.

An attractive collection of photographs accompanies the text of this book. Ranney
discusses the stonework of the Maya as part of the natural setting in which it stands.

681 **The Mexican muralists.**
Alma M. Reed.   New York: Crown, 1960. 191p.

An introduction to mural painting which contains potted biographies of more than
thirty Mexican artists who worked in this field, including José Orozco, Diego Rivera
and David Siqueiros. This work is intended for the general reader.

682 **Mexican manuscript painting of the early colonial period.**
Donald Robertson.   New Haven, Connecticut: Yale University Press,
1959. 234p. bibliog.

The author studies a group of manuscripts from the Central Valley of Mexico and
traces Spanish influence on Indian styles.

The Arts. Architecture, sculpture and other visual arts

683 **A history of Mexican mural painting.**
Antonio Rodríguez, translated from the Spanish by Marina Corby.
New York: G. P. Putnam and Sons, 1969. 571p.

One of the most distinctive of all art forms in which Mexicans have excelled is the mural. This is a political form of art, but the sheer excellence of Mexico's most important muralists should not be overlooked. Rodríguez starts his account with an analysis of pre-Columbian murals and pottery.

684 **Mexican interiors.**
Verna Cook Shipway, Warren Shipway.   New York: Architectural
Book Publishing Co., 1962. 257p.

A photographic collection of Mexican interiors, illustrating both surviving examples from colonial times and folk art used in restored colonial and modern homes. Details are emphasized. These include tiles, screens, ceramics, fireplaces and gardens.

685 **Mexican popular arts; being a fond glance at the craftsmen and their handiwork in ceramics, textiles, metals, glass, paint, fibres and other materials.**
Frances Toor.   Detroit, Michigan: Blaine Ethridge, 1973. 107p.

This work was first published in 1939, and the present volume is a revised update. Most of the popular arts and crafts of Mexico are covered.

686 **Art and time in Mexico.**
Elizabeth Wilder Weismann.   New York: Harper and Row, 1985.
284p. bibliog.

An illustrated study of Mexican colonial architecture and decoration. The work considers a range of buildings such as convents, churches, schools, universities, hospitals, houses and cathedrals. It examines various influences including Spanish, Flemish and Aztec which can be detected in the contruction. Sometimes more than one style is in evidence in a single building.

687 **The sculpture of ancient Mexico.**
Paul Westheim, translated from the Spanish by Ursula Bernard.
Garden City, New York: Doubleday, 1963. 69p. (Anchor Books).

A volume published for a general readership. The author discusses pre-Columbian sculpture and illustrates selected clay and stone objects in a series of ninety-four plates. The work was originally published in German, translated into Spanish and then into English.

Music, theatre and film

688 *Cantares Mexicanos*: **Songs of the Aztecs.**
Edited by John Bierhorst, translated by the editor.   Stanford,
California: Stanford University Press, 1985. 560p. bibliog.
The Aztecs took poetry and singing very seriously. This work includes not only
examples of the poems and songs themselves, but also an important analysis of the
literary and historical background to the songs. The works include some pre-
Columbian compositions but many were in fact composed shortly after the Conquest.

689 **Musical artefacts of pre-Hispanic west Mexico: towards an
interdisciplinary approach.**
Peter Crossley-Holland.   Los Angeles, California: Program in
Ethnomusicology. Department of Music, University of California,
1980. 45p. bibliog. (Monograph Series in Ethnomusicology, no. 1).
A short monograph providing information on musical instruments seen in their cultural
setting. They are interpreted using integrated musicological, archaeological and
historical data.

690 **Mexican theater of the twentieth century: bibliography and study.**
Ruth S. Lamb.   Clairemont, California: Ocelot Press, 1975. 2nd ed.
140p.
This is essentially a bibliography but it contains an introductory essay which discusses
the Mexican theatre in three stages: 'Emancipation – 1900-30'; 'Renovation – 1928-50';
and 'New Theatre – 1950-1975'. Also presented are a critical bibliography, and a list of
periodicals containing theatre criticism, bibliography and texts of plays.

691 **Mexican cinema: reflections of a society 1896-1988.**
Carl J. Mora.   Berkeley, California: University of California Press,
1989. 256p.
The author provides a detailed history of Mexican cinema which reflects to some extent
the social and political history of the country. The study begins with the silent movies,
moving on to the talkies and the growth of the industry in the war years, and looks at
the Golden Age of Mexican cinema from around 1947 to 1959. Thereafter the industry
became increasingly commercial, although the author is hopeful for the future.

692 **Music in Aztec and Inca territory.**
Robert Stevenson.   Berkeley, California: University of California
Press, 1968. 378p.
A general survey work, containing much of what was then known about the music of
central Mexico. Most of the material has been gleaned from documentary and native
pictorial sources.

693 **En su proprio espejo: entrevista con Emilio "El Indio" Fernández.** (In his own mirror: an interview with Emilio 'the Indian' Fernández.) Julia Tuñón Pablos.   Mexico: UNAM. 116p.

Biographical study of the life, personality, views and production of Emilio Fernández who is a famous Mexican film-maker. The work is largely based on interviews with the subject.

Folklore

694 **Mexican folktales from the borderland.**
Riley Aiken. Dallas, Texas: Southern Methodist University Press, 1980. 159p.
A collection of stories which the author gathered over a period of years from 1929 onwards. These represent the culture of the Mexican–Indian rural borderland.

695 **Ritual humor in highland Chiapas.**
Victoria Reifler Bricker. Austin, Texas: University of Texas Press, 1973. 257p. maps. bibliog. (Texas Pan-American Series).
A study of the ritualized humour found in songs, costumes and so forth used during the main festivals in Chiapas – carnivals, Christmas, New Year, and Epiphany.

696 **A guide to Mexican witchcraft.**
William Madsen, Claudia Madsen. Mexico City: Editorial Minutiae Mexicana, 1972. 96p. bibliog. (Minutiae Mexicana Series).
A popular account of folk medical practices in early and contemporary Mexico. Anecdotes show the relationship between concern with witchcraft and social mobility.

697 **Folktales of Mexico.**
Compiled by Americo Paredes. Chicago, Illinois: University of Chicago Press, 1970. 282p. bibliog. (Folktales of the World).
A collection of eighty tales, which includes a glossary and indexes of tale types and motifs.

698 **Mexican folk toys: festival decorations and ritual objects.**
Florence H. Pettit, Robert M. Pettit. New York: Hastings House,
1978. 185p. bibliog.

An examination of one folk art, which relates it to Mexican history and society. The book contains material on the techniques and materials used by the craftspeople. There is a calendar of Mexican festivals and holidays; a list of shops and museums where folk toys and ritual objects can be found; and there are some charming photographs.

699 **Amapa storytellers.**
Edited by Stanley L. Robe. Berkeley, California: University of
California Press, 1972. 108p. bibliog.

A collection of fifteen orally collected texts gathered in Amapa, Nayarit, in 1959. The tales are briefly summarized in English and notes give information on other versions of each tale, and identify tale types. The introduction describes the village, its population and tale-telling customs.

700 **Mexican tales and legends from Los Altos.**
Edited by Stanley L. Robe. Berkeley, California: University of
California Press, 1970. 578p. bibliog.

This book contains two hundred and nineteen tales. The texts are in Spanish but with English summaries. They are identified by tale type and theme. There is considerable background information on the Los Altos region of Jalisco.

701 **A treasury of Mexican folkways.**
Frances Toor. New York: Crown, 1971. 566p.

An illustrated collection of customs, legends, dances and songs (including music). This is very much a work for the general reader.

Costume and Design

702 **Riders of the border: a selection of thirty drawings.**
Jose Cisneros. El Paso, Texas: Texas Western Press, University of
Texas at El Paso, 1971. 64p. bibliog. (Southwestern Studies
Monograph, no. 30).

One of the few existing collections of renderings showing details of clothing worn
throughout history by various people in Mexico and the Spanish southwest of the
United States. All the types represented in this collection are riders on horseback, and
vary from the sixteenth-century Spanish conquistador to the twentieth-century Colima
rider.

703 **Mexican Indian costumes.**
Donald Cordry, Dorothy Cordry. Austin, Texas: University of Texas
Press, 1968. 373p. maps. bibliog.

A thoroughly illustrated, well-produced and very knowledgeable work on pre-Hispanic
and modern costume. Besides 261 black-and-white plates, there is information on
weaving, design, jewellery, and much else.

704 **Mexican costume.**
Chloe Sayer. London: British Museum Publications, 1985. 240p.

This is a thorough study of Mexican costume from pre-Hispanic times to the twentieth
century with particular reference in the contemporary period to the techniques used in
making clothes. There are many photographs. The author also looks at the social and
ceremonial rôle of the costumes, their symbolism and their importance in group
identification.

705 **Mexican patterns; a design source book.**
Chloe Sayer.   London: Studio Editions, 1990. 202p. bibliog.

This work is heavily illustrated and very informative. Design work is a traditional Indian art form which is traced back to pre-Columbian days. There are over one hundred colour plates, featuring a diversity of styles. The book will be of interest to the professional designer as well as to the general reader.

Cooking

706   **Authentic Mexican cooking: regional cooking from the heart of Mexico.**
Rick Bayless, Dean Groen.   London: Headline Book Publishing,
1989. 384p. bibliog.
The authors of this book are restaurateurs. The dishes described range from chili
sauces of various types to tortillas, salads, soups, tacos, enchiladas, tamales, moles,
and desserts and drinks. The book is comprehensive, informative and attractively
produced.

707   **Savoring Mexico: a travel cookbook.**
Sharon Cadwallader.   New York: McGraw-Hill, 1980. 207p. maps.
A sampling of regional cookery throughout Mexico. The author has provided details of
dishes whose ingredients are widely available outside Mexico.

708   **Mexican cooking.**
Caroline Dehnel.   London: Ward Lock, 1990. 96p.
A simple and useful introduction to Mexican cooking. There is a brief history and a
glossary of ingredients. The recipes start with the basics but also include a number of
more challenging savouries and other dishes.

709   **The cuisines of Mexico.**
Diana Kennedy.   New York: Harper and Row, 1972. 378p. bibliog.
A well-researched book, written by the wife of a *New York Times* correspondent who
lived for a number of years in Mexico and gathered recipes from local kitchens as well
as from ancient cookery books. There is an introduction by Craig Claiborne, and
colour photographs of some of the dishes.

Cooking

710 **Mexican cooking.**
Lourdes Nichols. London: William Collins, 1984. 240p.
Lourdes Nichols, herself a Mexican, presents a range of recipes with clear instructions, useful serving suggestions, a guide to pronunciation, and an index which includes both the Spanish and English names of the dishes.

711 **The complete book of Mexican cooking.**
Elizabeth Lambert Ortiz. New York: M. Evans, 1967. 352p.
Three hundred and forty recipes present the blend of influences in Mexican cookery, combining Aztec, Spanish and French cuisine.

712 **Flavours of Mexico.**
Mariena Spieler. New York: Harper Collins, 1991. 294p.
This is a an all-round introduction to Mexican cooking which includes a glossary, a list of sources and a historical introduction. The recipes are extensive, and the book well illustrated.

Museums

713 **National Museum of Anthropology, Mexico.**
Ernesto Orellana Villers, translated from the Spanish by Martha
Guzman Hope.   Mexico DF: Distribuidora Mesoamericana, 1984.
95p.
A simply conceived but clear and well-illustrated guide to the most famous of all of
Mexico's museums. The museum, opened in 1964, is located in Chapultepec park near
the centre of Mexico City.

714 **The National Museum of Anthropology, Mexico: art, architecture,**
archaeology, anthropology.
Pedro Ramirez Vazquez.   New York: Abrams, 1968. 257p. maps.
bibliog.
A full-length study of the National Museum of Anthropology, which offers an
introductory study of pre-Columbian art and architecture. There are many photographs.

Press and Mass Media

715 **Este país; tendencias y opiniones.** (This country; tendencies and opinions.)
Mexico DF: Editorial Abeja, 1991- . monthly.
The main focus of this monthly journal which began in 1991 is on Mexican politics, though there are some international issues discussed. The most distinctive feature of the journal is its intensive use of opinion polling and survey data.

716 **Mass media and society in twentieth-century Mexico.**
Elizabeth Mahan. *Journal of the West*, vol. 17, no. 4 (Oct. 1988), p. 41-50.
The author argues that, with certain exceptions, the market has been more important than political control in determining the way in which the media have developed in Mexico during the course of the century.

717 **Broadcasting in Mexico: reassessing the industry–state relationship.**
Elizabeth Mahan. *Journal of Communication*, no. 35 (Winter 1985), p. 60-75.
Mahan looks at the way in which politics and commercial considerations have conflicted in Mexican broadcasting, and how these conflicts have been resolved.

718 **Nexos.**
Mexico City: Centro de Investigaciones Cultural y Científica, 1977- . monthly.
A monthly publication covering political and cultural matters, edited by a group of intellectuals who are broadly sympathetic to the Left of the political spectrum. However, its cultural and intellectual importance extends well beyond its short-term political evaluations.

719 **Broadcasting in Mexico.**
C. Antonio de Noriega, Frances Leal.   London: Routledge and Kegan
Paul, 1979. 87p. bibliog.
This relatively short work provides a descriptive account of the early development of
the broadcasting media, including television as well as radio. There is a a good deal of
detail on the 1960s and 1970s.

720 **Proceso.**
Mexico City: CISA, 1977- . weekly.
This weekly magazine has been published since 1977. More important than the
editorial line, which is uncompromisingly oppositional, is the quality of the
investigative journalism in some of its articles.

721 **Dependent development and broadcasting: the Mexican formula.**
John Sinclair.   *Media, Culture and Society*, no. 8 (Jan. 1986), p. 81-
102.
In this article, Sinclair discusses the development, organization and political economy
of Mexican broadcasting. He is particularly interested in the large private con-
glomerate, Televisa, and its rôle in Mexican political culture.

722 **Televisa; el quinto poder.** (Televisa; the fifth power.)
Edited by Raul Trejo Delarbe.   Mexico City: Claves Latinoamericano,
1985. 237p. bibliog.
This is a collection of ten articles about Televisa which is Mexico's most important
privately owned television company. The articles are mostly critical and accuse the
company of a Right-wing bias in its coverage of national affairs, both political and
cultural. This is an important book, one of the first to treat systematically the rôle of
private ownership of the mass media in Mexico.

723 **Vuelta.**
Mexico City: Amigos del Arte A.C., 1977- . monthly.
Edited by Octavio Paz and Enrique Krause, *Vuelta* is a monthly which focuses mainly
on cultural, historical and literary topics. Some of its interpretative articles on Mexican
history are particularly impressive. There is some political coverage from an angle
which is broadly liberal and anti-authoritarian.

Statistics

724 **The Mexican economy.**
Bank of Mexico. Mexico City: Banco de Mexico. annual.
The annual report of the Bank of Mexico is the authoritative source for up-to-date information on the Mexican economy. Each report discusses recent developments and policies, economic activity by sector, the financial system, the balance of payments and particular economic issues.

725 **Mexico demográfico: breviaro 1988.** (Mexican demography: 1988 report.)
Consejo Nacional de Población. Mexico City, Conapo, 1988. 151p.
This work offers an extensive statistical profile of the Mexican population with estimates up as far as 1985. The population of Mexico increased from 25.8 million in 1950 to 77.9 million in 1985. It will have shown a further significant increase since then.

726 **México: encuesta nacional sobre fecundidad y salud, 1987.** (Mexico: a national enquiry into fertility and health, 1987.)
Dirección General de Planificación Familiar. Columbia, Maryland: Institute for Resource Development, 1989. 171p.
A comprehensive study of births, birth rates, birth control and related issues. The survey is based, in part, on questionnaire evidence.

727   **Anuario estadístico de los Estados Unidos Mexicanos 1988-1989.**
(Annual statistical report on the United States of Mexico 1988-1989.)
Instituto Nacional de Estadísticas, Geografía e Información.   Aguas
Calientes, Mexico: INEGI, 1989. 838p.

A comprehensive statistical series covering a very wide range of issues. These include
infrastructural provision, transport, housing and electricity. There are also socio-
demographic aspects such as health, education, migration and law and order.
Economic data are also evident in abundance.

728   **10 años de indicadores económicas y sociales de México.** (Ten years of
economic and social indicators for Mexico.)
Instituto Nacional de Estadísticas, Geografía e Información.   Mexico
City: SPP, 1986. 390p.

This is a very comprehensive set of statistics which deal mainly with economic issues
although there is also material on education, housing, migration and other social
issues.

729   **United States–Mexico border statistics since 1900.**
Edited by David Loney.   Los Angeles, California: UCLA Latin
American Centre Publications, 1990. 475p.

This work, as is to be expected, is mostly made up of some comprehensive statistical
data which relate mainly to the 1945-80 period. There are also three short essays which
attempt to place the material in context.

730   **Plan nacional de desarrollo 1989-1994.** (National development plan
1989-1994.)
Secretaria de Programación y Presupuesto.   Mexico City: SPP, 1989.
137p.

It is a legal requirement in Mexico that a national development plan should be
published and sent to Congress at the beginning of each six-year presidential term.
This sets out what the government intends to do, and is of value for reference
purposes.

Bibliographies and Reference Works

731 **Oaxaca: a critical bibliography of rare and specialised materials in the University of New Mexico's general library.**
Claire Lise Benaud, Oscar Dellepiani.   Albuquerque, University of New Mexico, 1992. 100p. (Occasional Paper Series, no. 5).

Five hundred and two items are listed here. There is a good deal on the Church, on Indian languages and tribes, and on literature. This is not just a listing, however, for most items carry a brief annotation.

732 **The historical dictionary of Mexico.**
Donald C. Briggs, Marvin Alisky.   Metuchen, New Jersey; New York: Scarecrow Press, 1981. 259p. bibliog. (Latin American Historical Dictionaries, no. 21).

A one-volume reference tool providing short entries on various aspects of contemporary and historical aspects of Mexico.

733 **Political and economic encyclopaedia of South America and the Caribbean.**
Edited by Peter Calvert.   London: Longman, 1991. 362p.

This encyclopaedia is organized alphabetically with themes, countries and historical figures entered in the appropriate order. There is a heavy emphasis on biographical data on particular individuals, although there is also a discussion of recent Mexican history and political evolution.

734 **Mexico.**
R. A. Camp. In: *Handbook of political science research on Latin America; trends from the 1960s to the 1990s*, edited by David W. Dent. New York; Westport, Connecticut; London: Greenwood Press, 1990, p. 25-47.
An annotated bibliography written by a leading authority on current affairs in Mexico.

735 **The Cambridge encyclopaedia of Latin America and the Caribbean.**
Edited by Simon Collier, Harold Blakemore, Thomas Skidmore. Cambridge, England: Cambridge University Press, 1992. 2nd ed. 481p. maps.
This work is organized mainly by theme. These include the physical environment, the economy, the peoples, history, politics, and culture. There is a historical introduction to Mexico, but most references to Mexico come in their thematic context.

736 **Latin America 1979-83: a social science bibliography.**
Robert L. Delorme. Santa Barbara, California: ABC–Clio Information Services, 1984. 169p.
Pages 109-41 cover Mexico. The 730 titles are listed rather than evaluated. They include articles and books in English and Spanish.

737 **Europa 1988. South America, Central America and the Caribbean.**
London: Europa, 1987. 683p. bibliog.
This is an extensive work which is aimed mainly at a business readership. There are sections covering particular themes, regional organizations, and country topics. Each country is given a historical and economic outline, which is backed up by considerable statistical data and a directory of companies, trade unions, ministries and so forth.

738 **An index to Mexican literary periodicals.**
Merlin H. Forster. New York; Metuchen, New Jersey: Scarecrow Press, 1966. 276p.
Sixteen Mexican literary periodicals are indexed. These publications cover the period from 1920 to 1960, and most of them are not indexed elsewhere.

739 **Mexican literature: a bibliography of secondary sources.**
David William Foster. New York; Metuchen, New Jersey: Scarecrow Press, 1981. 386p.
A bibliography of criticism of major Mexican literary figures. The book is divided into two parts: one is general references and the other, authors. The compiler states that the bibliography is selective and depends in part on the wealth or paucity of material available on each author.

740 **A bibliographhny of Chicano and Mexican dance, drama and music.**
Jorge A. Huerta. Oxnard, California: Colegio Quetzalcoatl, 1972.
59p.
This bibliography, which is in the form of a pamphlet, covers areas of dance, drama
and music. Each subject is divided according to pre-Columbian, Mexican and Azlan
people. The work provides a listing only.

741 **The art of pre-Columbian Mexico: an annotated bibliography of works
in English.**
Aubyn Kendall. Austin, Texas: Institute of Latin American Studies,
University of Texas, 1973. 115p. (Guides and Bibliographic Series,
no. 5).
This useful annotated bibliography has an appendix listing works which were received
too late to be included in the alphabetical arrangement.

742 **The art and archaeology of pre-Columbian middle America: an
annotated bibliography of works in English.**
Aubyn Kendall. Boston, Massachusetts: G. K. Hall, 1977. 324p.
(Reference Publications in Latin American Studies).
This bibliography contains material on Mexico as well as the countries of Central
America. Some items are reproduced from the earlier *Art of pre-Columbian Mexico*,
and there are some later works on Mexico included here for the first time.

743 **A bibliography of Latin American bibliographies 1980-84: social sciences
and humanities.**
Lionel V. Lorona. Metuchen, New Jersey; London: Scarecrow Press,
1987. 164p.
This work is mainly organized by subject although there are some general works listed
under country headings.

744 **European immigration and ethnicity in Latin America: a bibliography.**
Oliver Marshall. London: ILAS, 1991. 151p.
This listing of works is organized mainly by European country rather than by Latin
American recipient. Nevertheless, there are a significant number of references to
Mexico.

745 **Index of Mexican folktales, including narrative texts from Mexico,
Central America, and the Hispanic United States.**
Stanley L. Robe. Berkeley, California: University of California Press,
1973. 276p. bibliog.
A useful index of some fifteen hundred Hispanic-Mexican folktales, classified
according to the Aarne-Thompson system. The index does not include tales of purely
non-Hispanic origin.

746 **An annotated bibliography of the novels of the Mexican revolution of 1910-17, in English and Spanish.**
John Rutherford. Troy: Whitston, 1971. 180p.
This is a useful reference work, which includes brief essays on the novelists, critics, and editors. The text is provided in both English and Spanish.

747 **Latin American politics; a historical bibliography.**
Edited by Gail Schlachter. Oxford, England: Clio Press, 1984. (Clio Bibliographic Series, no. 16).
This work contains some 440 titles and annotations on Mexico, covering history and politics. Work in both Spanish and English is included.

748 *Maquiladoras*: **annotated bibliography and research guide to Mexico's in-bond industry 1980-1988.**
Compiled by Leslie Sklair, Karen Lindvall, K. C. Moor Harnis. San Diego, California: Center for US–Mexican Studies, University of San Diego, 1988. 217p. (Monograph Series, no. 24).
The work includes newspapers, magazines, books, articles and official documents. It is the most important work of its kind to have appeared to date.

749 **Mexico's international relations.**
Dale Story. In: *Handbook of political science research on Latin America; trends from the 1960s to the 1990s*, edited by David W. Dent. New York; Westport, Connecticut; London: Greenwood Press, 1990, p. 307-25.
An annotated bibliography by an acknowledged authority on the subject.

750 **Handbook of research on the illicit drug traffic: socioeconomic and political consequences.**
La Mond Tullis. New York; Westport, Connecticut; London: Greenwood Press, 1991. 611p. (Published in co-operation with the UN Research Institute for Social Development).
This book is organized by theme rather than by country, but there are more than fifty references to Mexico. Topics include patterns of production and consumption, consequences, and suggested solutions.

Indexes

There follow three separate indexes: authors (including editors, compilers, contributors, translators and illustrators); titles of publications; and subjects. Title entries are italicized and refer either to the main titles or to other works cited in the annotations. The introductory definite or indefinite article is omitted. The numbers refer to bibliographical entries, rather than page numbers. Individual index entries are arranged in alphabetical sequence.

Index of Authors

A

Abel, Christopher 524
Acevedo, Esther 34
Adair, Marta 35
Adams, Richard 105, 142
Aguilar Camín, Héctor 481, 617
Aguilar Barajas, Ismael 57
Aiken, Riley 694
Aisen, Judith 326
Aiton, Arthur Scott 163
Alba, Francisco 372-3
Albers, Anni 649
Alcalá, Graciela 293
Aldrich, Richard 650
Alisky, Marvin 732
Alonso, Antonio 590
Alduncín Abitia, Enrique 1
Alsberg, John L. 651
Alvarado, Arturo 410, 431, 442, 451-2
Alvarez del Villar, Jose 611
Andersen, John M. 61
Anderson, Arthur 164, 208
Anderson, Rodney 591
Anderson, William Marshall 12

Andres, E. Wyllys 119
Andrews, George F. 106, 652
Andrews, Greg 255
Andrews, J. Richard 176
Ankerson, Dudley 256
Anglade, Christian 517
Anna, Timothy 224
Anzaldúa, Ricardo 420, 470, 474
Applegate, Howard G. 597
Archer, Christon 184
Arias, Jose 558
Arizpe, Lourdes 294, 392
Armstrong, George 362
Arnold, Linda 185
Aronson, J. D. 551
Arreola Ayala, Alvaro 465
Arrom, Silvia 380
Arruza, Carlos 612
Arthaud, Claude 646
Aschmann, Homer 58
Ashby, Joe C. 592
Aspe, Pedro 354-5, 358-9
Auerbach, Ellen 349
Ault, Stephen 577
Austin, James 575
Aveni, Anthony 618

B

Baez Macias, Eduardo 653
Bailey, John 411
Baird, Joseph Armstrong 653
Baker, Don 460
Baklanoff, E. 550
Balán, Jorge 295
Baldwin, Deborah 257
Ball, Joseph W. 107, 112
Bamford-Smith, Clive 655
Bank of Mexico 724
Baquedano, Elizabeth 84
Barenstain, Jorge 355
Barkin, David 513, 576
Barquera, Luis 558
Barrett, Elinore 186
Barry, Tom 2
Basáñez, Miguel 412-13, 461, 482
Bastiam 225
Bath, C. Richard 598
Batra, Roder 576
Baúdez, Claude 13
Bayliss, Rick 706
Bazant, Jan 155, 226, 342
Bazdresch, Carlos 414, 595
Beacham, Hans 656
Beeley, George 258

163

Beezley, William H. 6, 227
Behar, Jaime 539
Bell, Betty 121, 318
Beltrán, Ulises 187
Benaud, Claire Lise 731
Benitez, Fernando 59
Benjamin, Thomas 259,
    268, 270, 363
Bennemann, Carlos 657
Bennett, Douglas 548
Berdan, Frances 85-6, 164,
    208
Berlo, Janet Catherine 147
Bermúdez, Antonio J. 559
Bernal, Ignacio 122
Bernard, H. Russell 296
Berrin, Kathleen 637
Berry, Charles Redman
    228
Bethell, Leslie 226, 239,
    281, 284
Bierhorst, John 688
Bilateral Commission on
    the Future of United
    States–Mexican
    Relations 488
Binford, Leigh 374
Birnbaum, Alexandra 36-7
Birnbaum, Stephen 36-7
Bizberg, Ilan 475, 593
Blanton, Richard 123, 143
Block, M. A. Gonzalez
    356
Blomstrom, Magnus 549
Bond, Mike 38
Bond, Peggy 38
Booth, John 415
Botz, Dan La 260
Box, Ben 39
Brack, Gene 229
Brading, David 182, 188,
    230, 261, 343
Bradley, Charles Henry
    327
Brainerd, George W. 117
Brandes, Stanley 297
Brannon, J. T. 262, 550
Bravo Mena, Luis Felipe
    470
Bray, Warwick 87
Bricker, Victoria Reifler
    298, 695

Briggs, Donald C. 732
Brockington, Lolita
    Gutierrez 189
Brown, Johnathan 560
Browning, Harley 295
Brundage, David C. 88
Brosnahan, Tom 40
Brotherston, Gordon 144
Bucay, Nisso 414, 595
Bullock, William 14
Burke, Michael 41
Bustamante, Jorge 393,
    416, 454
Butler, Edgar W. 72, 416,
    454
Buve, Raymond 231

C

Cadwallader, Sharon 707
Cal y Arena 480
Calderón de la Barca,
    Fanny 15
Calvert, Peter 156, 489,
    733
Camp, Roderick A. 263,
    417-19, 471-2, 734
Cancian, Frank 299
Carey, James C. 264
Campbell, Lyle 334
Campbell, Timothy 60
Carmichael, Elizabeth 300,
    646
Carpizo, Jorge 462
Carr, Barry 420-1
Carrasco, David 89
Carroll, Patrick 190
Carvajal, Luis de 191
Castañeda, Jorge 502
Celaya, Rene 42
Cervantes, Francisco 165
Chamberlain, Robert
    Stone 166
Chandler, D. S. 192
Chance, John 167
Chant, Sylvia 381
Chantikan, Kosrof 619
Charlot, Jean 638
Cheetham, Sir Nicholas 15
Chinas, Beverly 382
Choenhals, Louise L. 76
Cisneros, Jose 702

Cleaves, Peter 422
Clendinnen, Inga 90, 168
Clewlow, C. William 657-8
Cline, S. L. 193
Coatsworth, John 490
Cockroft, James 157, 265
Coe, Michael 108-9, 124-5,
    659-60
Coerver, Don M. 266, 271
Coggins, Clemency Chase
    110
Collier, George Allen 599
Collier, Simon 735
Conrad, Barnaby 612
Conrad, Jim 43-4
Consejo Nacional de
    Población 725
Cook, Scott 578
Cordova, Arnaldo 483
Cordry, Donald 661, 703
Cordry, Dorothy 703
Cornelius, Wayne 364-5,
    423-5, 428, 441
Corona Renteria, Alfonso
    402, 404, 505, 520, 541
Corrigan, Eileen 198
Cortes, Hernan 169
Cosio Villegas, Daniel 426,
    491
Costeloe, Michael 342
Couch, Christopher 91
Covarrubias, Miguel 16,
    639
Cowan, George 328
Cowan, Richard 657
Cowhey, P. F. 551
Cox, Norman 427
Craig, Ann 267, 423, 428
Crawford, Ann 232
Crennan, Robert 126
Crete, L. 242
Crossley-Holland, Peter
    689
Crumrine, Ross 301
Culbert, Patrick 111, 662
Cunninghame Graham,
    R. B. 33

D

Daly, John 329
Davies, Nigel 127, 145

Day, Christopher 330
Dayley, John Philip 331
Deans-Smith, Susan 194
Dehnel, Caroline 708
Delgado, Antonio 620
Dellepiani, Oscar 731
Delormoe, Robert L. 736
Dennis, Philip 302
Dent, David W. 734, 749
Díaz Briquets, S. 394-5
Diaz del Castillo, Bernard 18
Dickey, Thomas 146
Diehl, Richard 124-5, 147
Diguet, Leon 668
Dirección General de Planificación Familar 726
Dockstader, Frederick J. 640
Doolittle, William 148
Domínguez, Jorge 514
Dorner, Gerd 663
Duncan, Ann J. 620
Duran, Diego 92, 344
Duran, Esperanza 515, 561
Durand, Jorge 396

E

Eaton, David J. 61
Eaton, Jack D. 112
Earle, Peter 7
Edmunson, Munro 303
Edwards, Ernest Preston 77
El Gundi, Fadiva 304
El Mallakh, Ragaci 562, 574
Eliot, J. H. 169
Emmanuel, Victor 82
Enciso, Jorge 664-5
English, Nora 332
Enríquez, Rosario 516
Erb, Richard 360
Esbach, Cheryl 492
Escalante, Roberto 579
Escobar Latapí, A. 356, 364
Esteva, Gustavo 575
Evans, Margaret 563
Ewald, Ursula 552

Ewell, Peter T. 580

F

Fagan, Brian 93
Fagan, Richard 463
Falcon, Romana 268
Falk, Pamela 540
Farriss, N. M. 195
Fatemi, Khoscow 493
Favela, Ramon 641
Fedger, Richard S. 78
Fernández, Justino 642
Fernández, Raúl 397
Fernández del Castillo, Germán 435
Fitzgerald, Valpy 517
Fodor Trade Travel Press 45
Folgarit, Leonard 666
Fontana, Theodore 29
Forster, Merlin H. 738
Fortin, Carlos 517
Foster, David William 739
Foster, George McClelland 305
Foweraker, Joe 428
Franco, Jean 383
French, William 564
Friedlander, Judith 367
Friedrich, Paul 306-7
Fuentes, Carlos 621-2, 634

G

Gallenkemp, Charles 113
Gallop, Rodney 19
Gamio, Manuel 398
Garcia Alba, Pascual 518
Garcia Mora, Carlos 308
Garcia y Cubas, Antonio 68
Garcia Oropeza, Guillermo 49
Gardea, Jesús 620
Gardner, Glenn 565
Gardner, C. Harvey 174
Garner, Paul 270
Garner, Richard 196
Garrido, Luis Javier 429
Garza Tarazona de Gonzalez, Silvia 69

Gendrop, Paul 671
Gentleman, Judith 412, 424-5, 432, 441, 457-8, 519
Gerhard, Peter 62
Geroffi, Gary 553
Gibson, Lay James 402, 404, 505, 520, 541
Gil, Carlos 430
Gilbert, Alan 368
Gillespie, Susan D. 94
Ginnekin, Wouter van 521
Gonzalez, Luis 158
Gonzalez de la Rocha, Mercedes 356, 364, 384
Gonzalez Peña, Carlos 623
Grant, Campbell 668
Grayson, George 494
Greenberg, James 309
Greene, Graham 20
Greene, Stanley C. 233
Greene, Walter 399
Greenleaf, Richard 197
Gregory, Peter 594
Griffin, William 234
Grindle, Merilee 375
Groen, Dean 706
Grove, David 128
Grunwald, Joseph 541
Gruzinski, S. 198
Guaderrama, Graciela 431
Guevara Sanchez, Arturo 129
Gunther, John 21
Guzman, Humberto 620
Guzman, Oscar 565

H

Hale, Charles 235
Hall, Linda 266, 271
Hamilton, Nora 433, 484
Hammond, Norman 114
Hamnett, Brian 199, 236
Hanrahan, Gene 272-3
Hansen, Roger D. 522
Harding, Timothy 433, 484
Hardy, Robert William
Hale 22
Harlow, Neal 237
Harmon, Mary 624

Harniss, K. C. Moor 748
Harrison, Margaret 357
Hart, John M. 274-5
Harvey, H. R. 149
Harvey, Marian 669
Harvey, Neil 434, 473
Hassig, Ross 95, 170, 176
Haviland, John Beard 337
Heath, John 581-2
Hebert-Stevens, F. 646
Heer, David 400
Hellman, Judith Adler 435
Helms, Cynthia Newman
670
Hernández Jiménez, Abel
304
Hernández Medina,
Alberto 376
Hernández Rodríguez,
Rogelio 523
Herrera Sobek, Maria 385
Herzog, Lawrence Arthur
63, 401, 405, 408, 598
Hewitt de Alcantara,
Cynthia 310-11
Heyden, Doris 92, 97, 344,
671
Hileman, Sam 621
Hill, Jane 333
Hill, Kenneth 333
Hoberman, Louisa Schell
200
Hollenbach, Barbara 327
Hopkins, Joseph 312
Hopkinson, Amanda 3
Horcasitas, Fernando 92,
344
Humboldt, Alexander von
70
Hu Dehart, Evelyn 238
Huerta, Jorge A. 740
Humphrey, Roger R. 79
Hunt, Eva 625
Hunter, C. Bruce 150
Hurtado, Javier 435
Huxley, Aldous 23

I

Illades, Carlos 276
INEGI 71, 727-8
Ingham, John 345

J

Jacobs, Ian 277
Jacobsen, Nils 183
Jelin, Elizabeth 295
Jenkins, Philip 633
Jennings, Bruce 583
Johnson, Kenneth F. 436
Johnson, Lyman 196
Jones, Grant D. 115
Jones, Oakah 201-2
Jones, Richard 402
Joseph, Gilbert 262, 278
Joyce, Rosemary A. 116
Justeson, John 334

K

Kassell, John 203
Karttunen, Frances 335
Kaufman, Terence 334
Katz, Friedrich 159, 187,
239, 289, 495
Keen, Benjamin 181, 346
Kemp, Lysander 172
Kemper, Robert 403
Kendall, Aubyn 741-2
Kennedy, Diana 709
King, Mona 46
Kirby, Rosina Greene 672
Klor de Alva, J. Jorge 171
Knight, Alan 279-81, 524,
560
Konrad, H. A. 204
Kraft, Joseph 525
Kurbjulin, Kornelia 336
Kurjack, Edward Barns 69

L

Ladd, Doris M. 203-4
Lafae, Jacques 346
LaFrance, David 269, 613
Lajous, Adrian 437
Lamb, Ruth S. 690
Lanzer, Elizabeth L. 72
Latorre, Dolores 313
Latorre, Felipe 313
Laughlin, Robert 337
Leahy, Margaret 386
Leal, Frances 719

Leal, Juan Felipe 484
Leiby, John 207
León Portilla, Miguel 101,
172-3, 347, 626
Leopold, A. Starker 80
Levy, Daniel 438
Lewis, Colin 524
Lewis, Oscar 314-15
Lida, Clara 603
Liebman, Seymour 191
Lindenfield, Jacqueline 338
Lister, Florence C. 96
Lister, Robert H. 96
Lindvall, Karen 748
Litwak King, Jaime 151
Livingston, Jane 673
Loaeza, Soledad 414, 429,
439-41, 465, 485, 595
Lockhart, James 164, 208,
335
Lombardo de Ruiz, Sonia
130
Lomnitz, Cinna 240
Lomnitz, Larissa 240
Loney, David 729
López, Carlos Roberto 570
Looney, Robert 526
Loret de Mola, Carlos 464
Lorona, Lionel V. 743
Lozoya Thalmann, Emilio
358
Luiselli Fernández, Casio
584
Luke, Paul 527
Lumholtz, Karl Sofus 24-5
Lustig, Nora 414, 528, 595
Lynch, John 241

M

Machado, Manuel 282
Mackintosh, Graham 26
Maclachlan, Colin 209, 283
Madsen, Claudia 696
Madsen, William 696
Mahan, Elizabeth 716-17
Mallan, Chicki 47
Mares, David 496, 585
Markus, Joyce 131
Marquez, Enrique 442
Marshall, Oliver 744
Martin, Cheryl 210

Martínez Assad, Carlos
465-7
Martínez Logorreta, O.
497
Mason, Charles T. 81
Mason, Patricia B. 81
Massey, Douglas 396
Matesanz, Jose 603
Matos Moctezuma,
Eduardo 97-8
Maxfield, Silvia 470, 474
McAndrew, John 674
McDowell, John 404
McGuire, Thomas 316
McNeish, Richard S. 675
Meighan, Clement W. 132
Merida, Carlos 643
Meyer, Jean 284, 348
Meyer, Lorenzo 498-9, 511
Meyer, Michael 160, 211
Michaels, Albert 486
Middlebrook, Kevin 595
Miller, Mary 152, 644, 676
Miller, Robert R. 161
Minelli, Laura Laurencich
136
Minelli, Nelson 554
Mixto, Mauricio J. 173
Monsivais, Carlos 627
Montemayor, Carlos 620
Moorhead, Max 212
Mora, Carl J. 691
Morales, Isidro 566
Morales, Rebecca 405
Moriaty, James Robert 27
Morley, Sylvanius
Griswald 117
Morris, Stephen D. 443
Mountjoy, Joseph B. 677
Moser, Mary Beck 78
Mullen, Robert J. 678
Muller, Karl 49
Mumme, Stephen 500, 600
Murphy, Arthur 377
Murphy, Michael 213
Muse, Vance 146
Musgrove, Peggy 501
Myers, Bernard S. 645
Myers, Charles Nash 604

N

Nader, Laura 317

Nagao, Debra 134
Napoli, Ignacio Maria 27
Narro Rodríguez, Luis 376
Naylor, Thomas 214
Needler, Martin 444
Newall, Roberto 520
Nichols, Lourdes 710
Nicholson, H. B. 171
Noriega, Antonio de 719
Norman, William 334
Novelo, Victoria 378
Nunn, Charles 406
Nutall, Zelia 135
Nutini, Hugo 318

O

Och, Joseph 28
O'Connell, James F. 657
OECD 530
Offner, Jerome 99
Oliver, Luis Nicolau d' 173
Olivera, R. 242
Oliveros, Arturo 122
Olson, Wayne 531
O'Malley, Irene 285
Orellana Villers, Ernesto
713
Ortiz, Elizabeth Lambert
710
Ortiz de Montellano,
Bernard 100
Ortiz de Montellano,
Wendy 51
Oster, Patrick 4
Ouwened, Arij 286

P

Pacheco, Jose Emilio 620
Palmer, Colin 215
Pansters, Will 286
Paredes, Americo 697
Parnell, Philip 319
Parsons, Jeffrey 153
Pastor, Robert 502
Patch, Robert 216
Paz, Octavio 5, 619, 628-9
Paz Salinas, Maria Emilia
503

Peden, Margaret Sayers
630
Pellicier, Olga 504-5
Pérez Lizaur, Marisol 240
Pérez Nuñez, Wilson 555
Perry, Richard 50
Perry, Rosalind 50
Petshek, Rodolfo 651
Pettit, Florence H. 698
Pettit, Robert M. 698
Pfefferkorn, Ignaz 29
Philip, George 294, 427,
445-6, 515-16, 532,
543, 581-2, 601
Picasso, Sydney 13
Pick, James B. 72
Pina Chan, Roman 136
Pollock, Harry Evelyn 679
Polzer, Charles 214
Poole, Stafford 217
Porter, Eliot 349
Potter, Joseph 372
Powell, Philip 218
Powell, Thomas 506
Pozos Ponce, Fernando
320
Prescott, William Hickling
174
Price, Kitty 339
Prock, Jerry 399
Puhle, Hans Jurgen 183
Purcell, Susan Kaufman
447-8

Q

Quinones Keber, Eloise
171
Quirk, Robert 350

R

Raat, W. Dirk 6
Ramírez, Miguel 556
Ramírez de la O., Rogelio
507
Ramírez Vazquez, Pedro
714
Ramos, Samuel 7

Randall, Laura 568
Rankine, Margaret 243
Ranney, Edward 680
Read, John Lloyd 631
Redclift, Michael 601
Reed, Alma M. 681
Reid, Alastair 614
Reynold, Clark Winston 533
Ricard, Robert 175
Rello, Fernando 369
Rice, Don S. 111
Richardson, William 244
Rico, Carlos 490
Riding, Alan 8
Robe, Stanley L. 699-700, 745
Robertson, Donald 682
Robertson, Merle Greene 118
Robinson, Cecil 245
Rocca, Paul 351
Rodríguez, Antonio 683
Rodríguez, Victoria 449
Roett, Riordan 492, 508-9
Rollwagen, Jack 291
Romanucci-Ross, Lola 321
Romero, Matias 247
Ronfeldt, David 450, 468
Ros, Jaime 534
Ross, Stanley 360
Roxborough, Ian 475, 596
Rubin, Jerry 451
Rubío, Luis 529
Ruiz, Ramon 162, 246, 605
Ruiz, Vicky 387
Ruiz de Alarcón, Hernando 176
Rulfo, Juan 634
Rutherford, John David 632, 746

S

Salinas de Gortari, Carlos 359
Salinas Domínguez, Carlos F. 452
Salinas Pedraza, Jesús 296
Salvucci, R. J. 219
Sabloff, Jeremy 119

Sanderson, Susan Walsh 370
Sanderson, Steven E. 586-7
Sandstrom, Alan 352
Sandstrom, Pamela 352
Santa Anna, Antonio Lopez de 232
Saragoza, Alex 476
Saxton, Dean 340
Saxton, Lucille 340
Sayer, Chloe 300, 704-5
Schendel, Gordon 606
Scherer Garcia, Julio 453
Schiffrin, Ayna 51
Schlachter, Gail 747
Schmidt, Henri C. 9
Schoonover, Thomas 247-8
Schroeder, Susan 177
Schryer, Franz 322
Schultz, John S. 220
Schultz, Jutta 52
Schurer, Enid 633
Schwaller, John Frederick 221
Secretaria de Panificación y Presupuesto 74, 730
Seed, Patricia 222
Segovia, Rafael 429, 454, 465
Seligson, Ester 620
Seligson, Mitchell 415
Serra Puche, Jaime 518
Seyds, Manuel 615
Shaiken, Harley 542
Shane, Orrin C. 110
Sharer, Robert J. 117
Sharpe, Kenneth E. 548
Sheridan, Thomas 323
Sherman, William 160
Sherry, Norman 9
Shipway, Verna Cook 684
Shipway, Warren 684
Sigmund, Paul 354-5, 358-9
Simcox, David 407
Simonelli, Jeanne 388
Simpson, Lesley Bird 175
Sims, Harold Dana 249
Sinclair, John 721
Sklair, Leslie 408, 543-5, 748
Smith, Benjamin F. 27
Smith, Peter 424, 428, 441

Smith, Robert Eliot 120
Smith, Robert Freeman 510
Snoeck, Michele 569
Somers, Joseph 634
Sordo, Ana Maria
Soto, Shirlene 389
Soustelle, Jacques 137, 646
Spieler, Mariena 712
Spores, Ronald 138
Stallones, Lorann 360
Stallones, Reuel 360
Stark, Barbara 602
Stavenhagen, Robert 324
Stephens, John L. 13
Stepick, Alex 377
Sterner, Thomas 571
Stevens, Donald 250
Stevens, Evelyn Paniagua 455
Stevenson, Robert 692
Stewart, George E. 53
Story, Dale 456-7, 477, 749
Story, Rebecca 139
Stout, Joseph Allen 251
Strand, Mark 628
Stuart, George E. 75
Suárez, Luis 487
Swanson, Winfield 53
Szekely, Gabriel 551, 572

T

Tagle, Silvia Gómez 458
Tamayo-Sanchez, Jesús 405
Tandeter, Enrique 196
Taube, Karl 152
Taylor, Joshua C. 642
Teichman, Judith 459
Terrazas, Benito 616
Thompson, Catherine 54
thompson, Charlotte 54
Thompson, Guy 223, 252
Thompson, J. Eric 341
Thorp, Rosemary 534
Thorup, Catherine 545
Time-Life 10
Tiano, Susan 387
Toledo, Alejandro 573
Toor, Frances 685, 701
Torres, Blanca 540

Toussaint, Manuel 647
Townsend, Richard F. 102
Trejo Delarbe, Raúl 478, 722
Trejo Reyes, Saúl 557
Tuck, Jim 287
Tullis, La Mond 750
Tuñón Pablos, Julia 693
Tuohy, William S. 463
Turner, Frederick C. 11
Tutino, John 288
Tylor, Edward Burnett 31

U

Ugalde, Antonio 469
Upton, John 158
Urquidi, Marjory 373
Urteaga, Agusto 378

V

Valencia, Elicecer 409
Valliant, G. C. 103
Valliant, Suzannah B. 103
Vanderwood, Paul 253
Varley, Ann 368, 371
Vaughan, Mary Kay 607
Vázquez, Josefina 511, 608
Vernon, Raymond 535
Vigil, Ralph 178
Villanueva, Margaret 390
Vleugels, Rene 64

Von Winning, Hasso 141
Voorhies, Barbara 602

W

Walker, David 254
Walker, John 32
Walt, Billie R. De 576
Walt, Kathleen De 379
Ward, Peter 65, 449
Warman, Arturo 289
Warren, J. Benedict 179
Wasserman, Mark 259, 268, 270
Wasserstrom, Robert 324
Waters, Frank 353
Wauer, Roland H. 82
Waugh, Evelyn 33
Wayne, Scott 55
Weaver, Muriel Porter 154
Weigand, Phil 301
Weintraub, Sydney 396, 512, 546-7
Weisman, Elizabeth
    Wilder 647, 686
Westheim, Paul 687
White, Russell 479
Whitecotton, Joseph 140
Whitehead, Laurence 534, 536
Wiard, Leon 83
Wicke, Charles 648
Wieneck, Henry 146
Wilk, David 60

Wilkens, Gene 588
Williamson, Rodney 565
Willey, Gordon H. 114
Wilson, Fiona 391
Wilson, Jason 635
Wilson, Patricia Ann 66
Wionczek, Miguel 565, 609
Wirth, John 561
Witmore, Thomas 180
Womack, John 290
Wood, Richard 610
Wright, Angus 361

Y

Yáñez, Augstín 634
Yates, P. Lamartine 589
Young, James Clay 325
Young, Gay 67
Yuñez-Naude, Antonio 565

Z

Zaid, Gabriel 537
Zamba, Michael 56
Zantwijk, Rodulph van 104
Zedillo Ponce de León, Ernesto 536
Ziccardi, Alicia 467
Zogbaum, Heidi 636
Zorita, Alonso de 181

Index of Titles

A

After the storm: landmarks
of the modern Mexican
novel 634
Agrarian change in
eighteenth century
Yucatán 216
Agrarian struggle and
political power in
Mexico 577
Agrarian populism and the
Mexican state: the
struggle for land in
Sonora 586
Agrarian reform and public
enterprise in Mexico:
the political economy
of Yucatán's henequen
industry 550
Agrarian revolt in a
Mexican village 306
Agrarian warlord:
Saturnino Cedillo and
the Mexican
Revolution in San Luis
Potosí 256
Alienation of Church
wealth in Mexico:
social and economic
aspects of the liberal
revolution 1856-1875
342
Alonso de Zorita: royal
judge and Christian
humanist 1512-1585
178
Amapa storytellers 699
Ambivalent conquests:
Maya and Spaniard in
Yucatán 1517-70 168
Anahuac: or Mexico and
Mexicans, ancient and
modern 31
An American in
Maximilian's Mexico,
1865-1866: the diaries

of William Marshall
Anderson 12
Anarchism and the
Mexican revolution:
the political trials of
Ricardo Flores Magon
in the United States
283
Anarchism and the
Mexican working class
274
Ancient kingdoms of
Mexico 145
Ancient Maya 117
Ancient Maya writing and
calligraphy 109
Ancient Mesoamerica: a
comparison of change
in three regions 143
Ancient Mexico: Aztec,
Mistec and Maya
landscapes 53
Ancient Mexico, an
overview 151
Ancient sculpture from
western Mexico: the
evolution of artistic
form 651
Annotated bibliography of
the novels of the
Mexican revolution of
1910-17, in English
and Spanish 746
Anthropological
perspectives on rural
Mexico 310
Antonio de Mendonza, first
viceroy of New Spain
163
Antropología en México:
panorama histórico.
Tomo 1, los hechos y
los dichos 308
Anuario estadístico de los
Estados Unidos
Mexicanos 1988-1989
727

Apache frontier: Jacobo
Ugarte and the
Spanish–Indian
relations in northern
New Spain 1769-1791
212
Apportioning groundwater
beneath the
US–Mexican border.
Obstacles and
alternatives 500
Archaeological ceramics of
Becan, Campeche,
Mexico 107
Archaeology of West
Mexico 121
Archaeology of the Morett
Site, Colima 133
Architecture of Mexico
yesterday and today
656
Army in Bourbon Mexico
1760-1820 184
Arqueología del valle de las
cuevas 129
Art and archaeology of pre-
Columbian middle
America: an annotated
bibliography of works
in English 742
Art and time in Mexico 686
Art of Mesoamerica: from
Olmec to Aztec 644
Art of pre-Columbian
Mexico: an annotated
bibliography of works
in English 741-2
Art of the Huichol Indians
637
Arts of ancient Mexico 646
Assembling for
development; the
maquila industry in
Mexico and the United
States 544
Atencingo: the politics of

agrarian struggle in a
Mexican ejido 468
Atlas arqueológico del
estado de Yucatán 69
Atlas geográfico, estadístico
e histórico de la
república mexicana 68
Atlas nacional del medio
físico 71
Atlas of Mexico 72
Authentic Mexican
cooking: regional
cooking from the heart
of Mexico 706
Aztec arrangement: the
social history of pre-
Spanish Mexico 104
Aztec kings; the
construction of
rulership in Mexican
history 94
Aztec medicine, health and
nutrition 100
Aztec ruins on the Animas:
excavated and
interpreted 96
Aztec sculpture 84
Aztecs 85, 93, 98, 102
Aztecs, Mayas and their
predecessors:
archaeology of
Mesoamerica 154
Aztecs of Mexico: origin,
rise and fall of the
Aztec nation 103
Aztecs; the history of the
Indies of New Spain 92
Aztecs: an interpretation 90
Aztecs of central Mexico:
an imperial society 86
Aztec thought and culture:
a study of the ancient
Nahuatl mind 101
Aztec warfare: imperial
expansion and political
control 95

B

Baja California: a survival
kit 55
Being Indian in Hueyapan:

a study of forced
identity in
contemporary Mexico
367
Benito Juárez, early
liberalism and the
regional politics of
Oaxaca 1828-1853 236
Bernal Díaz chronicle: the
true story of the
conquest of Mexico 18
Beyond the codices: the
Nahua view of colonial
Mexico 164
Beyond the Mexique Bay
23
Bibliography of Chicano
and Mexican dance,
drama and music 740
Bibliography of Latin
American
bibliographies 1980-
84: social sciences and
humanities 743
Birnbaum's Ixtapa and
Zihuantenejo 1992 36
Birnbaum's Cancún,
Cozumel and Isla
Mujeres, 1992 37
Blacks in colonial
Veracruz: race
ethnicity and regional
development 190
Blood ties: life and violence
in rural Mexico 309
Book of the gods and rites
and the ancient
calendar 344
Broadcasting in Mexico 719
Broadcasting in Mexico:
reassessing the
industry–state
relationship 717
Broken spears: the Aztec
account of the
conquest of Mexico
172
Builders in the sun 655
Bureaucracy and
bureaucrats in Mexico
City 1742-1835 185
Bureaucrats, planters and
workers: the making of
the tobacco monopoly

in Bourbon Mexico
194

C

Cacaxtla: el lugar donde
muere la lluvia en la
tierra 130
California conquered: war
and peace on the
Pacific 1846-1850 237
Cambridge encyclopaedia
of Latin America and
the Caribbean 735
Campesinado y migración
392
Campo Mexicano 589
Canal irrigation in
prehistoric Mexico; the
sequence of
technological change
148
Cancún handbook, plus
Mexico's Caribbean
coast 47
Cantares Mexicanos: songs
of the Aztecs 688
Casa llena, bola roja. La
lucha de los peloteros
de la ANABE 616
Caudillo and peasant in the
Mexican revolution
261
Caudillos in Spanish
America 241
Causas y efectos de la crisis
económica en México
518
Cemote of sacrifice: Maya
treasures from the
sacred well at Chichen
Iztá 110
Centaur of the North:
Francisco Villa, the
Mexican revolution
and northern Mexico
282
Central desert of Baja
California:
demography and
ecology 58
Ceramic history of the

central highlands of Chiapas 662
Ceramics 675
Cerro Palenque: power and identity on the Maya periphery 116
Chalcatzingo: excavations on the Olmec frontier 128
Challenge of interdependence: Mexico and the United States 488
Chamalpahin and the kingdoms of Chalco 177
Change and uncertainty in a peasant community: the Maya corn farmers of Zinacantan 299
Changing boundaries in the Americas: new perspectives on the U.S.–Mexican, Central American and South American borders 401, 405, 408, 598
Changing networks: Mexico's telecommunications options 551
Chatino syntax 339
Chronicles of Michoacán 17
Churches of Mexico 1530-1810 654
City state in central Mexico at the time of the Spanish Conquest 87
Ciudad de México 1325-1982 59
Ciudad de México; áreas metropolitana y alrededores 73
Clases medias y política en México: la querella escolar, 1959-1963 439
Class and society in central Chiapas 324
Codex Nuttall: a picture manuscript from ancient Mexico: the Peabody Museum facsimile 135
Colegio de México; años de expansión e institucionalización 1961-1990 608
Colegio de México: una hazaña cultural 1940-62 603
Colonial art in Mexico 647
Colonial bureaucrats and the Mexican economy: growth of a patrimonial state 1763-1821 207
Colonial Culhuacán: a social history of an Aztec town 193
Colossal heads of the Olmec culture 657
Como somos los mexicanos 376
Complete book of Mexican cooking 711
Composición del poder: Oaxaca 461
Concise history of Mexico from Hidalgo to Cárdenas 1805-1940 155
Confesiones de un gobernador 464
Conflict, violence and morality in a Mexican village 321
Conquest and colonization of Yucatán 1517-1550 166
Conquest of Michoacán: the Spanish domination of the Tarascan kingdom in western Mexico 1521-1530 179
Conquest of the Sierra: Spaniards and Indians in Colonial Oaxaca 167
La contienda presidencial, 1988. Los candidatos y sus partidos 437

Cora Indians of Baja California: the relación of Ignacio Maria Napoli, September 20, 1721 27
Corruption and politics in contemporary Mexico 443
Counter-revolution along the border 272
Course of Mexican history 160
Crafts of Mexico 669
Criminal justice in eighteenth century Mexico: a study of the Tribunal of the Acordada 209
Crisis and social change in Mexico's political economy 531
Crisis of Cardenismo 486
Cristero rebellion: the Mexican people between Church and state, 1926-1929 348
Crónica del sindicalismo en México 1976-88 478
Crown and clergy in colonial Mexico, 1759-1821: the crisis of ecclesiastical privilege 195
Cuisines of Mexico 709

D

Debating Oaxaca archaeology 131
Debt and oil-led development: the economy under López Portillo 527
Demand, supply and politics in the Mexican salt industry 1560-1980: a study in change 552
Dependent development and broadcasting: the Mexican formula 721
Derecho indígena y

173

derechos humanos en América Latina 292
Design motifs of ancient Mexico 664
Designs from pre-Columbian Mexico 665
Después del Milagro 481
Development strategies and the status of women: a comparative study of the United States, Mexico, the Soviet Union and Cuba 386
Development banking in Mexico: the case of the Nacional Financiera S.A. 556
Diego Rivera: a retrospective 670
Diego Rivera: the Cubist years 641
10 años de indicadores económicas y sociales de México 728
Dilemma of Mexico's development: the roles of the private and public sectors 535
Directions in the anthropological study of Latin America 291
Disease and death in early colonial Mexico: simulating Amerindian depopulation 180
Disidentes: sociedades protestantes y revolución en México 1872-1911 225
Disorder and progress; bandits, police and Mexican development 253
Distant neighbours 8
Distorted development: Mexico in the world economy 513
Dollars over dominion: the triumph of Liberalism in Mexican–United States relations 1861-1867 248
Dominican architecture in sixteenth century Oaxaca 678
Dynamics of Mexican nationalism 11

E

Early stone pectoral from southeastern Mexico 659
Echeverría en el sexenio de López Portillo 487
Economía política del petróleo en México 572
Economía presidencial 537
Economic crisis and the decentralisation of health services in Mexico 356
Economic crisis, domestic reorganisation and women's work in Guadalajara, Mexico 384
Economic policymaking in Mexico: factors underlying the 1982 crisis 526
Economies of Mexico and Peru during the late colonial period 1760-1810 183
Edificio del Hospital de Jesús: historia y documentación sobre su construcción 653
Education and cultural development in Mexico 604
Edward L. Doheny: petroleum, power and politics in the United States and Mexico 260
Effects of receiving country policies on migration flows 395
Efrén Hernández: a poet rediscovered 624
Ejidos and regions of refuge in Northwestern Mexico 301
Electoral patterns and perspectives in Mexico 410, 431, 442, 451-2
Emergence of the modern Mexican woman: her participation in Revolution and struggle for equality 1910-40 389
Emilio Carballido 630
Empresarios, banca y estado: el conflicto durante el gobierno de José López Portillo 523
Energy efficiency and conservation in Mexico 565
Energy use in Mexican industry 571
En su proprio espejo: entrevista con Emilio "El Indio" Fernández 693
Entrepreneurs and politics in twentieth century Mexico 471
Environmental problems of the borderland 597
Escalating disputes: social participation and change in the Oaxacan highlands 319
Escenas de pudor y livianidad 627
Essays on the price history of eighteenth century Latin America 196
Estadistas, caciques and caudillos 466
Estado y sindicalismo en México 593
Este país: tendencias y opiniones 715
Ethnicity and class conflict in rural Mexico 322
Europa 1988. South America, Central America and the Caribbean 737
European immigration and

ethnicity in Latin
America: a
bibliography 744
Evaluation of industrial
estates in Mexico 1970-
85 57
Excelsiór 615
Exploraciones arqueológicas
en Dainzú, Oaxaca
122
Exploración, reservas y
producción de petróleo
en México, 1970-85
570
Exports and local
development. Mexico's
new maquiladoras 66
Explusion of Mexico's
Spaniards 1821-1836
249
Expropriacion petrolera y
el contexto
internacional 503
Edzna, Campeche, Mexico:
settlement patterns and
monumental
architecture 652

F

Festival cycle of the Aztec
Codex Borbonicus 91
Field guide to the birds of
Mexico; including all
birds occurring from
the northern border of
Mexico to the southern
border of Nicaragua
77
Fields of the Tzotzil: the
ecological bases of
tradition in highland
Chiapas 599
Fiesta del alarido y las
Copas del Mundo 615
Filosofía nuhuatl 101
Firewood versus
alternatives – domestic
fuel in Mexico 563
First agraristas: an oral
history of a Mexican
reform movement 267

First America. The Spanish
monarchy, Creole
patriots and the
Liberal state 182
Flavours of Mexico 712
Fodor's Acapulco, Ixtapa
and Zihuantejo: the
best of resorts, beaches
and hotels 51
Fodor's Mexico 45
Foder's 1993. Cancún,
Cozumel, Yucatán
Peninsula, with trips to
the Mayan ruins 48
Folktales of Mexico 697
Food policy in Mexico: the
search for self-
sufficiency 575
Foreign direct investment
and industrial
development in Mexico
555
Foreign immigrants to early
Bourbon Mexico 1700-
60 406
Foreign impact on lowland
Mayan language and
script 324
Formación de la política
petrolera en México
1970-86 566
Foundations of
international
agricultural research:
science and politics in
Mexican agriculture
563
Fray Bernardino de
Sahagún 1499-1590
173
From Calpizqui to
corregidor:
appropriation of
women's cotton textile
production in early
colonial times 390
From insurrection to
revolution in Mexico:
social bases of
agrarian violence 1750-
1940 288
Frommer's 93. Mexico on
$50 a day 35

Futuro de la política
industrial en México
557

G

Generals in the Palacio: the
military in modern
Mexico 419
Generative syntax of
Penoles Mixtec 329
God-kings of Mexico 146
Gods and symbols of
ancient Mexico and the
Maya: an illustrated
dictionary of
Mesoamerican religion
152
Good farmers: traditional
agricultural resource
management in Mexico
and Central America
588
Governing Mexico: the
statecraft of crisis
management 411
Government and private
sector in contemporary
Mexico 470, 474
Grammar of Mam, a
Mayan language 332
Great Temple of the
Aztecs: treasures of
Tenochtitlán 97
Great Tzotzil dictionary
and Santo Domingo,
Zinacantan 337
Guatemalan refugees in
Mexico 1980-84 409
Guía de murales del centro
histórico de la ciudad
de Mexico 34
Guide to Mexican art, from
its beginnings to the
present 642
Guide to Mexican
witchcraft 696
Guide to the ancient
Mexican ruins 150
Guide to the historical
geography of New
Spain 62

H

Handbook of Mexican roadside flora 81
Handbook of political science research on Latin America; trends from the 1960s to the 1990s 734, 749
Handbook of research on the illicit drug traffic: socioeconomic and political consequences 750
Harding and Mexico: diplomacy by economic persuasion 1920-23 258
Harmony ideology: justice and control in a Zapotec mountain village 317
Heaven-born Merida and its destiny: the book of Chilam Balam of Chumayel 303
Hippocrene companion guide to Mexico 41
Historia de las Indias de Nueva Espana e Islas de la Tierra Firme 92
Historical dictionary of Mexico 732
History of Mexican literature 623
History of Mexican mural painting 683
History of the Conquest of Mexico 174
Hope and frustration: interviews with leaders of Mexico's political opposition 430

I

Idea of the devil and the problem of the Indian: the case of Mexico in the sixteenth century 165
Ideología de la revolución mexicana: la formación del nuevo regimen 483
Ideological and structural integration of the compadrazgo system in rural Tlaxcala 318
Images of Mexico in the United States 490
Impacto de la industrialización en las comunidades rurales; el caso de Atequiza, Jalisco 1920-80 320
Incidents of travel in Yucatán 13
Index of Mexican folktales, including narrative texts from Mexico, Central America, and the Hispanic United States 745
Index to Mexican literary periodicals 738
Indian art and history: the testimony of prehispanic rock paintings in Baja California 132
Indian art in Middle America 640
Indian art of Mexico and Central America 639
Indian Christ, the Indian King: historical substrata of Maya myth and ritual 298
Industria de refinación en México 1970-85 569
Industria en los magueyales: trabajo y sindicatos en ciudad Sahagún 378
Industrialization and secondary cities in Central Mexico 64
Industry, the state and public policy in Mexico 477
Inside the volcano 8
Inside Latin America 21
Insider's Guide to Mexico 38
Intellectual precursors of the Mexican Revolution 1900-13 265

Intellectuals and the state in twentieth century Mexico 472
Intensification of peasant agriculture in Yucatán 580
Intervillage conflict in Oaxaca 302
Into a desert place: a 3000 mile walk around the coast of Baja California 26
In the land of the Olmec 124-5
Introduction to the orchids of Mexico 83
Irrigation and the Cuicatec ecosystem: a study of agriculture and civilization in north central Oaxaca 312
Irrigation in the Bajío region of colonial Mexico 213
Isthmus Zapotecs: women's roles in cultural context 382

J

Jacaltec language 330
Jade steps; a ritual life of the Aztecs 88
Jesuit hacienda in colonial Mexico: Santa Lucia 1576-1767 204
Judas at the Jockey Club and other episodes of Porfirian Mexico 227
Judicial review in Mexico: a study of the amparo suit 460

K

Key to the Mesoamerican reckoning of time: the chronology recorded in native texts 144
Kinship, business and politics: the Martínez

del Rio family in Mexico 1824-1867 254

L

Labyrinth of solitude: life and thought in Mexico 5

Laguna Verde nuclear? No gracias! 558

Land, labor and capital in modern Yucatán: essays in regional history and political economy 262

Land and politics in the valley of Mexico: a two thousand year perspective 149

Landlord and tenant: housing the poor in urban Mexico 368

Land reform in Mexico 1910-80 370

Las Truchas: historia de una empresa 554

Late lowland Maya civilization; Classic to post-Classic 119

Latin America: economic imperialism and the state 524

Latin America 1979-83: a social science bibliography 736

Latin American debt and the adjustment crisis 534

Latin American oil companies and the politics of energy 561

Latin American perspectives 433

Latin American politics: a historical bibliography 747

Law and market society in Mexico 362

Law and politics in Aztec Texcoco 99

Lawless Roads 20

Letters from Mexico 169

Let's go: Mexico 42

Leverage of labor: managing the Cortés hacienda in Tehuantepec 1588-1688 189

Liberal patriotism and the Mexican reforma 230

Liberators: filibusters expeditions into Mexico, 1848-1862 and the last threat of manifest destiny 251

Life and death in the ancient city of Teotihuacán: a modern paleodemographic synthesis 139

Life and labor in ancient Mexico: the brief and summary relation of the lords of New Spain 181

Life in a Mexican village: Tepoztlán restudied 315

Life in Mexico during a residence of two years in that country 15

Life in Mexico under Santa Anna 1822-1855 242

Life of Graham Greene. Volume 1, 1904-39 30

Limits to friendship: United States and Mexico 502

Literacy and basic needs satisfaction in Mexico 610

Living in Mexico: a complete guide 56

Llamado de las urnas 485

Lords of the underworld: masterpieces of classic Maya ceramics 660

Lost cities of the Maya: new horizons 13

Lucha por la hegemonía en México 1968-90 482

M

Making of a strike:

Mexican silver workers' struggle in the Real del Monte 205

M. Alvarez Bravo 673

Man-gods in the Mexican highlands: Indian power and colonial society 1520-1800 198

Map of the ruins of Dzibilshaltan, Yucatán 75

Maquiladoras: annotated bibliography and research guide to Mexico's in-bond industry 1980-1988 748

Maquila industry and the creation of a transnational capitalist class in the United States–Mexico border region 408

Marriage of convenience: relations between Mexico and the United States 512

Marxism and communism in twentieth century Mexico 421

Mary, Michael and Lucifer: folk Catholicism in central Mexico 345

Mass media and society in twentieth century Mexico 716

Maya 108

Maya archaeology and ethnohistory 114

Maya cities: placemaking and urbanization 106

Maya hieroglyphs without tears 341

Maya missions: exploring the Spanish colonial churches of Yucatán 50

Maya resistance to Spanish rule and history of a colonial frontier 115

Maya Road; Mexico, Beliza, Guatemala 44

Maya: the completed
catalog of glyph
readings 336
Maya: the riddle and
rediscovery of a lost
civilization 113
Medical choice in a
Mexican village 325
Medicine in Mexico, from
Aztec herbs to
betratons 606
Men and horses of Mexico.
History and practice of
Charreria 611
Men in a developing
society: geographic
and social mobility in
Monterrey, Mexico
295
Mesoamerica after the
decline of Teotihuacán
A.D.700-900 147
Mexica buried offerings: a
historical and
contextual analysis 134
Mexican–American border
region. Issues and
trends 397
Mexican art and the
Academic of San
Carlos 1785-1915 638
Mexican cinema: reflections
of a society 1896-1988
691
Mexican colonial copper
industry 186
Mexican churches 349
Mexican cooking 708, 710
Mexican corrido: a feminist
analysis 385
Mexican costume 704
Mexican economy 515-16,
532, 543, 581-2, 601,
724
Mexican economy:
twentieth century
structure and growth
533
Mexican elite family 1820-
1980: kinship, class
and culture 240
Mexican empire of Iturbide
224

Mexican folk art 663
Mexican folktales from the
borderland 694
Mexican folk toys: festival
decorations and ritual
objects 698
Mexican historical novel
631
Mexican immigration to the
United States: a study
of human migration
and adjustment 398
Mexican Indian costumes
703
Mexican Inquisition of the
sixteenth century 197
Mexican interiors 684
Mexican Kikapoo Indians
313
Mexican landscape
architecture: from the
street and from within
672
Mexican Left, the popular
movements and the
politics of austerity 420
Mexican literature: a
bibliography of
secondary sources 739
Mexican lobby: Matias
Romero in Washington
1861-1867 247
Mexican manuscript
painting of the early
colonial period 682
Mexican masks 661
Mexican migration to the
United States: a critical
review 396
Mexican mining industry in
the nineteenth century
with special reference
to Guanajuato 243
Mexican mosaic 19
Mexican muralists 681
Mexican nobility at
independence 1780-
1826 206
Mexican national
petroleum industry: a
case study in
nationalization 559

Mexican oil and dependent
development 519
Mexican painting in our
time 645
Mexican patterns: a design
source book 705
Mexican petroleum
industry in the
twentieth century 560
Mexican political
biographies 417
Mexican political
biographies 1884-1935
263
Mexican political system in
transition 423
Mexican politics in
transition 425, 432,
457
Mexican politics: the
containment of conflict
444
Mexican popular arts:
being a fond glance at
the craftsmen and their
handiwork in
ceramics, textiles,
metals, glass, paint,
fibres and other
materials 685
Mexican popular image of
the United States
through the baseball
hero, Fernando
Valenzuela 613
Mexican profit-sharing
decision: politics in an
authoritarian regime
448
Mexican republic: the first
decade 1823-32 232
Mexican rescue 525
Mexican revolution 279
Mexican revolution and the
Catholic Church 350
Mexican revolution in
Puebla 1908-13: the
Maderista movement
and the failure of
liberal reform 269
Mexican revolution in
Yucatán 1915-1924 264

Mexican revolution 1910-14: the diplomacy of Anglo-American conflict 489

Mexican ruling party: stability and authority 456

Mexicans; a personal portrait of a people 4

Mexican society during the Revolution: a literary approach 632

Mexican tales and legends from Los Altos 700

Mexican theater of the twentieth century: bibliography and study 690

Mexican trade policy and the North American community 546

Mexico 10, 54, 156

Mexico 1991-1992 530

Mexico and the Spanish Civil War 506

Mexico and the United States in the oil controversy 1917-42 498

Mexico and the United States: managing the relationship 508

Mexico and the United States: studies in economic interaction 393, 501

Mexico. APA insight guides 49

México: auge, crisis y ajuste 414

Mexico: a country guide 2

Mexico: a history 161

Mexico and Central American Handbook 39

Mexico City: the supply of a primary health care service 357

Mexico City 52

Mexico City: the production and reproduction of an urban environment 65

Mexico: class formation, capital accumulation and the state 157

México demográfico: breviaro 1988 725

Mexico: dilemmas of transition 434

Mexico: encuesta nacional sobre fecundidad y salud, 1987 726

Mexico from bust to boom: a political evaluation of the 1976-79 stabilisation programme 536

Mexico from the oil boom to the debt crisis: an analysis of policy responses to external shocks 1978-85 534

Mexico in crisis 435

Mexico in the global economy: high technology and work organisation in export industries 542

Mexico in transition: implications for US policy 447

Mexico mystique: the coming sixth world of consciousness 353

Mexico since Independence 226, 239

Mexico south; the isthmus of Tehuantepec 16

Mexico: the challenge of poverty and illiteracy 605

Mexico: the remaking of an economy 528

Mexico through Russian eyes 1806-1940 244

Mexico's agricultural dilemma 589

Mexico's alternative political futures 424, 441

Mexico's dilemma: the political origins of economic crisis 529

Mexico's energy resources: towards a policy of diversification 574

Mexico's external relations in the 1990s 492, 509

Mexico's foreign policy as a middle power: the Nicaragua connection 496

Mexico's international relations 749

Mexico's leaders: their education and recruitment 418

Mexico's merchant elite 1590-1660 200

Mexico's political economy: challenges at home and abroad 514

Mexico's recent balance of payments experience and prospects for growth 538

Mexico's trade policy: the US, GATT and the future of economic relations 540

Mexico views manifest destiny 1821-1846: an essay on the origins of the Mexican war 229

Mezcala stone sculpture: the human figure 667

Migration and adaptation: Tzintzuntzan peasants in Mexico City 403

Miners and merchants in colonial Mexico 1763-1810 188

Mining and the state in twentieth century Mexico 564

Missionary in Sonora: the travel reports of Joseph Och S.J., 1755-1767 28

Mixtecs in ancient and colonial times 138

Modernizing Mexican agriculture; socio-economic implications of technological change 1940-70 311

Modern Mexican artists: critical notes 643

Modern Mexican military: a reassessment 450

Modern Mexico: state, economy and social conflict 433, 484

Monte Albán: settlement patterns at the ancient Zapotec capital 123

Monterrey elite and the Mexican state, 1880-1940 476

Morir en el Golfo 617

Movimiento ferrocarrilero en México 1958-59 590

Multinationals and market structure in Mexico 549

Murals of Bonampak 676

Music in Aztec and Inca territory 692

Musical artefacts of pre-Hispanic west Mexico: towards an interdisciplinary approach 689

My life as a matador. The autobiography of Carlos Arruza 612

Myth of market failure: employment and the labor market in Mexico 594

Myth of ritual: a native's ethnography of Zapotec life-crisis rituals 304

Myth of the Revolution; hero cults and the institutionalisation of the Mexican state 1920-1940 285

N

Nahuatl in the middle years: language control phenomena in texts of the colonial period 335

National Museum of Anthropology, Mexico 713

National Museum of Anthropology, Mexico: art, architecture, archaeology, anthropology 714

Native ethnography: a Mexican Indian describes his culture 296

Native Mesoamerican spirituality 347

Naturalists' Mexico 82

New agrarian movement in Mexico 1979-1990 473

New poetry of Mexico 628

New Trails in Mexico: an account of one year's exploration in northwestern Sonora, Mexico, and southwestern Arizona 1909-10 25

Nexos 718

90 years and 535 miles: vegetation changes along the Mexican border 79

No frills guide to hiking in Mexico 43

North American sketches of R. B. Cunninghame Graham 32

Nueva Vizcaya: heartland of the Spanish frontier 201

Nutritional strategies and agricultural change in a Mexican community 379

O

Oaxaca: a critical bibliography of rare and specialised materials in the university of New Mexico's general library 731

Octavio Paz 635

Octavio Paz: homage to the poet 619

Oil and Mexican foreign policy 494

Olmec: an early art style of pre-Columbian Mexico 648

Olmec: mother culture of Mesoamerica 136

Olmecs: the oldest civilization in Mexico 137

On poets and others 629

On the viability of a policy for science and technology in Mexico 609

Open-air churches of sixteenth-century Mexico: atrios, posas, open chapels and other studies 674

Opposition politics, power and public administration in urban Mexico 449

Organised labor and the Mexican revolution under Lázaro Cárdenas 592

Origins of Church wealth in Mexico: ecclesiastical revenues and church finances 1523-1600 221

Origins of instability of early republican Mexico 250

Origins of Maya civilization 105

Outcasts in their own land: Mexican industrial workers 1906-11 591

P

Paisanos: Spanish settlers on the northern frontier of New Spain 202

Pancho Villa and John Reed: two faces of romantic revolution 287

Papago and Pima to English, English to Papago and Pima dictionary 340

Pedro Martinez: a Mexican peasant and his family 314

Pedro Moya de Contreras: Catholic reform and royal power in the New Spain 1571–1591 217

PEMEX: la caída de Díaz Serrano 567

Penetrating the international market: theoretical considerations and a Mexican case study 585

Pensar el 68 480

People of Sonora and Yankee capitalists 246

People of the desert and sea: ethnobotany of the Seri Indians 78

Pescadores de Tecolutla: el tiempo cotidano y el espacio doméstico en una villa de pescadores 293

Petróleo y ecodesarrollo en el sureste de México 573

Petroleum and political development: the cases of Mexico and Norway 562

Pharmaceutical industry and dependency in the Third World 553

Plan nacional de desarrollo 1989-1994 730

Planning for the international border metropolis: transboundary options in the San Diego–Tijuana region 63

Plans and planmaking in the valley of Mexico: the evolution of a planning process 60

Plotting women: gender and representation in Mexico 383

Poder presidencial 462

Poesia in movimiento, México 1915-1966 628

Policy and political implications of foreign indebtedness in Mexico 507

Policymaking in Mexico: from boom to crisis 459

Política exterior de México: desafíos en los ochenta 504

Política y gestión municipal 467

Political and economic encyclopaedia of South America and the Caribbean 733

Political conflict and land tenure in the Mexican isthmus of Tehuantepec 374

Political culture of authoritarianism in Mexico, a re-examination 415

Political development and environmental policy in Mexico 600

Political economy of income distribution in Mexico 354-5, 358

Political economy of Mexican oil 568

Political essay on the kingdom of New Spain 70

Political patronage and politics at the village level in Central Mexico: continuity and change in patterns from the late colonial period to the end of the French intervention (1867) 231

Politics and ethnicity in the Rio Yaqui: Potam revisited 316

Politics and privilege in a Mexican city 463

Politics and the migrant poor in Mexico City 365

Politics in Mexico 294, 427, 445

Politics of Mexican development 522

Popular aspects of liberalism in Mexico 1848-1888 252

Popular movements and political change in Mexico 428

Population and development in Mexico since 1940: an interpretation 372

Population of Mexico: trends, issues and policies 373

Pottery of Mayapan, including studies of ceramic material from Uxmal, Kabah and Chichen Itzá 120

Poverty of revolution: the state and the urban poor in Mexico 366

Power and conflict in a Mexican community: a study of political integration 469

Power and the Glory 20, 30

Power and persuasion: fiestas and social control in rural Mexico 297

Pre-Columbian architecture of Meso America 671

Pre-Columbian literature of Mexico 626

Pre-Columbian Mexican miniatures: the Josef and Anni Albers collection 649

Pre-Columbian population history in the Maya lowlands 111

Prehistoric coastal adaptations: the economy and ecology

of maritime middle America 602

Prehistoric Mesoamerica 142

Prehistoric settlement patterns in the Texcoco region, Mexico 153

Prehistoric social, political and economic development in the area of the Tehuacán Valley: some results of the Palo Blanco project 126

Presencia española en la Revolución mexicana 1910-15 276

Presidency in Mexican politics 446

Presidentes 453

Presidio and militia on the northern frontier of New Spain: a documentary history, volume 1: 1570-1700 214

Princes of Naranja: an essay in anthropological method 307

Proceso 567, 720

Professions and the state: the Mexican case 422

Profile of man and culture in Mexico 7

Prophecy and myth in Mexican history 343

Protest and response in Mexico 455

Protestants and the Mexican Revolution: missionaries, ministers and social change 257

Provinces of the Revolution: essays on regional Mexican history 1910-1929 259, 268, 270

Puebla de los Angeles. Industry and society in a Mexican city 1700-1850 223

Pulso de los sexenios: 20 años de crisis en México 413

Puuc: an architectural survey of the hill country of Yucatán and northern Campeche, Mexico 679

Q

Quetzalcoatl and Guadelupe: the formation of Mexican national consciousness, 1531-1812 346

R

Race and class in colonial Oaxaca 167

Ranchero revolt: the Mexican Revolution in Guerrera 277

Rappaccini's daughter 619

Rebellion of Felix Díaz 273

Reform in Oaxaca, 1856-76: a microhistory of the liberal revolution 228

Región mas transparente 621

Region, state and capitalism in Mexico: nineteenth and twentieth centuries 286

Regional and sectoral development in Mexico as alternatives to migration 394

Relación de Michoacán 17

Relations between Mexico and Canada 497

Remote beyond compare: letters of don Diego de Vargas to his family from the New Spain and New Mexico 1675-1706 203

Re-thinking the circle of poison: the politics of pesticide poisoning among Mexican farm workers 361

Revolutionary Mexico: the coming and process of the Mexican Revolution 275

Revolution from without: Yucatán, Mexico and the United States 1880-1924 278

Revolution on the border: the United States and Mexico 271

Rhetoric, reality and self-sufficiency: recent initiatives in Mexican rural development 375

Rich land, a poor people: politics and society in modern Chiapas 363

Riders of the border: a selection of thirty drawings 702

Riot, rebellion and revolution: rural social conflict in Mexico 159, 187, 289

Ritual humor in highland Chiapas 695

Robbery under law; the Mexican object lesson 33

Rock art of Baja California 668

Roots of insurgency: Mexican regions 199

Roots of lo-mexicana: self and society in Mexican thought. 1900-1934 9

Route to self-sufficiency in Mexico. Interactions with the U.S. food system 584

Rural industry, social differentiation and the contradictions of provincial Mexican capitalism 578

Rural society in colonial Morelos 210

Ruta maya 40

S

San José de Gracia: Mexican village in transition 158

Savoring Mexico: a travel cookbook 707

Sculpture of ancient Mexico 687

Sculpture of Palenque: the cross group, the north group, the olvidado and other pieces 118

Secret war in Mexico: Europe, the United States and the Mexican Revolution 495

Sellos del antigua México 664

Shaft tomb figures of west Mexico 141

Shoulder to shoulder? The American Federation of Labor, the United States and the Mexican Revolution 255

Sintesis geográfica de Coahuila 74

Sistema político mexicano: las posibilidades de cambio 426

Six months' residence and travels in Mexico 14

Skeleton at the feast: the Day of the Dead in Mexico 300

Sky in Mayan literature 618

Slaves of the white God: blacks in Mexico 215

Social assistance and bureaucratic politics; the Montepios of colonial Mexico 1767–1821 192

Social ecology and economic development of Cuidad Juárez 67

Social inequality in Oaxaca: a history of resistance and change 377

Social responses to Mexico's economic crisis of the 1980s 356, 364

Socio-economic groups and income distribution in Mexico 521

So far from heaven: David Alfaro Siqueiros. The march of humanity and Mexican revolutionary politics 666

Soldiers, Indians and silver: North America's first frontier war 218

Some aspects of the lexical structure of a Mazatec historical text 328

Some hypotheses regarding the petroglyphs of West Mexico 677

Sonora: a description of the province 29

Sorghum and the Mexican food crisis 576

Spain's colonial outpost 220

Spanish–English glossary of Mexican flora and fauna 76

Spanish Jesuit churches in Mexico's Tarahumara 351

Speaking Mexicano: dynamics of syncretic language in Central Mexico 333

Spiritual conquest of Mexico: an essay on the apostolate and the evangelizing methods of the mendicant orders in New Spain 1523-1572 175

Sporting scene. Mundial notebook: Ariel vs Caliban 614

State and capital accumulation in Latin America 517

State, education and social class in Mexico 1880-1928 607

State and henequen production in Yucatán 1955-80 579

State and peasantry in Mexico: a case study of rural credit in La Laguna 369

State, class and the nationalization of the Mexican banks 479

State of the Rio Grande/ Rio Bravo: a study of water resource issues along the Texas/ Mexico border 61

Stonework of the Maya 680

Structure and historical development of the compadrazgo system in rural Tlaxcala 318

Studies in the archaeology of coastal Yucatán and Campeche, Mexico 112

Studies in the syntax of Mixtecan languages 327

Style in Mexican architecture 650

Stylistic and chronological study of Olmec monumental sculpture 658

Sucesión presidencial: the 1988 Mexican presidential election 416

Su majestad británica contra la revolución Mexicana 1900-1950: el fin de un imperio informal 499

Sweaters: gender, class and workshop based industry in Mexico 391

T

Televisa: el quinto poder 722

Texas and the Mexican Revolution: a study in state and national border policy 1910-20 266

Textiles and capitalism in Mexico: an economic history of the obrajes, 1539–1840 219

The Eagle: the autobiography of Santa Anna 232

The Enlightened: the writings of Luis de Carvajal, el Mozo 191

The Immigration Reform and Control Act of 1986: its implications and prospects 399

The Puuc: an architectural survey of the hill country of Yucatán and northern Campeche, Mexico 679

The old gringo 622

Tlaxcalan actas: a compendium of the records of the cabildo of Tlaxcala 1545-1627 208

Tloltecs: until the fall of Tula 127

To change place: Aztec ceremonial landscapes 89

Todos santos in rural Tlaxcala: a syncretic, expressive and symbolic analysis of the cult of the dead 318

To love, honour and obey in colonial Mexico: conflicts over marriage choice 1574-1821 222

Trade and employment in Mexico 539

Trade tribute and transportation. The sixteenth-century political economy of the valley of Mexico 170

Traditional papermaking and paper cult figures of Mexico 352

Transformation of liberalism in late nineteenth century Mexico 235

Transformation of Mexican agriculture: international structure and the politics of rural change 587

Transformation of the Hummingbird: cultural roots of a Zinacantecan mythical poem 625

Transnational corporations versus the state: the political economy of the Mexican auto industry 548

Transportation of liberalism into late nineteenth century Mexico 235

Travels in the interior of Mexico in 1825, 1826, 1827 and 1828 22

B. Traven: a vision of Mexico 636

B. Traven: life and work 633

Treasures of the Sierra Madre 636

Treasury of Mexican folkways 701

Treatise on the heathen superstitions that today live among the Indians native to this New Spain, 1629 176

Triumph and tragedy: a history of the Mexican people 162

Twentieth century Mexico 6

Two boys, a girl and enough! Reproductive and economic decision making on the Mexican periphery 388

Tzintzuntzan: Mexican peasants in a changing world 305

Tzotzil clause structure 326

Tzutujil grammar 331

U

Undocumented Mexicans in the United States 400

Union locals in Mexico: the 'new unionism' in steel and automobiles 475

Unions and politics in Mexico: the case of the automobile industry 596

Unions, workers and the state in Mexico 595

United States and Mexico 511

United States and Mexico: face to face with the new technology 545

United States and revolutionary nationalism in Mexico 1916-32 510

United States–Mexican border statistics since 1900 729

United States relations with Mexico: context and content 360

United States versus Porfirio Díaz 491

University and government in Mexico: autonomy in an authoritarian system 438

Unknown Mexico: explorations in the Sierra Madre and other regions 1890-1898 24

Urbanization and agrarian law: the case of Mexico City 371

U.S. and Mexico: borderland development and the national economies 402, 404, 505, 520, 541

U.S. immigration in the 1980s: reappraisal and reform 407

U.S.–Mexican economic relations: prospects and problems 399, 493

US–Mexican industrial integration: the road to free trade 547

US–Mexican relations 1910-40: an interpretation 280

Utmost good faith: patterns of Apache–Mexican hostilities in north Chihuahua border warfare 1821-1848 234

V

Valores de los Mexicanos. México: entre la tradición y la modernidad 1

Vida política en la crisis 465

Vida política mexicana en la crisis 429, 440

View from Chapultepec:

Mexican writers on the Mexican–American war 1845-48 245

Voices, visions and a new reality: Mexican fiction since 1970 620

Vuelta 537, 723

W

Water in the Hispanic southwest: a social and legal history 1550-1850 211

Welcome to Mexico 46

Where the air is clear 621

Where the dove calls: the political ecology of a peasant corporate community in northwestern Mexico 323

Wildlife of Mexico; the game birds and mammals 80

Women and survival in Mexican cities: perspectives on gender, labour markets and low-income households 381

Women of Mexico City 1790-1857 380

Women on the US–Mexican border: responses to change 387

Work of Bernardino de Sahagún, pioneer ethnographer of sixteenth-century Aztec Mexico 171

World in view: Mexico 3

Y

Yaqui resistance and survival: the struggle for land and autonomy 1821-1910 238

Yaqui syntax 338

Z

Zapata and the Mexican Revolution 290

Zapotec princes, priests and peasants 140

Index of Subjects

A

Aarne-Thompson system 745
Acapulco 51
AFL *see* American Federation of Labor
Agrarian development 294, 550
Agrarian insurgency 261, 267, 288, 306, 468
Agriculture 14, 125, 154, 216, 299, 311-12, 359, 379, 524, 575-89, 601
see also Revolutionary period
Aguascalientes 57
Air quality 598
Alvarez Bravo, M. 673
American Federation of Labor 255
Amparo suit 460
ANABE [baseball union] 616
Anarchism 274, 283
Anasazi Indians 96
Anderson, William Marshall 12
Anglo-American conflict 489
Animas Perdidas, Río de la 96
Anthropology and ethnography 171, 291-325
Anticlericalism 342
Apache frontier 212, 234
Archaeological sites
  atlas 69
  see also Aztec; Indian heritage; Maya; *and sites by name*
Archaeology and prehistory 84-154, 639
Architecture 642, 646-7
  Aztec 85
  see also Arts, visual

Archivo General de la Nación 197
Army 184, 214, 419
Arthaud, Claude 646
Arts 10, 52
  Aztec 84, 98, 644, 665
  bibliographies 741-2
  music, theatre, film 688-93, 740
  Olmec 136
  painting 637-48
  visual arts 649-87
Atencingo 468
Attitudes 1, 376
Authoritarianism 415, 425, 448, 455, 484, 522, 590
Automobile industry 514, 548, 596
Avila Camacho, Manuel 21
Aztec civilization 53, 84-104, 145-6, 154, 172, 193, 333
  art 644, 665
  medicine 606
  music 692
  religion 344
  songs 688
Aztec expansionism 95
Aztec landscapes 53
Aztec sculptured gods 84

B

Bajío 188, 213
Baja California 22, 26-7, 55, 58, 132, 469, 668
Baker Plan (1986) 515
Balance of payments 530, 538
Banking 254, 525, 556
  nationalization 523
  privatization 474, 479
Barragan, Luis 655
Baseball 613, 616
Becan, Campeche 107
Belief systems

Aztec 90
  pre-Columbian 176
Belize 42
Benito Juárez dam 374
Bibliographies and reference works 731-50
Biotechnology 545
Birds 77, 80
Birth rate 372
  statistics 726
Black people 190, 215
Bonampak 676
Border policy 266, 397, 401, 405, 408
  public health 360
Bourbon Mexico 184, 194, 406
British relations with Mexico 489, 495, 499
Broadcasting *see* Mass media
Bullfighting 612
Bureaucracy 185, 194, 207, 607
Business élite 431, 471, 474, 476-7, 482, 523
Business–government relations *see* Government–business relations

C

Cacaxtla, Tlaxcala 130
Caciquismo see Leadership
Calendar
  Aztec 344
  Mayan 353
California 222, 237
Calles, Plutarco Elias 281
Calles–Morrow agreement (1927) 280
Campeche 107, 112, 652
Canada 497, 546
Cancún 37, 47-8

Candelar, Felix 655
Capital accumulation 157
  see also Economy
Car industry 475, 514, 545,
  547-8, 555, 596
Carballido, Emilio 630
Cárdenas, Lázaro 155, 281,
  486, 503, 592
Cardenismo 281, 486
Carillo, Juan Rodríguez
  220
Carvajal, Luis de 191
Caste War 298
Catholicism 33, 343, 345,
  389
  see also Roman Catholic
  Church
Caudillo see Leadership
Caves 129
Cedillo, Saturnino 256
Ceramics 130, 153, 662,
  675, 677, 684-5
  Mayan 107, 120, 660
  Olmec 124
Ceremonial centres
  Aztec 89
  Olmec 137
Chalcatzingo 128
Chalco 177
Chapultepec 245
Charismatic leaders 198
Chatino language
  Yaitepec dialect 339
Chiapas 20, 129, 324, 326,
  330, 363, 599, 602,
  662, 695
Chichen Iztá 110, 120
Chichimeca Indians 218
Chihuahua 201, 234, 351
Chilam Balam 303
Child rearing 388
Chimalpahin 177
Church, the 20, 33, 195,
  197, 221, 342, 348, 350
Churches 50, 349, 351,
  653, 674, 678
Cinema 691, 693
Ciudad Juárez 67
Ciudad Sahagún, Hidalgo
  378
Class formation 157
Class structure 295, 322
Clergy 195, 221

Clientelism 231
Climate 71
Clouthier, Manuel 441
CNPA [peasant league]
  473
Coahuila 12, 74, 201, 212,
  313
Codex Borbonicus 91
Codex Nuttall 135
Cold War 492
Colegio de México 603,
  608
Colima 133, 651
Colonial churches 50, 650,
  654, 674, 678, 686
Colonial period (1570-
  1820) 182-223
Colonization 12
Colorado River 79
Computers 547
Confederación Regional
  Obrera Mexicana 255
Confederation 12
Conquest 17-18, 115, 174,
  179
Conquistadores 18
Constitution see Legal
  system
Contreras, Pedro Moya de
  217
Conurbations 63, 65, 67
Conversion of Indians 175
Cooking 706-12
Coparmex 470
Copper industry 186
Cora Indians 27
Corn farming 299
Corrido see Folk songs
Corruption 443
Cortés, Hernán 18, 169,
  172, 174-5, 220
Costume and design 702-6
Cozumel 37, 48
Criminal justice 209
Cristero revolt 348
CROM see Confederación
  Regional Obrera
  Mexicana
Cuba 386, 439
Cuernavaca 64
Cuicatec people 312
Culhuacán 193
Cults

Aztec 88
Cultural history 9-10, 18,
  54, 160
  Aztec 86, 103
Cultural values 1, 5-7, 9
Culture see Arts; Cultural
  history; Literature;
  Music
Cunninghame Graham,
  Robert 32
Customs see Life and
  customs

D

Dainzu, Oaxaca 122
Day of the Dead 300, 318
Debt 8, 488, 493, 507-8,
  511-12, 529, 532, 534,
  562
Delgado, Antonio 620
Demography 72
  statistics 725
  see also Population
Depopulation 180
Díaz, Felix 273
Díaz, Porfirio 239, 257,
  491, 499
Díaz del Castillo, Bernal
  18
Diplomatic relations
  with USA 447
  see also Foreign relations
Disease 61, 180
  control 360
Dissidence 225
Doheny, Edward 260
Domestic fuel 563
Dominicans 92
Drama 623, 626, 630, 740
Drugs 488, 493, 508, 750
Dumbarton Oaks
  Robert Wood Bliss
  collection 659
Dynastic history 108
  see also Genealogy
Dzibilshaltan 75

E

Ecclesiastical privilege 195

Echeverría Alvarez, Luis 487, 566, 586
Ecology 599, 601
  pre-Columbian 148
  problems 60
  see also Environmental problems
Economic crisis, responses to 4, 8, 525, 531, 534
Economic history 262, 533
  see also Economy
Economic policy 513, 515-18, 526-32, 535-6, 724
Economy 2, 4, 8, 72, 143, 183, 207, 233, 362, 433-4, 447, 513-38, 735
  Aztec 86, 98, 181
  statistics 724, 727-8
  see also Agriculture; Industry; Migration; Revolutionary period; Trade
Education 7, 9, 233, 354-5, 438-9, 603-10
  statistics 727-8
Ejidos 294, 301, 369, 371, 468
Elections 410, 412, 416, 425, 432, 435, 437, 454, 458
Electoral fraud 458
Electoral reform 440, 458
Electronics industry 555
Elites 200, 263, 268, 270, 275, 363, 408, 423, 446, 461, 482
  see also Interest groups and pressure groups
Employment 64, 521, 539, 557
Energy 493, 512, 558-74
  statistics 727
  see also Mining; Oil
Enseñada, Baja California 469
Environmental problems 513, 547, 573, 597-8, 600
  see also Ecology
Equestrian sports 611
Ethnic diversity 19
Ethnicity 322

Ethnography *see* Anthropology and ethnography
Evangelism 175
  see also Missionaries
Exports 66, 541-2, 562, 585
Expropriation *see* Oil

F

Fall, Albert 258
Fauna *see* Flora and fauna
Fernández, Emilio 693
Festivals 91, 698
  ritualized humour 695
Fiction 620, 623, 631
  bibliography 746
Fiestas 297
Film *see* Music, theatre and film
Firewood 563
Flora and fauna 55, 76-83, 124, 296
  see also Wildlife
Flores Magon, Ricardo 283
Folk songs 385, 701
Folk tales 694, 697, 699-701
  index 745
Food imports 513, 547
Food strategies 575, 581, 584
Food subsidies 354
Foreign investment 354, 488, 491, 519, 555
Foreign policy 414, 434, 444, 488, 494
Foreign relations
  with Britain 499
  with Canada 497
  with Central America 492, 504
  with Europe 495
  with Nicaragua 496
  with USA 488, 493, 495, 498, 501-2, 510-12, 598
  bibliography 749
Franciscans 50
Frontier, northern 212, 218, 234
Fruits and vegetables 580
Fuentes, Carlos 621-2, 634

G

Gardea, Jesús 620
GATT *see* General Agreement on Tariffs and Trade
Genealogy 94, 135
General Agreement on Tariffs and Trade 540
Geography 41, 57-67, 296
  historical 62, 68, 70
Geology 71
Goeritz, Mathias 655
Gomez family 240
Government and politics 2, 410-512
Government–business relations 411, 440, 457, 477, 523
Green Party 601
Guadalajara 368, 384
Guanajuato 188, 243
Guatemala 42, 115, 330, 363, 401
  refugees in Mexico 409
Guerrero 277, 667
Guzman, Humberto 620

H

Hacienda system 189, 204, 216
Harmony ideology 317
Hazardous wastes 598
Health
  Aztec 100
Health care and welfare 56, 354-61, 519
  statistics 727
Hebert-Stevens, F. 646
Henequen industry 550, 579
Hernández, Efrén 624
Hidalgo 155, 296, 322
Hieroglyphics 652
  Mayan 108, 336, 341
Higher education 603
Historical geography 62, 68, 70
History 6, 8, 41, 52, 54, 155-62, 735, 747

History *continued*
  Aztec 85-6, 93
  Colonial period 182-223
  Independence to
    Revolution 224-54
  Olmec 136
  Revolutionary period
    255-90
  Spanish Conquest 163-81
Hospital de Jesús 653
Housing 354, 368
  statistics 727-8
Huasteca, Hidalgo 322,
  352
Huerta, Victoriano 272-3,
  499
Hueyapan 367
Huichol Indians 637
Human rights 2, 292
Human sacrifice
  Aztec 88, 90
Humour 695
Hunting and gathering 125
Hydrocarbons 565, 574

I

Iconography 130
  Mayan 108, 118
Idols
  Aztec 88
Illiteracy 605
Immigration 409, 744
Immigration Reform and
  Control Act (1986)
  399-400
  see also Migration
Income distribution 354-5,
  358-9, 377, 402, 513,
  519, 521, 557
Income Distribution and
  Employment Project
  521
Independence to
  Revolution (1820-
  1910) 224-54
Indian heritage 10, 19, 24
  see also Indian peoples
  by name
Industrial estates 57
Industrialization 64, 320,
  378, 531, 548-57, 571
Industry *see* Car; Oil; Steel

*and other industries by
  name*
Inflation 196
Inquisition 191, 197, 217
Instability 250
Institutional Revolutionary
  Party 412, 427, 429,
  440, 456
Intellectuals 265, 472
Interest groups and
  pressure groups 411,
  444, 470-9
International Labour
  Office
  World Employment
    Programme 521
International Maize and
  Wheat Improvement
  Centre 583
Irrigation 148, 213, 312,
  323
Isla Mujeres 37
Iturbide, Agustín de 224
Itzcoatzin 104
Ixtapa 36, 51
Izapa people 105

J

Jacaltec language 330
Jalapa, Veracruz 463
Jalisco 267, 320, 651, 700
Jesuits 17, 27-9, 238, 351
Juárez, Benito 12, 236,
  247-8
Juchitán 451
Justice system 209, 253

K

Kabah 120
Kickapoo, the 313
Kinship 240, 254, 321
Krause, Enrique 723

L

Labour 189, 205, 274, 423,
  448, 455, 475, 560,
  564, 587, 590-6

costs 541
  organization 255, 478
  see also Trade unions
Lagos de Moreña, Jalisco
  267
Laguna Verde nuclear
  power station 558
Land tenure 323, 370-1,
  374
  see also Agrarian
    insurgency; *Ejidos*
Land use 71
Language and linguistics
  18, 24, 326–41
Las Truchas steel plant 554
Law and order 727
Leadership 241, 261, 307,
  466
Left-wing politics 420-1,
  428, 430, 451
Legal system 56, 209, 253,
  362, 470-9
  Aztec 99
  Zapotec 317, 319
León 381
Liberalism 230, 235, 248,
  252, 342
Life and customs 16, 24,
  293
  Aztec 85-7, 93
Lifestyles *see* Life and
  customs
Linguistics *see* Language
  and linguistics
Literacy 610
  see also Illiteracy
Literary criticism 619, 623,
  632
Literature 617-36
  bibliographies 738-9
  pre-Columbian 626
Living conditions 15-16
Local politics and
  government 208, 231,
  319, 431
  see also Legal system
López Portillo, José 459,
  487, 523, 527, 584

M

Machismo 321

Maderista movement 269
Madero, Francisco 272-3
Madrid, Miguel de la 414, 427, 595
Mam language 332
Manufacturing 57, 64, 223, 549
Manuscript painting 682
Maps and atlases 68-75
Maquiladora sector 66, 408, 493, 543-4
  bibliography 748
Marriage 222, 380, 382
Martínez del Rio family 250
Masks 661
Mass media 441, 472, 715-23
Maximilian 12, 226, 248
Maya civilization 40, 53, 75, 105-20, 143, 146, 154, 168, 298, 301, 303, 341, 652, 660, 676
  see also Language and linguistics
Mayan literature 618, 626
Mayan ruins 44, 48, 679-80
Mayan writing 109
  see also Hieroglyphics
Mayapan 120
Mazatec language 328
Mechuacan *see* Michoacán
Medicine 180, 325, 355-8, 360, 606
  pre-Hispanic 100, 606
Mendicant orders 175
Mendonza, Antonio de 163
Merchant élites 200
Mexic-Zoque people 105
Mexica people 134
Mexicano language 333
Mexico City 10, 52, 60, 64-5, 365, 371, 403, 461, 608, 621
  evolution 59
  murals 34
  plan 73
  World Cup venue (1986) 614-15
Michoacán 17, 186, 463
  conquest 179

Migration 271, 364-5, 373, 392-409, 447, 488, 493, 508, 512, 594
  bibliography 744
  statistics 727-8
Military careers and politics 419, 450
Military recruitment 184
Militia 214
Mining 186, 188, 205, 243, 246, 564
Missionaries *see* Catholicism; Dominicans; Franciscans; Jesuits
Mistec civilization *see* Mixtec
Mixtec civilization 135, 138, 146
Mixtec languages 327, 329
Modernization 1, 388, 454, 576
Monarchy 182, 195
Monte Albán 123
Montemayor, Carlos 620
Montepios 192
Monterrey, Nuevo León 295, 539
Monterrey group 476
Morelia, Michoacán 57
Morelos 277, 315, 321, 345
Morett Site, Colima 133
Moya de Contreras, Pedro 217
Multinationals *see* Transnational corporations
Murals 34, 676, 683
  see also Rivera, Diego; Siquieros, David
Museum of Anthropology 713-14
Music, theatre and film 49, 688-93, 740
Myths 24, 343, 347

N

Nacional Financiera S.A. (Nafinsa) 556
NAFTA *see* North American Free Trade Area

Nahuatl language 101, 164, 171-2, 335
Naranja 306-7
Narcotics *see* Drugs
National Action Party 430, 436, 440-1, 449, 451, 457, 474
National Autonomous University 438
National identity 7, 9
National Museum of Anthropology 713-14
National Plan for Science and Technology (1976) 609
Nationalism 11
Nationalization 559, 561
Navista movement 442
Nayarit 651, 699
New Mexico 203
Nicaragua 496
Nobility 206
North American Free Trade Area 502, 540, 546
Norway 562
Novel, the 620, 623, 631, 634
Nuclear power 558, 574
Nueva Vizcaya 201
Nutrition 379
  Aztec 100

O

Oaxaca 131, 135, 138, 143, 167, 228, 236, 270, 286, 302, 312, 319, 339, 461, 578, 675
  bibliography 731
Obrajes 219
O'Gorman, Juan 655
Oil 514-15, 519, 527, 559-62, 570, 574
  and politics 260, 494, 498, 503-4
  see also Pemex
Oil boom 8, 375, 477, 505, 534, 566, 572, 617
Olmec civilization 105, 124-5, 136-7, 145-6
  art 644, 648

Olmec civilization *continued*
sculpture 657-8
Orchids 83
Orozco, José 681

P

Pacheco, José Emilio 620
Paez 241
Painting *see* Arts
Palenque 116
sculpture 118
PAN *see* National Action
Party
Pani, Mario 655
Papago–Pima language 340
Paper images 352
Paquime culture 129
Party of the Democratic
Revolution 430
Party rule 9-10
Patronage 231, 240, 321
Paz, Octavio 619, 628-9,
635, 661, 723
Peabody Museum 135
Peasants 261, 267, 289,
299, 314, 323, 369,
428, 473, 577, 580, 587
see also Migration
Pemex 559, 561, 567-8,
572-3
Pensions 192
Peru 183
Pesticide poisoning 361
Petrochemicals industry
547
Petroglyphs 677
Petroleum industry *see* Oil
Pharmaceuticals industry
545, 547, 553, 555
Photography 673
Planning, urban 60, 730
Poetry 619, 623, 625-6,
628-9
Political biographies 263,
417
Political culture 415, 715
Political élite 417-18, 459,
482
Political leadership 198
Political parties *see by*
name
Politics 2, 7-8, 10, 41, 72,

143, 179, 254, 410-59,
735
Aztec 85-6, 99, 181
bibliographies 735, 747
historical interpretations
480-7
see also Revolutionary
politics
Ponietowska, Elena 52
Popular images of Mexico
490
Population 139, 372-3
Aztec 100
growth 61, 64, 131, 183
see also Demography;
Depopulation
Porfiriato 227, 239, 275,
288, 308
Positivism 235, 308
Pottery 112, 120, 130, 133,
663
Poverty 365-9, 605
Power *see* Elites;
Leadership; Politics;
Presidency
PRD *see* Party of the
Democratic
Revolution
Prehistory *see* Archaeology
and prehistory
Presidency 435, 446, 453,
462, 537
Presidio 214
Press *see* Mass media
Pressure groups *see*
Interest groups and
pressure groups
PRI *see* Institutional
Revolutionary Party
Prices 196, 553, 557
Private sector 470, 474, 535
Professional status and
politics 422
Property ownership 157
Protestants 225, 257
Public investment *see*
Agriculture; *and*
industries by name
Public opinion 412-13
Puebla 223, 269, 333, 368
Puerta Vallarta 381
Puerto, Carillo 264, 278
Puuc, Yucatán 580, 679

Q

Queretaro 64, 381
Quetzalcoatl 346

R

Racism 190
Rancheros 277
Real Del Monte 205
Rebellion 199, 204
relation to economic
cycle 187
Recreations 227
Recruitment of political
leaders 418
Redfield, Robert 315
Reed, John 287
Reference works *see*
Bibliographies and
reference works
Reform 228, 230
see also Agrarian
insurgency
Regional government 461,
463-7, 469
Regionalism 259
see also Revolutionary
period; *and regions by*
name
Religion 1, 9, 20, 41, 152,
175-6, 226, 300, 342-53
Aztec 85-6, 88-91, 93,
101-3
Mexica 134
Olmec 136
Spanish theology 165
Revolution (1910) 11, 489,
632, 636
see also Revolutionary
period
Revolutionary Constitution
(1917) 483
Revolutionary period
(1910-40) 9, 255-90
Rio Grande 61, 79
Rivera, Diego 641, 670,
681
Rock paintings 132, 137,
668
Roman Catholic Church
175, 182, 342, 346, 350

see also Catholicism
Romero, Matias 247
Rosas, Juan Manuel de 241
Royal Academy of San
    Carlos 638
Ruíz de Alarcón,
    Hernando 176
Rulfo, Juan 634
Rural development bank
    369
Rural history 159
    see also Agriculture;
    Agrarian insurgency;
    Peasants
Rural social conditions
    159, 210, 261, 267,
    288, 309-10, 314-15,
    321, 369-70, 374-5, 473
Russian view of Mexico
    244

S

Sahagún, Bernardino de
    171, 173
Salinas de Gortari, Carlos
    437, 518
Salt industry 552
San Diego–Tijuana
    conurbation 63
San José de Gracia 158
San Lorenzo, Tenochtitlán
    124
San Luis Potosí 64, 256,
    268, 286, 442
San Miguel Allende 188
Sandinista regime 496
Santa Anna, Antonio
    López de 232, 241-2
School books controversy
    439
Science and technology
    583, 609
Scott, General 232
Sculpture see Arts, visual
Self-sufficiency see Food
    strategies
Seligson, Ester 620
Seri Indians 78
Settlement patterns 130,
    153
    Aztec 86

Shaft tomb figures 24, 141
Shaman 352
Sierra Madre 24
Silver 186, 205, 218
Sinaloa 585
Siqueiros, David Alfaro
    666, 681
Slave trade 190
Slavery 215
Soccer 614-15
Social administration 192
Social change 253, 372-9
    see also Revolutionary
    period
Social identity 182
Social sciences 603
    bibliographies 736, 743
Social security 358
Social services 354-61
Social stresses 196
Society 2, 14, 41, 72, 143,
    160, 233, 239, 362-71
    Aztec 85-6, 91, 98, 103,
    181
    Zapotec 123
    see also Revolutionary
    period
Soil types 71, 125
Sonora 25, 28-9, 156, 201,
    238, 246, 284, 323,
    338, 340, 388, 431, 586
Sorghum 576
Soviet Union 386
Spaniards in Mexico 249,
    276
    see also Spanish
    Conquest
Spanish Civil War 506
Spanish Conquest (1519-
    70) 86-7, 93, 102-3,
    138, 163-81
Spanish language 82
Spanish settlers 202
    see also Colonial period
Sport 49, 611-16, 627
Stabilising Development
    policy 516, 522, 535-6
State development bank
    556
State enterprise see
    Agriculture;
    Industrialization; and
    industries by name

Statistics 724-30, 737
Steel industry 475, 554
Stelae 652
Strikes 205, 455, 590, 592
Student movement (1968)
    455, 472, 480
Sugar 210
Superstitions 176

T

Tabasco 20
Tamaulipas 452
Tarahumara 351
Tarascan Indians 17, 179,
    297, 301, 325
Tarascan literature 626
Taxation 354
Technology 542, 545, 576,
    609
    pre-Columbian 148
    transfer 493
Tecolutla, Veracruz 293
Tehuacán 126
Tehuantepec 16, 189, 374,
    602
Telecommunications 551
    see also Mass media
Televisa 721-2
    see also Mass media
Tenochtitlán 97, 124-5, 134
Teotihuacán 139, 145-6
    decline 147
Tepoztlán 315
Texas 61, 232, 237, 266,
    402
Texcoco 99, 134, 153
Textile industry 219, 254,
    390-1, 547
Theatre see Music, theatre
    and film
    see also Drama
Tijuana 63
Time, Mesoamerican
    reckoning 144, 618
    see also Calendar
Tlacopan 134
Tlaxcala 130, 208, 286,
    318, 333
Tloltec people 127, 145
Tobacco planters 194
Toltec people 333, 665

Tourism 33, 71
see also Travel guides;
and resorts and sites by
name
Trade 14, 128, 271, 488,
501, 504, 508, 512,
530, 539-47
agricultural 514, 587
Aztec 102
16th-century 170
Trade unions 475, 590-6,
737
see also Labour
Transnational corporations
548-9, 553
Transportation
16th-century 170
statistics 727
Travel guides 34-56
Travellers' accounts 12-33
Traven, B. 633, 636
Tribunal of the Acordada
209
Tula 127
Tzeltal rebellion 298
Tzintzuntzan 297, 305, 403
Tzotzil language 326, 337
Tzotzil people 599
Tzutujil language 331

U

Ugarte, Jacobo 212
Undocumented migration
see Migration
Unions see Labour
United States of America
see USA
Universities 438

UNORCA [peasant
league] 473
Urbanization 59-60, 73, 84,
87, 123, 139, 365-6,
368, 371, 378, 403,
405, 557
Mayan 106
USA 66, 235, 258, 260,
271, 280, 283, 386
cultural influence 1-2
fear of 229
war against 226, 234,
245, 251
see also Border policy;
Migration; Trade
Uxmal 120

V

Valenciana 188
Valenzuela, Fernando 613
Vargas, Diego de 203
Vegetation changes 79, 125
Veracruz 190, 293, 602,
617
Villa, Francisco (Pancho)
282, 287
Violence 309, 321

W

Wages 196
Warfare
pre-Hispanic 102
Water pollution 598
Water rights 211, 323, 397,
504

Water supply 61, 213, 500
Weaving 663, 669, 703
Wildlife 26, 80
see also Birds; Fauna
Wills 193
Witchcraft 696
Women 380-91, 428, 434,
545
World Cup (1986) 614-15

Y

Yaltepec dialect 339
Yáñez, Agustín 634
Yankee capitalists 246
Yaqui culture 238, 301, 316
Yaqui language 338
Yautepec 210
Yucatán 13, 50, 69, 112,
115, 464, 550, 579–80,
679
Revolutionary period
262, 264, 278
Spanish conquest 166,
168

Z

Zapata, Emiliano 198, 289-
90
Zapatismo 289, 315
Zapotec Indians 123, 131,
140, 304, 317, 382
literature 626
Zihuantejo 36-7, 51
Zinacantan 299, 337
Zinacantecan poetry 625
Zorita, Alonso de 178, 181

Map of Mexico

This map shows the more important towns and other features.

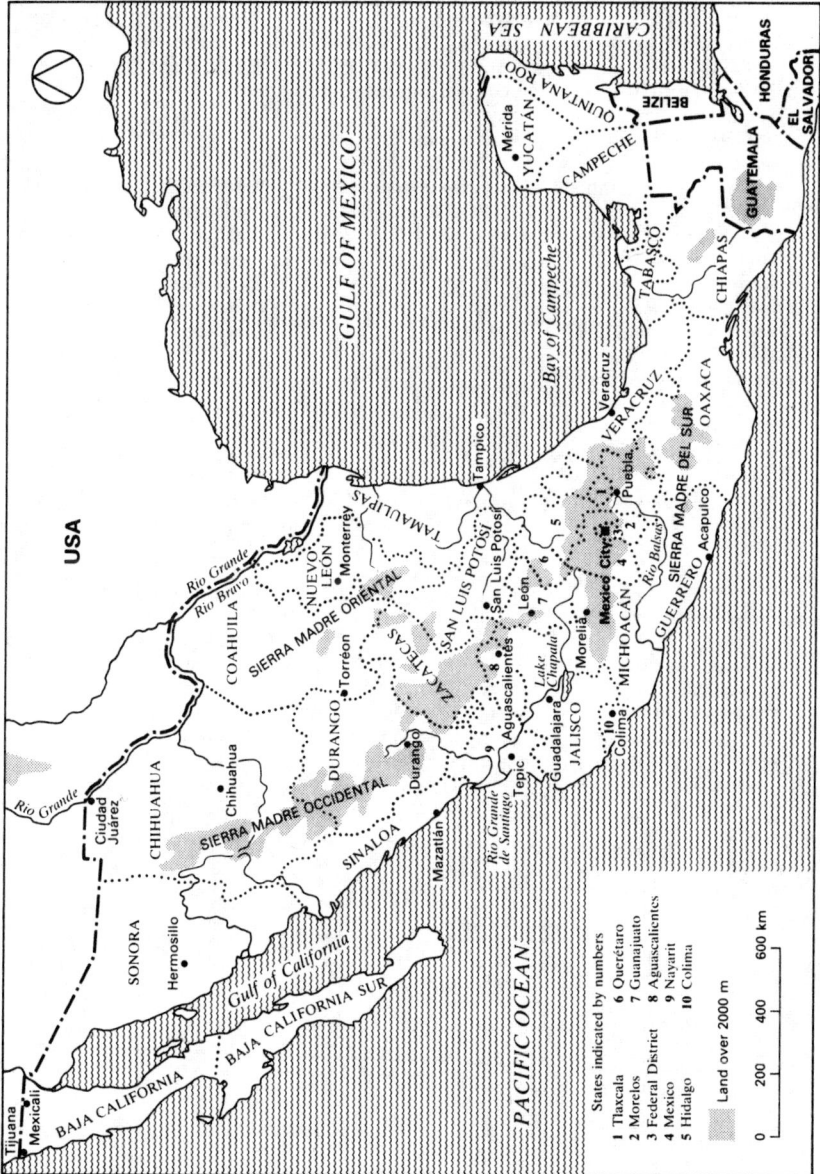

States indicated by numbers

1 Tlaxcala	6 Querétaro
2 Morelos	7 Guanajuato
3 Federal District	8 Aguascalientes
4 Mexico	9 Nayarit
5 Hidalgo	10 Colima

Land over 2000 m

0   200   400   600 km